Magic Words that Bring You Riches

Magic Words that Bring You Riches

Ted Nicholas

The single most important activity of your life is your ability to communicate. Unlimited success and wealth is as simple as using the right words as revealed herein. These words work as if by magic!

NICHOLAS DIRECT, INC.

Nicholas Direct, Inc., P.O. Box 877,
Indian Rocks Beach, FL 34635

Printed in the United States of America

First Printing July 1995
Second Printing Revised May 1996

ISBN 1–887741–00–3

Dedication

This book is dedicated to my sweetheart of seven years and my best friend, who helped me edit this book—Bethany Waller—the only person I've ever personally known on exciting planet Earth who has proven through her actions that she is completely 100% loyal to her values.

This book is written for seven special friends, 5 men and 2 women. Their ages vary from 29 to over 70. The oldest is 77. All of them after coming to my seminar told me how much they had accepted conventional wisdom and sunk into conformity. How they felt unalive—numb to all of life's possibilities. They finally had all stopped dreaming—and lost the fire. But at my seminar they felt I'd helped re-ignite their passion. Their zest for life.

I remember that when John, the 77 year old, spoke to me from his soul, I was moved to my depths. Instead of John accepting the kind of gray existence lived by most of his contemporaries, he chose to live.

I saw a man who changed his life—and who can now do anything on which he sets his mind. I realized playing some part, however minor, in any single human's development enriches my life beyond what I ever imagined as a communicator.

So, dear reader, if this book touches you in some special way you will have richly rewarded me more than you could ever know.

Ted Nicholas

About this book

This book is divided into three parts.

Part I involves 21 situations we all experience in life. In order to improve your results, I reveal the specific "magic words" which have made an extraordinary difference in my life. Once mastered, these words will produce huge changes in yours as well. You will better position yourself to get everything you have ever wanted.

Part II reveals "magic words" which will bring you financial riches. Discover the words, strategies, and techniques that have helped me profitably market over $500,000,000 worth of products and services both for my own and clients' products and services.

Part III—Should you wish to enhance your "magic word" skills, you are provided information on how to obtain more advanced materials and training. I'll also provide answers to commonly asked questions about the basis upon which I work with clients.

Contents

Part I

Magic Words That Get You Everything You Want in Life

Magic Words

How to get everything you've ever wanted in life by saying the right words.

The words with which you communicate determine the quality of your life.

This is true whether communicating with others or with yourself. Especially with yourself.

The impact of words actually causes measurable biological changes in ourselves. And in others. Words are stored in our conscious and subconscious minds. We think in words.

Certain words incite many emotions and subsequent actions. Words have the power to induce someone to laugh, to cry, to be kind, to be loving, to be cooperative, or to buy. Or be unkind, angry, irrational.

Whether words are written or spoken, they have enormous power. Of course, when words are spoken, the added factors of voice timbre, emphasis, emotion . . . all have the potential to cause even more impact.

This book offers many concrete examples of using simple words to produce certain results. This may sound like a form of manipulation. Actually, it is. But, here is the important distinction that needs to be made.

Manipulation can be either positive or negative. I define negative manipulation in this context: the use of words that causes others to act for the benefit of the communicator.

Positive manipulation is when certain words tend to cause responses that are of mutual benefit to the speaker or writer and the person with whom you communicate.

The techniques I'll reveal to you have all been developed in a win/win context.

Here is what few people seem to realize: People all over the world really want to accommodate their fellow humans. But they must be approached properly.

It's my experience and observation that many people do not give much attention to the people we all meet in life and who have positions on the lower end of the job scale. In fact, some people not only ignore them, they are rude and insensitive to them.

Here is a big mistake. I believe every human being should be treated with dignity and respect. Reason? People in service occupations, for example, such as waiters and waitresses, the health club attendants, golf and tennis assistants, hotel desk clerks, rental car agents, office clerks, etc. have an ongoing power to add so much quality and meaning to our lives. Little people mean a lot.

So, Rule Number One: Treat the "little" people in your world with dignity and respect. Learn their names and background information by asking questions. Think about it. Who do you think will get special consideration when it is requested? The open and kind caring person? Or the person who treats the "little" people as though they were invisible? The answer is obvious.

I've found the "little" people who I've taken time to know have enormous power to make my life more enjoyable—to add real quality to each day. Plus, it's fun to make lots of new friends.

It's been proven by the experts that body language communicates with as much impact as the words we speak. Therefore, to enhance their power, practice saying the secret words with:

- a smile (you can even hear a smile on the telephone);
- a warm, rich tone to your voice;
- enthusiasm in what you request;
- good eye contact;
- a firm handshake;
- sincerity—you can't fake friendliness;
- a purposeful posture—standing tall; and
- a manner that communicates an expectation that you deserve and expect to get what you request.

I submit that with each person we come in contact, we have in a certain sense the opportunity to market ourselves. To be liked or disliked. Of course, the more people like us, the happier they are to be helpful.

I use "magic words" every day of my life. Here they are revealed to you, dear reader, for the very first time anywhere.

Self-Communication

Unless you first learn to communicate with yourself, you will not be very effective communicating with others.

The silent words we all say to ourselves produce feelings. These can be positive, happy and life-enhancing, or negative, unhappy and detrimental to us.

Silent Words Are Heard!

You literally affect and change your nervous system by your internal dialogue.

While I will focus mainly on the silent words, it's important that I at least touch on another vital aspect of communication to ourselves and to the outside world.

We communicate both to our inner self with the world outside as much by the way we use our body as in our words. And our body messages, along with words spoken or silent, help create our emotion. Of course, we also hear silent words in the voice pitch and quality we choose, for our unspoken voice is heard. We hear a whiny, sleepy, apologetic voice, or we hear a rich, strong energetic voice when we speak to ourselves through internal dialogue.

In addition, if you sit slouched and speak softly and slowly with a yawning voice tone, tell yourself you are learning about communication as you begin to feel a lack of energy and drowsiness.

Any doubts? Try this test. Read the previous paragraph and see how you feel. Let yourself really experience the feelings your actions produce within you.

Now try this standing up. Walk briskly and purposefully across the room—head back, good posture. Sit comfortably, but keep your back straight as you sit in your chair. Speak silently to yourself in a strong voice with energy. Tell yourself you are learning about self-communication as you feel growing excitement about all the new benefits your new knowledge brings to your life. Let yourself really experience the emotions. See the difference!

The way we use our body muscles, facial muscles and posture is critical to our self-communication. Even how you use your eyes. It's almost impossible to feel up if you continually look downward, especially with a frown on your face. And it's almost impossible to feel down when you are looking straight up with a smile on your face.

Try it!

In summary, communication with the outside world, written or spoken, first starts with self-communication.

Self-communication starts with the way we use our body along with the silent words we say to ourselves. The loudness of the inner words, along with the richness of tone used when we say them combine to produce our inner emotional state. Interestingly, our communication to others reflects this inner state. It can't be hidden, at least not for long.

Personal Notes

How to get the very best table in any restaurant

Key words are: *"Celebrating Tonight"*

When calling for a reservation, say, "I'd like the very best, most special table you have. We're celebrating tonight. What can you do for us?"

If you bring your spouse on a date instead of a client or friend, say instead, "I'd like the most romantic table you have in the corner, so we can sit side by side. We're celebrating tonight."

If the maitre d' asks what you are celebrating (unless, of course, it's a birthday, anniversary, sales achievement, asset purchase, or other special event) say, "We're celebrating our existence!" Indeed, each day in our lives deserves to be celebrated.

Restaurant owners and managers always enjoy sharing the celebratory mood.

I've never failed to get the very best table. The restaurant is delighted to provide it, and it's never cost me a penny in gratuities.

Often get first class, business class seats on an airplane, even though you have coach tickets

Key Words are: *"Courtesy Upgrade"*

Upon check-in, ask, "Is it possible to obtain a courtesy upgrade to first class or business class?"

If you happen to fly the airline often and are in a "frequent flyer" program, be sure to mention it. Even if you are not a frequent flyer but are a passenger on the airline periodically, indicate you are a good customer.

Two other strategies can also be very effective.

If you are traveling as a couple and are in a close romantic relationship say, "We are on our honeymoon. Can you upgrade us on this special occasion?"

You must be comfortable saying these words. And as with all magic words, it must sound and actually be truthful.

You've heard of a second honeymoon. When I travel with my companion, the love of my life, I'm always enjoying continual "honeymoons," 3rd, 4th, 5th, etc. Ticket agents really enjoy helping honeymooners if they can. Remember that "the whole world loves a lover!"

If you are an investor in stocks, here is another tip. Simply buy some shares or even a single share in the airline. I own shares in several airlines individually and via mutual funds. Then you can truthfully say at the ticket window: "I'm a shareholder in your airline. Of course, you can check this if you have

access to shareholder records. Can you provide me a courtesy upgrade?"

Often, the ticket agent will upgrade you. On those occasions when they say only a supervisor can upgrade you, ask to see them. They are usually in the check-in area and are normally very nice to talk with.

This statement results in a great seat at no extra cost at least 50% of the time.

You are bound to enjoy your future flying trips a lot more when you are provided the luxury of first class service at coach rates. Bon voyage!

WE'D LIKE TO
HIRE YOU
JOB OFFERS

Have employers call you with job offers!

Key words are: *"Honest, hard working, experienced, immediately available, talented, competent, great references. 'I'll help you build a more profitable business' "*

Forget classified ads, resumes, employment agencies, and other traditional job sources. Jobs are rarely obtained by these methods in today's difficult times.

The best source of jobs in any town is in one place. And almost no one utilizes it. It's in the Yellow Pages. That's where the jobs are. And most of these businesses do not advertise in the classifieds. They are just too busy.

Here is what you do. Look under the business field in which you wish to work. This is a procedure employment agencies often follow. But why pay them?

For example, let's say you'd like a job as a graphic designer. Look up graphic designers and make a list of them and send them all a giant-sized postcard, 5½ by 8½, on shocking pink or goldenrod card stock, so it will stand out.

You will then proceed to write what is the equivalent of a radio commercial on yourself. You'll be amazed and delighted with the results.

Assuming the above all suits you, your card would read:

Graphic Designer Extraordinaire

Could you use a talented, honest, hard working, experienced, competent graphic designer with great references? Given the chance, I'll help you build a more profitable business! Available Immediately. Call me at 555-0000 Or Write: 123 Main Street, Anytown, USA.

Personal Notes

Slash the Cost of Lodging at First Class Hotels

Key words are: *"Is this the lowest rate you have?"*

Hotels and motels set room rates that are the very highest prices they can expect to get. If you say nothing and accept any rate, they will be delighted.

Here is my recommendation. Regardless when you book the reservation, including the time of day, day of week, season of the year, ask for the lowest price.

When the price is given, repeat: "Is this the lowest rate you have?" One response you'll hear goes like this:

> "Oh, so sorry. Did you want that rate?" Upon their reply, you can ask for more options from there. I've frequently gotten rates at 50 to 75 percent of the previously quoted rate for first class rooms, and so will you!

Before you accept any room, it's prudent to look at it first to be sure you like it.

Also, when you have time, look at more than one hotel, look at the room and get the lowest rate quotation.

Tell the desk clerk you'll get back to them. Another powerful technique is to get two or three quotations and tell the desk clerk at the hotel in which you are most interested that so-and-so has given you the special rate of "X" dollars! The hotel will often meet that rate. So you'll often wind up with the room you really want at the most favorable rate!

WITH
YOUR
INVESTMENT
$

Attract All the Money You Need for Any Business Venture You'd Like to Start

My key words are: *"Sophisticated Investor"*

Other important words are:

- Local business person with excellent track record and reputable history . . .
- Start-up business opportunity, limited investment, high potential return . . .
- References available—Call or write Tom Smith, your telephone and address.

Every successful professional, such as a prosperous doctor or lawyer, likes to think of himself/herself as sophisticated. You can often attract these prospects to invest in your business.

You can run above as an ad in your local newspaper. In many cases, you'll get several investors who will talk with you.

Of course, you'll need to check them out because they certainly will verify your background.

Other suggestions are to incorporate your business and sell up to 49 percent of your company because this allows you to keep control.

CAVEAT: The above procedure is recommended only if there is no other way to get your business off the ground. It's much better to start very small—out of your home at first to keep overhead down. Use your own savings or even a credit card loan. If the business works in a small way, it will work in a big way. And you'll own it 100 percent yourself, without partners!

Approach a Member of the Opposite Sex and Immediately Generate Interest in You

Key words are: *"Sincere Compliment and/or Question about an area of common interest, such as work, hobby, or sport"*

To establish immediate rapport with any human being is easy. All you need do is find something of interest to that person or of common interest to both of you.

A gentle and warm comment, such as, "This is such a great place to swim . . . or read . . . or play tennis . . . isn't it?" Or, "Do you find this field as interesting as I do?" Or, "How did you ever get interested in sky diving?" Or pay them a small but sincere compliment if there doesn't seem to be an area of common interest.

This approach, while also powerful, is more delicate.

It's very important that the compliment not be overstated. For example: If you walk up to a complete stranger and say, "You are the most beautiful/handsome woman/man I've ever seen," you've lost credibility. They just won't believe you.

Instead, be observant. All of us like compliments on the smallest things. Here are some examples, but remember—you must really mean them.

- "What a sharp tie. I really like that. Do you mind telling me where you got it?"
- "That shoe and handbag combination is really attractive. I bet it's from Europe."

- "That color is very unusual. What is it called?"
- "That pin is very special. Is it from a family collection?"
- "You have a nice tan. I'll bet you just returned from a vacation."
- "What a nice hat. I wish more people wore them."

Attractive people all over the world are often lonely and want to talk.

Verbal communication is the beginning of any relationship. Men and women you want to meet may seem aloof and uninterested, even from afar. After all, this is just a habit or defense. Approach them correctly and they will open up to you. This approach can often lead to a friendship or a romantic relationship.

The worst that can happen is that the person has no interest in speaking with you. But, you'll rarely find that to be the case.

Personal Notes

CAR
RENTAL
RENTAL

Rent a Mercedes for the price of a Ford anywhere in the world

Key words are: *"Courtesy upgrade"*

Here is how I do it. I always call and reserve a mid-sized car before I travel anywhere.

I call Hertz, Avis, Dollar, or National and choose the one offering the best rate. These companies vary in offering specials, as you may be aware.

I always request a mid-sized car.

When I arrive at the service desk, I say, "Do you have a Mercedes or other luxury car available?"

They say "yes" nearly all the time.

I then say, "I'm a good customer of your company. May I have a courtesy upgrade to the Mercedes for the price of the mid-sized car I reserved?"

The number of times you get the luxury car for the low rate is delightfully high.

Just this past summer I had the pleasure of driving a Mercedes in Switzerland for the same rate as a Ford. And in that country, the normal Mercedes rate is about five times the rate of the Ford.

Try it. You'll be very pleased.

Find a Great Gourmet Cook To Prepare Low Cost Meals for You

Key words are: *"Gourmet Cook"*

My life and health have been greatly enriched by having three wonderful cooks at different times over the last 25 years.

I used two techniques to find these gems. The first is to look in the Yellow Pages in the employment section. Look for a source that provides household help. I found a small firm with the slogan: "Nannies Indeed For Families in Need."

I called them and said that I wanted to locate a person who enjoyed running a household and was a good cook. I found a delightful person who had experience as a chef and had formerly owned her own restaurant. She prepared delicious gourmet meals for my family for several years, both on a full-time and a part-time basis.

We even sent her to Chinese, Italian, and French cooking classes to learn how to prepare gourmet foods nutritionally. She also did all our shopping for the ingredients in the recipes for organically grown fruits and vegetables and chemical-free meat, etc.

The other technique I've used is to run this classified ad, which produced dozens of qualified people:

> **Gourmet Cook**
>
> If you enjoy the art of cooking really special meals as well as running a household for a busy professional couple, you may wish to apply for an ideal position. Duties include shopping for nutritionally sound ingredients and helping to supervise gardener and repair people. References are necessary. Submit resume and salary history in confidence to (your name and address).

How to Get Invited to Speak Before Any Group You Choose and Enhance Your Business Career

Key words are: *"What are your group's strongest areas of interest?" Or "What are your group's biggest problems?"*

Once the president or program chairperson provides you with these answers, plan a presentation matching much of your knowledge and/or experience with the organization's needs. Create a provocative title for your talk.

Recently, for example, I asked the office manager of a large insurance company these questions. Not surprisingly, he said, "Our representatives approaching cold prospects and getting an appointment."

Since I have so much direct marketing experience, I suggested that I do a seminar for his top producers entitled: "Seven Secrets of Using Direct Mail to Successfully Make Appointments With Qualified Prospects."

Needless to say, as a by-product of my helping the company, the exposure resulted in many thousands of dollars in sales of my books, seminars, and videos.

Companies, civic groups, and other organizations are always looking for people who can help their members. By focusing on their needs and wants, you can continually enhance your business career.

Receive Free Expert Consulting Help for Your Business

Key words are: *"I have a business problem and need expert assistance"*

A completely underutilized source of assistance for any small business owner is available from S.C.O.R.E. (Small Business Council of Retired Executives).

Affiliated with the Small Business Administration, S.C.O.R.E. experts are retired volunteer executives who donate their time and talent to assist small business owners. There is no fee whatsoever charged for services, unless, of course, out-of-pocket expenses are necessary.

I've been absolutely delighted with the quality of assistance provided to me on several occasions. Of course, everything depends on the particular individual counselor who is assigned to you.

If you would like to try the consultant without risk, call your local SBA office.

Be specific about the kind and type of help in which you are interested.

Is your problem in the area of marketing? Finance? Research? Manufacturing?

S.C.O.R.E. will put forth their best effort to get you the kind of help you really need.

Of course, as with all expert assistance, when you meet with the consultant, the better you've defined the problem, the more meaningful will be the feedback.

Buy Beautiful Jewelry, Including Gold Rings and Watches, at Below Wholesale Prices

Key words are: *"Bargain Lover"*

I've gotten terrific bargains in jewelry in New York, Philadelphia, Clearwater, and throughout Europe.

Here is the procedure:

Go to at least two leading jewelers in the town or city in which you happen to be located.

Tell them you are interested in the possibility of buying jewelry. Say, "I'm a bargain lover. I always buy at wholesale or below everywhere I travel. Please show me items in which you may be interested in doing business on that basis."

Almost every time you will find at least one jeweler who is happy to offer you some great deals.

HOW
TO
MAKE
A
MILLION

Earn over $1,000 a day . . . everyday . . . in the most profitable business in the world. It's the best home-based business of all. And you can start it for under $600

Key words are: *"Information Publishing"*

The hottest, very best way to get rich is selling an information-based product.

We live in the information age. Opportunities abound for entrepreneurs, writers who produce books, special reports, newsletters, "guerilla" videos, cassette tapes, and floppy disks, to make a fortune!

The ways to make a great deal of money in information publishing are almost limitless. All my adult life has involved a search for the ideal business.

I started 18 companies before I was 35. Then I discovered publishing. My first publishing venture began with a $90 classified ad for the first book I wrote, HOW TO FORM A CORPORA-

TION WITHOUT A LAWYER FOR UNDER $75. That book has sold over a million copies.

I've since written 13 other books of my own and sold two and a half million copies. In addition, I've published 39 books written by others, as well as numerous special reports, newsletters, and video and audio tapes.

The lifestyle you can have as a publisher operating from home anywhere in the world is unsurpassed. I do my work in Florida and Europe, depending on the season.

There is also no more profitable profession in the world as publishing, and none as satisfying, because you can really have an impact on people's lives with valuable ideas and information.

So many people have asked me how I've done it. I've put together a complete program to help those who wish to enter this field and succeed. Everything is provided, including showing you how to get financing.

If you would like a free information packet (of course, without obligation) call 1-813-596-4966 or fax 1-813-596-6900 and request "complete information on Information Publishing."

Personal Notes

SOUTH WEST
CHAPTER

Find world famous people to speak before your group—free

Key words are: *"We do not have a speaker budget"*

If your organization or group is like most, you don't have the funds to pay huge speaking fees for top people. Top speakers charge $5,000 to $25,000 and up.

However, if you approach them in a certain way, over 90 percent of the time world-class experts will speak at your meeting or event absolutely free.

If travel is involved, that might be your only cost; but I've invited top speakers who have even paid their own way. But, minimally, you do need to at least pay travel costs.

Of course, in many cases, speakers do it to gain exposure to self-market their personal services, book, newsletter, etc. Or, often to have their talk publicized. Or because they just love the opportunity to speak!

Here is what you do: Call the speaker you would like as far in advance as possible, because, of course, well-known people are in demand and are booked well in advance.

Say, "We'd love to have you speak before our group, consisting of (name of group) on (date). However, we do not have a speaker budget. Would you consider speaking to our group at that time? We would be very honored to have you be our featured speaker!"

Usually the speaker's service, book, tapes, or seminars may be of interest to the organization. Of course, be sure to communicate to the speaker that he/she is free to offer these services.

You'll be surprised and pleased with the quality and number of people who will accept this offer.

Personal Notes

SECRETARY
OF THE
YEAR

Attract the world's best employees to help your business really prosper

Key words: *"Have everything to do with how you describe the job"*

In most employer's minds, even in a one-person business, recruiting employees is thought of as a personnel function.

I believe the main reason I have been able to attract dozens of excellent employees is because I treat recruiting people as a marketing function.

I've had the best success using classified ads in local newspapers for both management and support people. Classified ads have proven to be far more effective and less costly than through the use of employment agencies.

For example, my most recent hire was for an executive secretary.

I sat down and described the position from the secretary's point of view. Here is the ad:

EXECUTIVE SECRETARY

> Best secretary on Gulf Coast sought by busy writer/publisher. Excellent office skills including computer and bookkeeping are necessary. References required. Please send resume and salary history in confidence to Ted Nicholas, PO Box 877, Indian Rocks Beach, FL 34635.

I received over 100 resumes from highly qualified people for this position.

You will find top job candidates for your needs by using this direct approach.

CLASSIFIED BOARD
VOLUNTEERS NEEDED

How to Get Capable People to Work Free

The magic words are: *"Volunteers Needed." And: "Piece of the action"*

If you are involved in a small business or a project, often you can gain volunteer help from people who have free time. These people may be bored and/or have income from various sources.

A bookstore I ran a few years ago was basically run with volunteers. You may be able to do the same. You can put notices at church, or your community bulletin board, describing the type of person you'd like to respond.

The second method is applicable to more situations. Many of the best performing people are happy to work for a percentage of sales or profits.

Instead of paying a fixed salary and benefits, which involve overhead you may not want to incur, you run ads or contact people and offer them one of several options, including:

- Hourly rate for services rendered.
- Percentage of sales.
- Percentage of profits.
- Royalty on sales.
- Percentage of savings.
- Fixed payment for units produced.

Individuals with strong entrepreneurial instincts will be attracted by such an approach. In fact, they prefer it because there is no limit on their income and they are more independent and can set their own hours, etc.

The best way to structure such an arrangement is with a simple letter agreement wherein the individual working with you invoices you periodically as an "independent contractor." Of course, use caution that these people are actually independent, so you won't be forced by the IRS to classify them as employees. (For complete information on this topic, I refer you to my special report entitled, "How to Gain Financial Freedom.")

I utilize arrangements like these in my current business activities for various people who provide service, such as:

- Shipping
- Selling
- Authors who write books and reports for my company
- Editors
- Lawyers
- Accountants
- Consultants

Of course, as with all people who provide service to you, I recommend you ask for and check out their recommendations before you hire them.

Personal Notes

TIMES
A PUBLICATION OF NEWS
SECTION A PAGE 1
LOCAL WRITER HITS IT BIG.
TAXES LOWER
WEATHER

Get Free Advertising by Becoming a Celebrity, First Locally—Then Nationally

The key words are: *"Local Author"*

Writing a book is the best way to get gobs of free publicity. The best advertising there is—word of mouth. It's amazing how much attention you get locally and then nationally, just by getting a book published.

While there are some opportunities writing fiction, there are far more in non-fiction.

A good place to start seeking a subject is to reflect on what you've been doing with your life for the last 10-15 years. Often others will gladly pay you the price of a book to learn what you know.

If you need help in preparing your book, or special report, or video or audio tape, plenty is available. You can contact graduate students through a university or advertise for editorial assistance with an ad in your newspaper. It's surprising how many people, including teachers, professors and other experts who enjoy writing, will contact you.

You can arrange compensation to collaborators, including editors, ghostwriters, or proof readers in a variety of ways. These include an hourly rate, price per word, or per typewritten page. Another way, which I favor and have often used, is payment on a royalty basis after the book is published and on the market.

If you have difficulty in finding a publisher for your book or other product, you can self-publish. Does self-publishing work? I've sold over 3,000,000 copies of books using this strategy!

You can do the same.

FOR ONLY
$9.95
INTERNATIONAL
Markets
DAILY NEWS
BUSINESS TODAY
FOR ONLY
$9.95
INTERNATIONAL
Markets
STOCKS
& BONDS
FOR ONLY
$9.95
INTERNATIONAL
Markets

Obtain the U.S. Rights to Market Best Selling Products From Around the World for as Little as $250

The key words are: *"Exclusive direct marketing rights"*

It's amazing but true.

There are all kinds of profitable products, including best-selling books, to which you can obtain valuable rights for next to nothing.

When you locate a successful product that you'd like to sell, contact the owner. Look for things that are selling in retail stores or via mail order both in the U.S. and around the world. Use this approach:

"I'm interested in marketing your product, (name the product). I will undertake a market test to sell your product via direct response methods, including mail, print ads, and possibly TV and/or radio.

"I will produce the product under a license from you where I pay costs to produce it. Here is an advance in the sum of $250 to $1,000 to show good faith.

"After the test, I will pay you a continuing royalty on sales of (offer 5% up to 15%) on all revenue for exclusive direct marketing rights for the United States.

You continue to sell your product as you wish. In fact, my marketing may help to increase your sales due to the added advertising and publicity I will generate for the product."

Because the owner of a product has everything to gain and nothing to lose by such an arrangement, you should be able to obtain rights to numerous profitable products using this strategy.

I've obtained the rights to several best-selling books using the above techniques.

Personal Notes

BUY & SELL PROPERTY WITHOUT A LAWYER.
TAX LAWS
FORMS FOR A
ASY DIVORSE
FORMS TO FORM
A CORPORATION

Reduce or Eliminate Legal Fees in Your Business and Personal Life

The key words are: *"Ready-to-use-forms"*

You can document most important actions in your life by using stock forms and agreements. All you do is fill in the blanks. In this way, you can both protect yourself and save hundreds, even thousands, in legal fees.

Standard form and agreements can be found in books, as well as in stationery stores.

I like the usefulness of forms so much I've written several forms books, including:

- HOW TO FORM YOUR OWN CORPORATION WITHOUT A LAWYER FOR UNDER $75
- COMPLETE GUIDE TO BUSINESS AGREEMENTS
- COMPLETE GUIDE TO "S" CORPORATIONS
- COMPLETE GUIDE TO NON-PROFIT CORPORATIONS
- COMPLETE BOOK OF CORPORATE FORMS

There are many good form books by other authors, as well. Even divorce when it's simple! When the couple has accumulated few assets, a divorce can be done via ready-to-use forms.

You might ask, "Should you ever use a lawyer?" The answer is, Yes. A good rule to follow is when the agreement form matter you wish to document is complex, by all means, hire an experienced, competent lawyer.

Examples of complex legal matters include:

- A corporate merger
- Holding a public stock offering in a corporation
- Buying or selling a business
- Filing a lawsuit
- A complicated divorce case

However, for simple legal actions use forms and do it yourself to save time and money.

Personal Notes

500.00

Buy Valuable Antiques at Huge Discounts

The key words are: *"Open to negotiation"*

If you love antiques, you no longer have to pay the listed price. You'll find that antique dealers almost anywhere in the U.S. or Europe are receptive to this approach.

After you find something in which you are interested, regardless of the listed price, ask this question: "Are you open to negotiation?"

Invariably, the answer is "yes." The door has now been open. The seller will listen to your offer.

You can begin negotiations at a level wherein you are comfortable. It can be 25%, 40%, 50%, or 75% of the list price.

I frequently buy antique furniture, jewelry, and original art at huge discounts using the above techniques.

I get a lot of pleasure negotiating good deals. I'm always surprised when I see other customers paying the listed price. Of course, antique dealers are happy to accept the full price when prospective buyers simply do not ask for a discount.

STOCK

Get Valuable Financial Interests in Other People's Companies Without Investing One Red Cent

The key words are: *"Small financial interest"*

If you have skills which are helpful to entrepreneurs, you can often trade your expertise for a stock portion or percentage of a company.

This can also be very appealing to the entrepreneur founder if he/she is "cash starved," as are most business owners. It's often easier to pay those who help build the company in stock rather than cash.

Offer to trade your services for a small financial interest in the company. Indicate you are willing to work for a "piece of the action" and invest your time and skills to help the entrepreneur grow. This type of interest can be anything you negotiate, usually 5% to 25%.

Another variation of this technique I often use with clients is to work on a percentage of sales. This usually runs 5% of sales on projects on which I'm engaged.

A good way to present this, especially if you are able to help build sales, is to say, "If I can help you generate income you would not otherwise earn, are you willing to pay me an agreed upon percentage?" Almost always this kind of offer is accepted. Clearly, there is no downside whatsoever to the business owner and the chances to make more profit is irresistible.

$
PROFITS

Earn From $100,000 to $250,000 a Year and More as a Consultant by Making an Offer Almost No One Can Turn Down

The key words are: *"Increase sales or you owe nothing"*

There are many small companies that have good products that are under marketed.

When you find one that meets this criteria and you are willing to invest some time, make an offer.

Here is the basic offer you make:

"I'll present some marketing ideas to you. If you choose to use them, you pay me a percentage of increased sales. (I recommend 2.5% to 5% as a workable percentage.) Your payments to me will continue as long as the plans and ideas are used. If you stop using them, you have no further obligation to me. If for any reason the sales do not increase, you owe me nothing.

"All I ask you to do is to send me a letter agreeing that if you use my recommendations, you will pay me as per the above terms and conditions."

As you can readily see, the client has everything to gain and nothing to lose on this basis.

Each month, I'm paid thousands of dollars by hand-picked clients I enjoy helping. I currently have a waiting list. You can do the same, using the above plan of action.

Part II

Magic Words That Bring You Riches

How to Write Headlines that Make Sales Soar!

Includes the 27 most powerful magic selling words in the English language

Save money, time and hassles

This chapter features writing **effective headlines**. Reason? Ninety percent of the success or failure of any sales offer, whether in a space ad or sales letter, is the **headline**.

Teaser copy on an envelope and the **title** of a book are as crucially important as is the headline in a sales letter or ad.

So I feel headline writing is the best place to start. I'll show you how to ignite your sales by creating headlines with amazing power!

What the legends in advertising say . . .

In case you have any doubt about the importance of headlines, here is what two of the greats in advertising have to say:

> "Advice to copywriters: When you are assigned to write an ad, write a lot of headlines first. Spend hours writing headlines—or days if necessary. If you happen to think of a headline while walking down the street or while riding the bus, take out pencil and paper and write it down."
>
> **John Caples**

> "On the average, five times as many people read the headlines as read the body copy. It follows that, unless your headline sells your product, you have wasted 90 percent of your money."
>
> **David Ogilvy**

Headline writing is an area in which everyone, including professional copywriters, can be stronger. But, I'm unaware of anyone in the world today who teaches the art of the headline effectively.

Unfortunately, many direct marketing seminar speakers have learned from a book instead of the real world. Often they teach mythology that doesn't work.

What does a headline do?

An effective headline is important for many reasons. It:

- Attracts attention;
- Communicates a strong benefit;
- Appeals to the self-interest of the reader. It answers the question, "What's in it for me?";
- Sets the tone for the offer.

A headline acts like a marquee does for a movie theatre and

- Selects the right audience.

Based on hundreds of tests conducted, a good headline can be as much as 17 times more effective than a so-so headline. And this is with *exactly* the same body copy!

Because it is so important, I always write many headlines for an ad or book title. For instance, for *How To Form Your Own Corporation Without a Lawyer for Under $75*, I wrote 217 titles before I published the book. And the final title also became the headline for my first ad. Here are some guidelines I use for the way a headline is written and presented.

- The promise must be believable.
- Never use more than 17 words.
- Use quotation marks because it is more memorable.
- Use reverse type sparingly, because it is hard to read.
- Use upper and lower case letters—not all caps—for reading ease.
- If a large photograph is used, place the headline below it.
- Do not vary type size.

How to start writing great headlines . . .

On any product, including an information product—book, special report, newsletter, tape, floppy disk . . . re-review the product, element by element.

Step back from the product. If you have written or created the product, take off the producer's cap and look at it with a "marketer's eye." Identify all the **benefits** and **features** of the product—from the *buyer's* point of view.

Benefits are the real hot buttons

Benefits are those elements of the product that provide the answer to, "So what?".

Use strong action verbs. For example: "Discover how to slash your taxes by 95%". The word *slash* is a strong action word.

A feature is a fact about the product that builds credibility: "It's 11 × 17 inches, 244 pages and has 13 illustrations."

Both features and benefits are necessary in your copy. But benefits are where to place the emphasis. Benefits close the sale. Reason? People act 90 percent on their emotions. Benefits help bring out emotions. Everyone then justifies their decisions by using logic.

The best strategy to capture benefits

Here is a great technique. Using 3 × 5 cards, write one benefit or feature on each card. If, for example, the product is a book or tape, from some pages or segments you will write several benefits and features. On others, only one or even none. Do this throughout the review of the product.

When you have completed this process, review the 3 × 5 cards. Sometimes you will have 50, 75, 100—up to 200 and even more. In some cases **the strongest benefit you can find on a card is also the best headline**.

It can just pop out at you sometimes! A benefit you have isolated on your 3 × 5 card can become what sometimes is called your "unique selling proposition"—your USP.

The obvious can be your key to wealth

When you isolate the obvious benefits, you will start building wealth. You will immediately start earning a great deal of money as a marketer. Why? Many marketers miss isolating the obvious benefits of their product.

You will have many headline choices. And the benefits you have isolated will help you write the rest of the body copy. Your entire message needs to be filled with benefits. Put the strongest ones first in order of priority when you get into writing body copy.

Put drama, power and passion into your benefits.

Here is a special technique that can be even more powerful than the procedure I have just described.

A technique NOBODY teaches—
originated by me so only *I* know it.
I call it . . .

Finding the hidden benefit

I often create headlines that do not arise from studying the product itself. Yes! That is not a misprint. By using this special strategy, I've written some of the most successful headlines in direct marketing history.

Here is how it works . . .

Ask yourself this question, "If I had unlimited, god-like powers and could grant my prospective customer the biggest benefit I can possibly imagine he or she would ideally want from my product, what would that be?" Write down your answer.

Here is a specific example. While writing *The Complete Book of Corporate Forms*, to sell it I naturally wanted to dramatize the book and excite my prospects about its benefits. How could I possibly do that? Numerous publishers sold legal form books. Not as good as mine, mind you, but still form books. (Mine was, and still is, the easiest to use.) What could I do to differentiate my product? How could I make a book of forms (sounds dull, doesn't it?) exciting!?

So I stood back and asked myself that question. I quickly realized that entrepreneurs don't care a whit about forms. Most abhor paperwork. What they want is the benefit from *using* the forms.

I knew entrepreneurs, more than anyone else, hate to pay taxes. And what every entrepreneur desperately wants is to preserve the corporation's tax shelter status. No one wants to lose that precious benefit.

So it came to me. I wrote the headline, **"What Will You Do When the IRS Suddenly Wipes Out Your Corporation's Tax Shelter Benefits?"**

Of course, the book has narrative information about the importance of keeping good records to maintain the corporate protection. But, while it happens all the time, there is nothing whatsoever in the book about the IRS taking away benefits. That is why I call it a **hidden benefit**.

The rest of the copy for the ad was easy to do once I had the lead. You too will find your copywriting task will be simpler.

I used this headline for a 7 × 10 inch space ad. Later I used the same headline for a successful sales letter. A card deck offer selling the book on a postcard was also very successful.

Wow! Did it work!

Results? Since 1979, 350,000 copies of the book have been sold at $70 per copy. That's **24.5 million dollars** worth of product sales. And it is *still* selling just as well today! Selling a million copies of this book in the next few years is easily within reach!

One caveat on the "hidden benefit" headline strategy. Make sure your product actually delivers on the headline's promise. If you have the slightest doubt, here is what to do: change or revise the product! Result? You will both deliver the benefit and greatly add to the product's sales appeal!!

Other examples of headlines I have written that have nothing whatsoever to do directly with the product, but nonetheless have set sales records, include the ads I did for my book *How To Form Your Own Corporation Without a Lawyer for Under $75*:

"The Eighth Wonder of the World"

"Wage Your Own Personal Tax Revolt"

"Only Way Left For Little Guy to Get Rich"

And the most successful headline I ever wrote for that product . . .

"The Ultimate Tax Shelter"

Another example of the technique is the headline:

"What Will You Do When Your Personal Assets Are Seized to Satisfy a Judgment Against Your Corporation?"
—Product: *The Complete Book of Corporate Forms*

Use the "hidden benefit" technique when you are writing headlines and watch your sales explode. And remember:

Write as many headlines as you can.

Test, test, test

You will undoubtedly want to test more than one headline or "teaser" before you choose your final "control" headline. And even after you have a control, it is imperative to keep running new headline tests against it for two reasons:

1. to see if you can beat it, and . . .
2. every headline eventually becomes tired and you need to change it. But not too soon!

You will tire of a headline much faster than will your customers. If it is working—never, never, never, never change it—until, or unless, you beat the results with a new headline.

Using photography to boost sales

A new trend affecting the art of writing headlines is the **increased use of photography** in ads and sales letters. People are influenced more than ever before, probably because of the increased watching of video and TV.

Think visually about your headlines. If your headline message can be depicted visually, try using a photograph for up to 1/3 of the first page of a letter or ad. Do at least one variation of the ad with a photo. The old saying is true: "A picture is worth a thousand words". But here is the key. The headline and the photography **must** work together. Ideally the photography emphasizes the headline.

An example of the headline supported by a photo

A project I am currently doing for a client uses a photo.

The product is a wonderful manual designed for business people and leaders of all kinds who want to improve their public speeches, as do nearly all of them who want to get ahead. (Did you know that 54 percent of Americans would rather face death than make a speech?!)

The headline I wrote is **"How To Get Enthusiastic Applause—Even a Standing Ovation—Every Time You Speak".**

The ad photo depicts an audience smiling, clapping and giving a standing ovation as the speech ends. I bet you can even feel the attention-getting pulling power of the ad as you read this description. Can't you? Doesn't that knock your socks off?

A photograph cannot replace a headline

But no matter how good the photograph, the headline has even more responsibility. The goal? To get readers into the body copy. And the copy should be directly under the photograph, right after the caption.

On the ad for the public speaking book, the headline's promise is not specifically mentioned in the product, as such. It is another example of a "hidden benefit". However, the excellent information contained in the product delivers on that promise. I know because it kept the promise for me in a recent speech.

Powerful headline words

Here are my favorite headline words. The safest headline begins with "How To". It immediately appeals to the reader's self-interest. It piques curiosity. If the benefit is powerful, the reader will move on to the body copy. You are involving the reader immediately.

Did you know there are over 7,000 books in print with titles that start with "How To"? This phrase **cannot** be overdone.

Here are 26 other provocative words and phrases I like to use in a headline:

1. announcing
2. secrets of
3. new
4. now
5. amazing
6. facts you
7. breakthrough
8. at last
9. advice to
10. the truth of
11. protect
12. life
13. here
14. discover
15. do you
16. bargains
17. yes
18. love
19. how much
20. how would
21. this
22. only
23. sale
24. hate

And finally, the two most powerful headline words:

25. free
26. you

Other important headline points

Avoid headlines that merely create curiosity. If the headline does not tie to the product or to the benefit derived from using the product, the reader will feel deceived and will stop reading. And, of course, your product will not be ordered.

A good headline is the first step in prompting an action on the part of a reader.

The headline must stir an emotion. It must get the reader excited or fearful or protective. It must motivate.

Use present tense, not the future tense, for added power and life. It adds more "juice" to the promise and makes the promise more credible and believable. The present tense is also far more emphatic. Use the first or second person.

Use verbs which are colorful, vital and strong. Use short words that create images or pictures. Eliminate most adverbs and adjectives; they belong in longer body copy where you can support them.

Do not try to be "catchy" or "cute" as do many copywriters. Instead of dramatizing the product, they call attention to the copy itself which is distracting. Make the product the "hero", not the copy.

How to Create Ads that Bring in Millions in Sales

In this chapter, I'm going to dissect for you a successful ad containing the **hidden benefit** technique. The purpose? To clarify and make it easier for you to use.

But a word of caution. The hidden benefit technique, properly applied, is the most powerful marketing strategy in the world bar none. You stand a good chance of increasing sales so much that you'll experience unwanted shipping delays. Be sure you can promptly fulfill the extra orders you are bound to generate!

A quick review

First, a quick review of the process of writing an ad or sales letter. Study your product. Write down all the **obvious** benefits from the prospect's point of view on 3 × 5 cards. Write as many as you can. Often you'll have the best headline you could ever find from this procedure. If so, prepare your ad with the obvious benefit headline.

But then you'll want to try a hidden benefit ad to test against the obvious benefit ad.

To create the hidden benefit, answer this question: "If I had unlimited god-like power, what would be the single most compelling benefit my prospects would like to gain from my product?"

Often the hidden benefit has nothing directly to do with the product itself. The answer to the previous question can become your most powerful benefit. And thus your headline. And also the main theme of your offer.

In this chapter is a successful ad recently prepared for a client. Look at the headline. It consists of a powerful hidden benefit.

Don't you agree the headline captures exactly what every speaker wants deep down? When you speak, isn't enthusiastic applause and possibly a standing ovation what you want? Of course! Everyone who speaks wants these results.

I'm also going to comment on the key elements that help the ad succeed. Some of the points may surprise you even if you are an experienced marketer.

Add power to headlines

Notice that the headline is in quotes. Why? Studies show that an ad headline draws 28% more attention if quotation marks are around it! It appears much more important because someone is being quoted. Therefore, it should be read. And that is your first task. If the ad is not read, you have no chance of a sale.

The first sentence

The first letter of the ad, the P, is oversized and bold. It's called a "drop letter." It increases readership. Why? The reader's eye is drawn toward the left. The likelihood of the first sentence being read is much higher.

Look carefully at the first sentence: "Picture yourself enjoying the smiles and the pleased look of excitement on the faces of your audience."

The above sentence is powerful. It's strong enough to be a headline. Or a sub-headline.

There are three important reasons for this:

1. The sentence helps set the tone of the rest of the ad.
2. The headline is reinforced by the first sentence.
3. The reader is induced to read the second sentence.

The next paragraph and the rest of the copy amplifies the headline theme.

Read the ad. Can you pick out the benefits and features? A great exercise is to find those benefits and features in a successful ad.

Here is a great tool in learning to write copy that sells. Sit down and copy by hand a successful ad you particularly like. Hand write it on a yellow pad. You'll start getting a feel for sentence construction and flow. Long sentences. Short sentences. Bullets. Subheads. You'll actually get into the mindset of the author when it was written! Then have it set in type so you actually experience the whole process.

Typefaces are important

The featured ad employs the old classic, a Times-Roman typeface in the headline. Either serif or sans serif typefaces can be used for the headline.

In the body copy, the typeface is also Times Roman. Reason? It's easy to read. Never, never use a sans serif typeface in body copy. Strive for an editorial look. The ad should appear similar to an article in the magazines or newspapers in which your ads will run. I call it an "advertorial." Five times as many people read editorials than messages that scream out "I'm an ad!" If an advertorial is prepared in accordance with the techniques that follow, it can do 500% more in sales!

Photograph

The sample ad was tested both with and without a photograph. Results were mixed. In some publications the photo adds response. In others it works better without a photo.

Photos often lift response. But remember to always use a **caption**; many marketers overlook this.

Column Width

The size of the columns in your ads is also very important. Your prospects' reading habits are largely found through reading magazines and newspapers. Therefore, your column width should be approximately the same size as the editorial columns where you run the ad.

Set your 7 × 10 ads in a **three column** format. The right side can be "justified" or "ragged" right. I have found no difference in results either way.

Free bonus

Results from any offer can be improved with an attractive **free bonus**. Add bonuses to successful offers and watch sales dramatically increase.

There is one exception. The bonus must be highly desirable. When I first began direct marketing, I tried using slow moving or even failed products as bonuses. But it doesn't work. If you can't sell it, you can't give it away!

Ask for the order

Unsuccessful marketers are reluctant to ask for the order. For any offer to be successful, you must be clear and explicit as to **how** you ask for the order. Include every detail. Make it easy for the prospect to buy.

It's also important **when** you ask for the order. The prospect must be primed for the close. The sequence is crucially important.

In your sales letters, wait until the end of the message to reveal the price and ordering instructions. If your offer includes a brochure and an order form, separate them from the letter. This strategy will increase response. Put the brochure and order form in a sealed envelope. On the outside of the envelope say "Please don't open until you have read my letter."

Your guarantee

Offer a money-back guarantee. A guarantee increases your credibility and your response will be higher, no matter if you market a product or service.

I notice The Hampton Inns, a hotel chain, is using this guarantee:

Money-back Guarantee
If you are not completely satisfied
with your accommodations, just let us know,
and you will be issued a full refund or credit.

Someone asked me whether or not Hampton Inns has been influenced by my ads. Frankly, I don't know. However, I do know this. A money-back guarantee increases orders on any offer. Especially for any service business that depends completely on customer satisfaction, feedback, and referrals to build their business.

Length of guarantee

I've found 10-day, 21-day, 30-day, 60-day, and one year guarantees are all effective. Once again you should test to be sure.

What about returns?

In direct marketing, highly successful offers with quality products tend to run less than 5% returns.

Do you need a coupon?

It's usually a good idea. However, results from my coupon versus no coupon tests have been inconclusive. Sometimes one outpulls the other and vice versa. Therefore, sometimes I use them and sometimes not. A lot depends on how "tight" I am for copy, as a coupon usually takes slightly more space.

When you do use a coupon, **keep the dotted line surrounding it thin**. Reason? You don't want the reader's eye to be drawn to the coupon too early. Remember you must stage your offer in a sequence.

Most graphics people tend to use a heavy coupon, unless instructed otherwise.

The role of graphics

Graphics, even in all-copy ads, are very important. Choose a graphics designer who understands the "marriage" needed between graphics and copy. They are important to your success.

This is the principle that only one in a hundred graphics people have grasped:

The role of graphics is to support, embellish, and strengthen the copy!

The most important ad element is the copy. The graphics can help create the tone, set the stage. The mood of the offer.

The big ad agencies sometimes waste a fortune on graphics that do not support the copy. Instead, the graphics fight with, or are in conflict with, the copy, thus reducing power and effectiveness of the ad.

Copyright your ad

When you create winning ads and sales letters, others will copy you. The best, no cost, easy form of protection is to use the proper copyright notice.

Here it is: © Copyright (Year) (Your company name)

Use it on all your ads, brochures, and sales letters. All your printed material. The above is what is known as the common law copyright protection.

You can also register everything you create with the Copyright Office for even more protection if you so choose.

When someone steals your ad copy, sending a "cease and desist" letter usually stops them.

Pricing your product

Here is a really powerful tip that will increase your profits. You may have noticed that the price of my books and tapes ends in seven. There is a good reason for this.

Remarkably, with the same copy and offer for a given product, you can increase sales simply by changing the price to one ending in seven.

Recently, at a seminar at which I spoke, my co-speaker, Gil Good, who was in charge of promotions at the *Wall Street Journal* for many years, discussed that subscription offers ending in seven outpulled all others.

At my last seminar, an attendee, a biblical scholar, pointed out the number seven was often used in the Bible. Remember the phrase, "70 × 7"? Seven may be a number that is truly blessed!

The most effective magazine subscription offer, made many years ago, was by *Life Magazine* for $7.77.

Test price this way. If your current price is $19.95, try $19.97. If you now sell at $69, test $67 or $77; or if your price is $99, try $97, etc.!

Creative plagiarism

I hate copycats. Besides being against the law, it's also immoral. But there is a huge difference when you "model" others' success. Or improve other people's ideas with a superior product and advertising campaign. I call that creative plagiarism. It's completely moral and ethical. Modeling success is the least risky way to success. Why? Because pioneering new products, while sometimes highly profitable, is also very risky.

Ideas are not copyrightable. You can take an idea originated by someone else that has been tested and proven and change it. Often you can improve it. Perhaps, make a more compelling offer at a better price with a strong premium.

How to hire a copywriter

The best copywriter for your product is often you or the entrepreneur founder. No one has the understanding of the product and market or the passion as does the originator. A few examples include Joe Sugarman of JS&A; Bud Weckesser, Green Tree Press; William Bonner, Agora Publishing; and Christian Godefroy, Edi-In-ter, S.A. And these entrepreneurs are not available for hire.

The first thing to decide is whether to write your own copy. Don't treat the decision lightly. However, writing your own copy may be the most profitable way for you to invest your time.

But even if you do your own copywriting, you should be hiring other copywriters as well! Why? To provide fresh new ad appeals that pull and improve on results. And because ads eventually get "tired" and have to be replaced.

Hiring copywriters or ad agencies

Here is how to hire a copywriter or ad agency, while avoiding the biggest mistakes most often made:

1. Hire the best writer you can afford. The best copywriters are freelancers 99% of the time. The top ones tend to not stay with ad agencies very long.
2. When retaining an ad agency, be sure you know which specific writer will be doing your copy. Don't be over influenced by a big name firm. A relatively untested copywriter may be assigned to your work.
3. Ask for samples of the writer's "controls." (A "control" is a sales letter or ad that is the most profitable sales piece a company uses to sell a given product.)

4. Ask for references. Check out the references provided by the copywriter. Call and verify that the writer actually created the "control." Unfortunately, some copywriters who may have contributed a small part of a marketing project or in some cases, contributed nothing, claim full credit.
5. Ask the copywriter's clients how easy or difficult the writer is to work with. Are deadlines met? Any problems of which you should be aware?
6. Audience compatibility. Find writers who have written other successful offers to your target audience. It's crucially important for the writer to understand the mindset of your market.
7. Make sure the writer has done the control in the **medium** you plan to use, i.e., space ad, sales letter, card deck, TV, radio. For example, most copywriters are far more effective in crafting sales letters than space ads.
8. Make sure the copywriter is prepared to do the necessary homework. Research can take from 33% to 75% of the time involved in the marketing project. You want a writer who studies the product, as well as the current and past ads that have worked and that haven't worked.

If the writer says he/she doesn't need to study your product, do any homework, etc., run, don't walk away! Success is no accident. You must dig in and work at writing copy. If you or the copywriter don't, time and money will be wasted on an unsuccessful campaign.

What will be the fee for a good copywriter?

Of course, fees vary. For direct marketing champions, up front fees are usually from $4,500 to $20,000 for a space ad or sales letter. By and large, you get what you pay for. The best writers usually charge a royalty in addition. 2 1/2 cents to 5 cents per letter mailed or 5% of sales are typical. I charge $15,000 plus 5% of sales. A low-cost copywriter can be very expensive! While fees seem high for the best, they can often be your best investment as you will save enormous quantities of the biggest asset of all—time!

What can you expect in results?

No copywriter in the world is successful every time out. The very best copywriters will write a successful ad for a new, viable product perhaps 20% to 40% of the time. If the task is to improve a winning product offer, the success can be 50% and more. So your odds of success with the help of a real pro can be as low as one-in-five to one-in-two.

Today's Best No Cost Low Cost Marketing Strategies

Here is a strategy that sells products like crazy and doesn't cost a dime.

I call it **direct marketing public relations**, DMPR. It's the best no cost, no risk way to sell any product or service. This is where a magazine, newspaper, TV show, or radio program features your product in the form of a **story**.

If the wire services, such as Associated Press, pick up the story, sales can be phenomenal. You can be featured in hundreds of newspapers overnight. Radio and TV can also help move a lot of product. But print media pickup is usually best because it lasts longer than any other form.

Sometimes you can luck out. A story can run without any action on your part. But it's far more likely to occur if you make it happen. How? By providing one of three things. And sometimes all three.

1. News release
2. Camera-ready article
3. Sample of your product

Send the news release to magazines, newsletters, newspapers, and radio and TV stations that are the most likely to be interested in your product.

When a story is run that also includes, as a public service, information about price and **how** and **where** to obtain your product, you can generate substantial sales.

Recently, a self-published book called HOW TO MAKE YOUR PAYCHECK LAST was featured in a large circulation magazine. The magazine editor fell in love with the book.

According to Jerry Buchanan, who writes the TOWERS Club Newsletter, the author received $3,650,000 in cash orders within 60 days of when the article appeared!

Using the DMPR technique, I've had hundreds of major news stories written or picked up with various products I've marketed. These include fudge in 77 flavors, cosmetics, newsletters, and exercise equipment. And, of course, the 53 books I've authored or published.

I'm currently helping a client with a product using DMPR. This product is perfect for a major publicity campaign. Why? It's particularly newsworthy.

What is the product? A charger which makes any battery last for life! It's really an important breakthrough. Just imagine the potential for news stories!

The secret of getting media to run your story is making the introduction of a new product . . .

A major event

Here is what to do. Prepare a news release. Write it yourself. Or hire a journalist who will prepare it for you if you prefer.

If you like the writing style of any reports in your local paper, contact them first. This can be a good place to find the needed skills. And usually reporters like earning extra cash.

Another option is, once completed, have the story set in type. Then if the editor to whom you submit the article likes the story, all the publication has to do is run it exactly as submitted! It's amazing how many periodicals will run a well written camera-ready story as submitted. It's easy for them. They don't have to do anything.

When stories or reviews are run based on your news release or camera-ready story, request permission to reprint.

On the next page is an example of a story which ran in the Santa Rosa Sun Newspaper. The reviewer wrote a review about my book, HOW TO PUBLISH A BOOK AND SELL A MILLION COPIES. This review is currently being used exactly as written in tens of thousands of successful "tear sheet" mailings for the book and has helped to greatly increase sales!

About

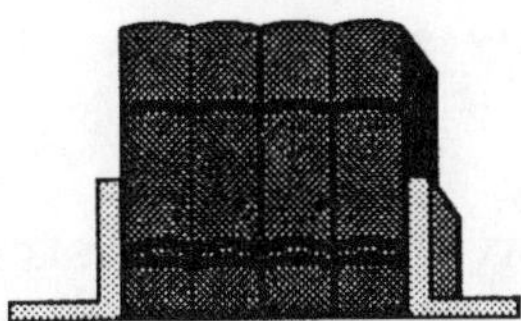

Book Review

How To Publish a Book and Sell a Million Copies

by Bill English
Sun Newspapers

With the advent of desktop publishing almost anyone can get their book in print today. Computer technology has slashed the price of creating product and opened new avenues for small presses. But getting the book printed is only half the battle. In America censorship still exists in the form of distribution. You may have the greatest book in the world to offer—but if the public never sees it they can't buy it.

In HOW TO PUBLISH A BOOK AND SELL A MILLION COPIES, noted author and lecturer Ted Nicholas reveals how to market your book and get it out to a vast readership. Nicholas clearly demonstrates that there are huge profits to be made from "how to" books, special reports, videos, or audio tapes. Nicholas himself is a college dropout who has made millions of dollars from such famous titles as HOW TO FORM YOUR OWN CORPORATION WITHOUT A LAWYER FOR UNDER $75. If you read newspapers or magazines you've seen his ads everywhere.

But do they work?

According to Nicholas, his P.O. Box is crammed with checks.

And that sure beats a mailbox full of rejection slips from the major New York publishing houses.

The key to Mr. Nicholas' success is to take complete control of your product and its distribution. If you have a good idea then you should have the guts and determination to back it with your own time and money.

HOW TO PUBLISH A BOOK AND SELL A MILLION COPIES tells you exactly what to do so you won't fail or spin your wheels. You learn how to pick where to advertise. You learn how to get a cut rate; what pages of a magazine give the best results. Even how to get free advertising.

Nicholas reveals the truth behind the publishing myth. There is no mystery to the book business. Books are a great product because they are relatively cheap to manufacture and distribute and have a fantastic markup. It is not uncommon for a book to sell for ten times the cost of production. And each book is unique. No one else has exactly what you are selling.

Books are bucks!

But this is just the start of the benefits to self-publishing. As the publisher of your own book you are more apt to go out and push it. Many major publishers have too many titles and let many good books slip between the cracks. But when the author is in control of publicity and distribution this is not likely to happen.

Nicholas also points out that once you self-publish and have had some success, New York may well become interested in your work. This happened to Mr. Nicholas—but he chose to remain independent; he was simply making too much money to turn over any of his rights. After all, he had done the work and deserved the profits.

He was in control.

HOW TO PUBLISH A BOOK AND SELL A MILLION COPIES gives you extremely detailed instructions on what types of ads to run and where to run them. Nicholas advises you to start small and work your way up. The book comes with an audio and one of the most fascinating things about it is the development of the ad copy for HOW TO FORM YOUR OWN CORPORATION WITHOUT A LAWYER FOR UNDER $75. Nicholas began with a tiny ad in the Wall Street Journal that soon blossomed to a full page. Never satisfied, he refined his copy until he had a selling tool that was almost impossible to resist.

But you don't have to waste the time he spent on trial and error. Nicholas gives you all the secrets in the cost of the package.

Ted Nicholas is the kind of guy who is going to survive in the America of the future. He doesn't sit on his hands and wait for a corporation to feed him a check. He goes out in the world and sells a product of his own creation. He makes money from his own ideas. He pays mega taxes and helps to fuel the economy. This country needs more guys like Mr. Nicholas. Big Brother and Uncle Sam can no longer be counted on to take care of us. One thing is for sure—Ted Nicholas isn't losing any sleep over the health of Social Security.

He won't be needing it.

HOW TO PUBLISH A BOOK AND SELL A MILLION COPIES by Ted Nicholas $19.97. Call 813-596-4966 to order.

Offer a special report

Another effective marketing strategy is to prepare a special report. Make sure it provides useful and valuable information to prospects for your products or seminars. It should be closely related to your business or profession.

For example: Let's say you run a plumbing business. Your report could be something like this:

"How To Do Your Own Minor Plumbing Repairs . . . Save $50 or More Per Service Call."

Your report would show the layman how to do basic things like repairing leaky faucets or water closets. Make it easy to use by providing step-by-step instructions.

Or suppose you own a restaurant. You could create a special report that everyone wants:

"How to Get Delicious Low-Fat, Low-Cal Meals in Any Restaurant

Another example. Suppose you sell computer products. Offer a special report on *"How to Clean Computers,"* which, if not put into effect, ultimately leads to 94% of computer failures.

Now, in these examples, it would be relatively easy to get the news media interested in writing a story about you. Clearly, you really are providing useful information. You could sell these reports at low cost, in the $5 to $20 range. But it's more effective to give them away **free**.

It's not necessary to promote your company directly in the report. Just the fact your company is mentioned as the distributor of the report is enough due to the good will that is created. Who do you think the person will call when they need a service in your field?

Sample News Release

new book information

FOR IMMEDIATE RELEASE CONTACT: Sandi Turja 813-596-4966

PUBLISH YOUR OWN BOOK AND MAKE A FORTUNE

Bestselling author reveals insider secrets and shortcuts to self-publishing success

For many would-be authors, the most difficult part of getting published is not the actual writing of a book. It's finding an agent or publisher who will do the work justice and recompense the author fairly.

According to prolific author and seasoned self-publisher Ted Nicholas, "The conventional publishing route is simply not open to the majority of writers, especially new ones. It is becoming more and more difficult to even get an editor interested enough to look at your manuscript, much less see the day when it rolls off the presses."

Nicholas knows a better road to publishing fame and fortune, revealed in his new guide, HOW TO PUBLISH A BOOK & SELL A MILLION COPIES (Enterprise • Dearborn, $19.95). The surprising truth is that authors can benefit more from self-publishing. Once they learn the ropes, they can put in the time and hard work to promote their product that publishing companies just aren't prepared to devote to an unknown author. Even better, once their work starts selling, authors can look forward to reaping all the profits.

Those ready to cash in on their labors of love need only consult Nicholas' book. Filled with the kind of inside information and tips that can make the difference between a best seller and a flop. HOW TO PUBLISH A BOOK & SELL A MILLION COPIES gives readers the tools and techniques to:

- Earn $1,000 a day from their publishing activities
- Develop their work — be it a book, newsletter, special report, video, audio tape or software
- Get it printed or produced at the best price
- Get free publicity
- Market and direct mail their product

An extensive appendix of resources and contacts the author has personally cultivated through the years will help readers get the additional assistance they need — worth the price of the book alone!

Nicholas himself launched Enterprise Publishing Company in 1972 with his first self-published title, HOW TO FORM YOUR OWN CORPORATION WITHOUT A LAWYER FOR UNDER $75. That book has since sold nearly one million copies, and Nicholas has been approached by just about every major publisher to buy its rights.

Nicholas obviously knows what works and how to sell it and HOW TO PUBLISH A BOOK & SELL A MILLION COPIES is the summation of his hard-won publishing smarts. From filling orders to reducing risks to building a self-publishing venture into a profitable publishing business, readers can learn first-hand from this master marketer how to publish their own works—and profit handsomely from them.

Ted Nicholas, a successful author and independent publisher, has written 14 books on business and finance since his writing career began in 1972. Total sales of his books exceed 2.5 million copies.

HOW TO PUBLISH A BOOK & SELL A MILLION COPIES ($19.95 plus $4 S&H, 217 pages, 8½ x 11, soft cover, ISBN: 0-79310-620-6) is available at local bookstores or by mail order. The book can be ordered by calling Nicholas Direct, Inc. at 813-596-4966 or writing 19918 Gulf Blvd. #7, Indian Shores, FL 34635.

Information products boost sales

We're in the middle of the information age. Regardless of what you sell, if you don't use information products to enhance the value of products and services you market as well as your own image to your customer, you are missing a great opportunity. Create a good information product and watch your sales skyrocket!

Suppose you sell information products

As a publisher of books, newsletters, special reports, tapes, software, and other information products, you are already in a unique position. Reviews and stories about your products can be gotten just by sending a "review" copy to a good list.

However, very few publishers, in my view, take full advantage of their opportunities. Why? For several reasons:

1. Failure to make your product newsworthy. Along with the product, include a powerful hard hitting, exciting story about why your product is news. Most product stories are dull, poorly written, and uninspiring. They are boring. It's no wonder publishers often struggle to get media attention.
2. The product title or name is weak. The name or title to any product must be as good as a headline. Make sure your name is strong enough to **sell** the products all by itself! Examine your product titles. Be honest. Are they powerful enough to do the job by themselves? If not, there is only one solution. Change the title!

Continuously review and change book titles to improve their strength and selling power. Here are two examples of how I retitled books:

1. Original title: HOW TO GET OUT IF YOU ARE IN OVER YOUR HEAD

   New title: HOW TO GET OUT OF DEBT

People in bookstores at first thought the original books was about swimming, not debt management!

The new title was responsible for making the book, which failed at first, into a winner. (Originally, I sold three copies, as I recall, to my mother-in-law and two friends, and that was about it.) With the new title, I sold over 25,000 copies!

2. Original title: MANAGEMENT FOR ENTREPRENEURS

   New title: SECRETS OF ENTREPRENEURIAL LEADERSHIP

The new title has improved sales by 500%!

Lessons learned? **Do not** be cute or oblique with a product title.

Today's best advertising strategy

The best low-risk advertising method today is through the use of small display ads. And it's ideal for those on limited budgets. It's what many refer to as two-step selling. The strategy is in two steps:

1. **Capture an inquiry.** The first step is to sell the concept of the customer contacting you by phone, fax, or mail. Your goal is to capture the name and address and/or phone number. Then convert the person who has raised their hand into a buyer for your product. How?
2. **Send a sales letter** that sells the dickens out of your product! Keep sending follow-up letters until it is no longer profitable. How long should the letters be? The simple answer is long enough to tell the entire sales story. Many people ask me if long sales letters pull. The fact is a two-page letter outsells a one-page letter. A four-page letter outsells a two-page letter. An eight-page letter outsells a four-page letter. I've written 16 page letters that sell like crazy. Where it will stop, I don't know.

Here is the point. If someone is a serious prospect for your product, they want to know everything about it. If they are not interested, they won't even read three paragraphs! But here is the secret. You just don't write for length. Every word of copy must be **relevant**.

Use small display ads

Notice I recommend small display ads, **not** classified ads. In fact, most marketers should forget classified ads. You can lose a fortune fast buying classified ad space in hundreds of newspapers. Why? Because classified sections do not apply to most products and services.

Your prospects do not read classified ads often enough to give you a flow of prospects.

Unless your product is related to a home, car, employment, or business opportunity, do not invest in classified ads.

The biggest nonproductive use of money in all advertising is waste circulation. Powerful small display ads best deal with the waste circulation problem and also will:

1. Target that relatively small percentage of people in a given publication who are genuine prospects for your product.
2. Provide a steady flow of new prospects.
3. Build what will become the most valuable asset in your business—your mailing list of buyers and prospects.
4. Test headlines! Another great benefit of running small display ads at costs in the range of $100 to $500.

Take a look at some examples of fractional page ads on the next page which currently run and pull a continual flow of leads.

Fractional Display Ads

Instant Incorporation While-You-Wait

Often it's urgent to form a corporation immediately. Reasons include closing a deal, tax savings or to limit personal liability. Now, all you need do is pick up the phone and have your credit card ready. No lawyer necessary. You can be incorporated—including name reservation—while you hold the line! Patented system makes it easy for you. Your cost? Only $45 (plus filing fees, usually $74).

Your incorporation will be handled individually, with care. Nationally known corporate service organization is established for over 15 years. We've set up over 70,000 corporations and incorporate in any state, specializing in the well-known Delaware corporation. Call toll-free now: **1-800-228-2677.**

IN 8 MINUTES

You Can Have Your Own Corporation

You can now incorporate, including name reservation, instantly by telephone while you hold the line. Think of it. In 8 minutes or less you'll be the owner of a corporation, without red tape, large legal fees, or hassle. Incorporation can often take weeks through law firms at costs from $500 to $2,500 or more, through us your total costs are as low as $45 (not a misprint) plus filing fees — usually $74.

The Company Corporation (TCC) has been established since 1972, and during the last 20 years has set up over 90,000 corporations TCC is the number on organization of its kind and nationally know for its ability to establish corporations in any state, including the well-known corporate have — Delaware.

Just decide on a corporate name, have your credit card ready, and call:

1-800-542-2677 ext. W1653
THE COMPANY CORPORATION
Three Christina Centre, Dept. W1653
201 N. Walnut St.
Wilmington, DE 19801

You A Millionaire Writer?

Earn at least $1,000 a day. Ted Nicholas, author and self-publisher of 14 best-selling books of his own and 53 others, reveals all his inside secrets of success at his forthcoming Tampa seminar. Call now for free details without obligation.
813-596-4966

"Best Selling Author Reveals Secrets Of Making $1,000 A Day Publishing Books!"

Publish books, special reports, videos, audios, software, or newsletters. Cash-in on selling information in the hottest business opportunity in today's booming information age.

Turn your love of writing or publishing into your own profitable and enjoyable business. We can provide everything you need to start and can even show you how to get financing. For free information, call us at **1-813-596-4966** (9-5 M-F EST), **1-800-648-3733** (24 hours a day) or fax to **1-813-596-6900**. Or write Ted Nicholas, Dept. , 19918 Gulf Blvd. #7, Indian Shores, FL 34635.

Important tips

Notice the small display ads employ telephone, mail and telephone, and fax response options. Claude Hopkins, an excellent marketer, found that, even 50 years ago, the best way to obtain the highest level of response is by offering one option only!

Telephone!

Marketing guru, Gary Halbert, notes that by recently adding an 800 number for inquiries, his telephone response increased inquiries by 300%!

For most offers, the telephone-only response with an 800 number will draw the most responses.

On recent ads we're using the telephone-only option, but, of course, each offer to each market audience needs to be tested as there can be differences.

Catalogs build sales without risk

Another under-used method of boosting sales without advertising cost is by having your product included in catalogs.

Of course, you can easily generate sales for your product in your own catalogs. Here I'm referring to other people's catalogs.

If you have a product proven to be a winner in space ads, direct mail, or TV, results can be spectacular. Sales can be truly massive. But even if you don't advertise heavily at present, catalogs can still be a good source of sales for you.

If you do advertise extensively now, add the words "as seen on TV" or "nationally advertised." Or "as advertised in The Wall Street Journal, Forbes, Playboy," etc.

What discounts do you offer the catalogs? 50% to 65% is common.

There are 3,700 significant catalog companies in America. There are about 250 great ones. These include: Sharper Image, Spiegels, Tweed, and Avon. And they are all looking for new products to sell.

What you do is this. Put together a package containing a sample of your: **Product, Flyer, News Release,** and **Photograph**.

Send this package to a target list of catalog producers.

Some will want you to drop ship. Others want to take the product into inventory.

My products have profitably and steadily sold for years through other people's catalogs. Marketing consultant Dan Kennedy reports that one of his clients produced $39,000 in sales during the first four weeks in Playboy's catalog. Over the next year, from the single catalog, over $500,000 in catalog sales were generated.

Once you appear in one major catalog, many others will be after your product!

You can get a complete lists of catalogs by doing some research and by getting on mail lists. You can also get leads from major mail houses, mailers who are listed in SRDS (Standard Rate & Data Service, 1-708-574-6000). Oxbridge Communications Inc. publishes an annual called The National Directory of Catalogs. Their number is 1-212-741-0231.

Another way to contact catalog producers is through an agent. Their fee is usually about 10% of sales. One well-known agent who has a good reputation is Jess F. Clarke, Jr. with Catalog Solutions at 1-203-454-1919.

How to Get Marketing Rights to a Hot Product for as Little as $250

The first step to financial success is a saleable product. Before you can proceed to build any income you must first have a **product** to sell.

There are two ways to get a product.

1. Develop it from scratch, or
2. Acquire the rights to sell a product.

In this chapter I'm going to show you how to acquire the direct marketing rights to hot products. You'll be given a workable strategy I've developed that consistently works for me as well as my clients.

But first let's zero in on the first decision every entrepreneur needs to make . . .

How to get the product

Produce a product from scratch? Or acquire a product that has already proven its sales appeal?

Let's face it. It's a lot of fun developing a brand new product. Most people prefer the process, including me. It can be a terrific way to achieve success. But it also can be one of the most risky, time consuming, and costly endeavors known.

Do you know what the success percentage of new product launches is by the best marketing minds in America? Companies like Proctor and Gamble, 3M, and Microsoft? Less than 25%!

What choice do most entrepreneurs make? They develop products from scratch. And often without a well-defined market.

Then they ask themselves, "How can I sell it?" This approach ends in disaster at least 75% of the time.

Is there a better approach which lowers the risks and increases the chance of success? Yes! And done correctly, it's practically foolproof. But few people in the world know how it's done.

First, let's dispel some conditioning to which we've all been exposed.

Remember your teachers, professors, and books all proclaiming that the way to a fortune is to find a need and fill it?

More people go bankrupt trying to fill needs than any way I know.

The way to a fortune in business is to find a **want** and fill it. It's simple. Just find out what people want and give it to them. This is the main role of an effective marketer.

If you market a product that is already selling, you are benefiting from someone else's costly market research. Customers have demonstrated they want it through paid orders.

That's why the most direct way to business success is to obtain the rights to sell a proven product.

Define goals that assure success

1. Find an undermarketed product or product category.
2. Acquire the rights to the product or an improved version of the product.
3. Sell it using a superior marketing plan.

Notice I said superior marketing plan. Your goal should never be to copy or plagiarize someone else's work. It's also illegal to do so. But ideas are not copyrightable. What you want to do is rise above the marketing plan now being employed. Sometimes you can also improve the product too.

But how are you going to make this happen? Isn't it difficult to find a product and successfully negotiate the rights to sell it?

Most people think it's tough. But in a moment, I'm going to reveal a strategy to you that is remarkably easy! But first we must . . .

Find a hot product

Where? The best places are:

1. **Catalogs:** Get on as many catalog mailing lists as you can and study the products being offered. There are over 3,700 catalogs! Products would not be repeated unless there was a proven market.
2. **Mail offers:** Products sold through the mail on a repeat basis are excellent lead sources for products.
3. Products sold in **space ads:** When you see the same product repeated over and over in a space ad, you know it's a winner.
4. **Best seller lists:** Go to a good library. Look up the Sunday *New York Times* non-fiction best seller lists for the last two years. You'll not only find books but many other ideas for non-book products. What best seller lists tell you is what people want.

   Book stores look upon books more like "fashion statements" with as little as a three-month life. Often you can pick up hot products no longer featured which a huge number of people still want!
5. **Book stores:** Hang out in a good book store. Make friends with the owner/manager. Ask about what subjects people are particularly interested in. This can be excellent market research, regardless of what business you are in now. You really get "hands on" insights as to what consumers are asking for. If you listen with a "marketer's ear," you'll be able to spot hot categories. Obviously, if books are the product which most interests you, find the new winners.
6. **Active listening:** Listen carefully to what people are griping about. The solution can often fill pent-up want and demand for a product. For years, I listened to entrepreneurs gripe about getting "ripped off" by lawyers for routine work, forms, etc. So I created a multi-million dollar publishing company based largely on do-it-yourself legal books. It all began with HOW TO FORM YOUR OWN CORPORATION WITHOUT A LAWYER FOR UNDER $75,

a book which is still selling thousands of copies each month.

7. **Newspapers and magazines:** Good places to spot trends (which are really wants) include *Reader's Digest, Wall Street Journal, People, Washington Post, New York Times,* and *USA Today*. One of my favorites is *The International Herald Tribune*.

A word of warning. Don't get so busy you forget to read for an hour a day minimum. Many marketers stop devoting the necessary reading time.

Products to look for

What you should be looking for are products that fill **perennial wants** and will sell year after year forever. I don't like fad products. They are very risky and sales can stop overnight. This can put you into a financial bind or even cause you to go under fast.

If you are looking at books as a product, concentrate on "how to" books. Why? They sell!

Whether or not you sell information products now, perhaps you should, regardless of your current business. Reasons are many. They include:

- Books and other information products make appealing **premiums** or **free bonuses**, which can really enhance sales of any product.
- Books and other "paper and ink" products, like special reports, have a **high margin of profit**. Customers are not buying the paper and ink, tape, or diskette, but the information.
- We are in the middle of the booming information age.

When you supply valuable information, you add value to any product or service you sell.

Some of today's hottest product categories and markets include:

- Income Opportunities
- Fitness
- Diet
- Nutrition
- Environment
- Cosmetics
- Senior Citizens
- Software
- Self-defense
- Family Cost Cutting Programs

How to negotiate direct marketing rights

Now I'll reveal exactly how to acquire the rights to virtually any product.

For purposes of this example, the product will be a book. However, the same exact principles apply to all products.

The approach is a **win/win** situation for all concerned. The **author-publisher** (creator-producer) and the biggest beneficiary of all—the **consumer**.

Your negotiating goal is twofold:

A. Buy the product at favorable cost.
B. Get as much exclusivity as possible.

However, exclusivity is not as important as you might think. Reason? The successful marketing plan and copy which you create, and to which you own the copyright to, is the most important asset you have in selling any product.

Let's assume you've found a product you'd like to acquire the rights to and sell. The next step is to find the manufacturer or owner of the product. That's usually quite simple. It's printed on the product itself or on the sales literature. Now you are ready to telephone the product owner.

When you call you need to establish rapport. Then you create a "yes momentum." Once the person gets used to saying yes to you, it's much easier to conclude a successful negotiation.

Here is an example of a typical conversation between you and a mythical publisher named Random Horse:

You: "Hello. Random Horse (R.H.). This is Bob Smith calling. I'd like to speak with the person who handles rights for your non-fiction business books."

RH: "That's Dave Jones. I'll connect you."

You: "Hi Dave. This is Bob Smith. I understand you handle rights negotiation to non-fiction business books, isn't that true?"

RH: "Yes."

You: "I may be interested in direct marketing rights for one of your titles, KILL ALL THE LAWYERS, by Frank Shakespeare. You do publish that book, don't you, Dave?"

RH: "Yes. We sure do!"

You: "Great! Well I'm a direct marketer. We sell throughout the U.S. through mail order and space ads. Our methods can move a tremendous amount of product. I'm sure you would like to dramatically increase sales of that book, wouldn't you Dave?"

RH: "Yes, I'd love to do that."

You: "Well, of course. I can't make any promises. But here is how we operate. We'll do a marketing test entirely at our expense. If it's successful, we'll then go forward on a national campaign. And here is the best part for you, Dave.

We'll generate sales beyond what is now being done. For each sale by direct response, studies show two people go into a bookstore (or retail store) to get the product. You just keep doing what you're doing and our efforts will enhance your sales. Doesn't that sound good to you, Dave?"

RH: "Yes. It sure does! But how would the deal work?"

You: "We'd like exclusive direct mail rights. We will buy the book in a similar way as a book club. Basically at manufacturing cost, plus a royalty* on all income we receive to compensate the author and/or publisher."

(*Usually this figure is from 5% to 15% of revenue. If the book is used as a premium or bonus, a fixed amount, such as $1 up to $5 is not unusual.)

"If the test is successful, we then will continue buying in much bigger quantities or print our own edition of the book as called for in the agreement I'll send you. Dave, are you with me so far?"

RH: "Yes. I see now what you have in mind. Sounds like we have everything to gain, nothing to lose.

You: "If the book moves in a big way, your royalties will be very substantial indeed!"

RH: "Can you give me an estimate of sales?"

You: "I could, but it would really be guesswork at this stage. After the marketing test, and at first we'll buy just enough books for the test, I'll be in a much better position to give you some projections. I can tell you this. Some of our books sell in the hundreds of thousands of copies."

RH: "There may be one problem. We've got two companies, ABC Corp. and XYZ Corp., who do a little bit of direct marketing of KILL ALL THE LAWYERS through their catalogs. Does that hurt what we could do together?"

You: "Absolutely not. I'll send you our agreement for your review. We'll exclude the two dealers who are now doing some marketing. Does that solve the problem?"

RH: "Yes, it sure does!"

Rights Agreement

An Agreement made this ______ day of ___________ 1993 between _________________,(the "Licensee") and ___________________, ("the Licensor") in respect of a literary work entitled ____________________________, (the "Work").

1. Licensee is granted exclusive direct marketing rights and coupon advertising rights throughout the world (Licensee is also granted worldwide publishing rights for translations outside the United States.); and Licensee is further granted non-exclusive rights to offer the Work for sale through any bookstore, catalogs, or any other means. Any rights not specifically granted hereunder shall remain with the Licensor.
2. As the purchase price for the rights granted, Licensee agrees to pay Licensor the sum of ________, which shall be non-refundable, and shall be deemed an advance against any amounts otherwise due Licensor hereunder. Said payment shall be payable within _____ days following the date of this Agreement.
3. Licensee shall pay to Licensor a royalty amounting to the _____ of the sales revenue on every copy sold by Licensee. No royalty shall be due for books which are returned to the Licensee by the purchaser. On foreign rights sold by Licensee, _____ percent of all such revenues shall be paid to Licensor.
4. Any amounts payable to Licensor under Paragraph 3 shall be payable within ___ days following _________ and _________ in each year with respect to the 6 month period preceding each of said dates. Licensee agrees that Licensor shall have the right, on 48 hours notice, to examine the Licensee's accounting books and records which relate to the Work.
5. Licensor shall deliver ____ copies of the Work to Licensee and charge Licensee $______ per copy, which represents Licensor's manufacturing costs. Licensee may elect to have further copies of the Work manufactured by another manufacturer of its own choice. Licensee may use Licensor's plates, negatives, and artwork for the purpose of manufacturing its edition of the Work and Licensor shall, without charge to Licensee and if available to Licensor without charge, deliver all plates, negatives, artwork, and other similar materials necessary or useful for the manufacture of the Work.
6. If Licensee shall determine to remainder any portion of its edition, it shall first notify the Licensor of such intention and give Licensor written notice of any offer which would be acceptable to Licensee. If Licensee remainders its edition of the Work, all rights granted under this Agreement to Licensee shall revert to Licensor.
7. If sales of the Work, under this Agreement, shall amount to less than 1,000 copies for any calendar year, either party shall have the right to terminate this Agreement on 30 days written notice to the other party.
8. The Licensor warrants and represents that it legally controls all the rights to the Work herein granted and has full right and power to make this Agreement; that the Work is not a violation of any copyright, proprietary, or personal right; that Licensor has not in any manner granted any of the rights herein granted to the Licensee or any rights adverse to or inconsistent therewith; that there are no rights outstanding which would diminish, encumber, or impair the full enjoyment or exercise of the rights herein granted the Licensee; and that no part of the Work is libelous, obscene, or unlawful, or violates any rights of privacy.
9. The Licensor agrees to defend, hold harmless and indemnify the Licensee against any claim, demand, suit, action, proceeding, recovery, or expense of any nature whatsoever, including costs and attorney fees, arising from any claim of infringement of copyright or other proprietary right, libel, obscenity, unlawfulness, invasion of privacy, or based upon or arising out of any matter or thing contained in the Work or any breach of the warrantees or represented herein contained.
10. Any dispute between the parties to this Agreement which involves interpretations of the terms of this Agreement shall be submitted to arbitration under the rules of the American Arbitration Association, and the findings of the Arbitrator shall be binding on all parties. Any other dispute concerning fulfillment of this Agreement shall be litigated in a court of competent jurisdiction. Legal interpretation of this Agreement shall be governed by the laws of the State of Delaware.

IN WITNESS WHEREOF, the parties hereto have caused this Agreement to be executed by their respective duly constituted officers, as of the day and year first written above.

BY: ____

BY: ____

New Growth Financial
"The Distressed Property Experts"
(510) 837-2106 Fax (510) 743-0926

Dear Ted:

...In the past year, your ideas and writings have influenced and inspired me many times and I want you to know of a recent achievement — thanks to you.

I certainly got my money's worth at your seminar — just one technique which you generously gave me in your seminar will change my life. Briefly, here's the story of how you saved me two years of work.

For the past two years, I've been researching and writing a manual on negotiation. As most authors will testify, writing a book is a major undertaking in terms of time and discipline. That book is finished, but I need a sequel... back end/follow-up sale.

With your easily learned technique of buying "rights", I've managed in a few hours on the telephone to accomplish what otherwise would have taken another two years. I telephoned Prentice Hall, used your techniques, and saved myself thousands of hours of hard work. The cost savings in time alone will pay for your seminar 100 times or more.

Your instructions have been sincere, learnable, down to earth and easy to follow. Thank you.

Sincerely,

Ted Thomas

Ted Thomas
Vice President

You: "One more thing I'm sure you'll like. To show good faith, we will send you an advance against royalties of $250. But remember, it's only an advance. The important factor is getting the product successfully direct marketed."

RH: "Sounds terrific. I'll look forward to getting the agreement and getting it signed real fast."

(We've been successful many times with advances of $250, even for "best sellers." In no case have we paid more than $1,000.)

This dialogue is typical of such a negotiation. Do you see the full significance? You capture the rights to a proven product without a big investment of time or money.

You can also give the product away as a premium to induce sales of other products.

Use successful products as free bonuses and premiums freely in marketing. Your sales greatly increase when you do so.

One book I negotiated the rights for is called WRITE YOUR OWN WILL—THE LAST WILL AND TESTAMENT by Daniel Sitarz. I saw the book on the best seller list in the *Chicago Tribune* and felt it would make a nice premium. And it has greatly increased sales of the main product.

I've never been turned down by either small or major publishers using the strategy just revealed. Once you learn the technique, you too will be highly successful in getting products. You could even build an entire business with products acquired in this manner.

Remember, while I've used a book as an example, the strategy works with virtually any product. Why? All manufacturers are happy to sell more of their product.

Recent successes

My clients and seminar participants who have learned this strategy are finding great success in getting product. On the previous page is a letter from Ted Thomas. He shares his successful experience negotiating rights to a book with one of the world's largest publishers, prentice Hall.

Also included in this chapter, on page 107, is a sample agreement you or your lawyer can use as a model to set up a rights agreement for virtually any product.

How to Triple the Sales Power of Successful Ads

Once you start using the technique revealed here, you'll multiply sales results from ads or sales letters by 300% or more. How? By going successfully from one print media to another.

You'll be able to convert space ads to direct mail and vice versa. You'll also see how to prepare successful card deck offers and fractional page ads.

Learn this strategy and the net result will be to get far greater sales from your copy. This will give you a huge edge over competition. Reason? Not one in a thousand marketers knows how to do it.

Ideally, start with a "Full Blown" offer

The recommended strategy begins with a sales letter or space ad. Prepare the offer, incorporating as many benefits and features as you can. Compellingly tell the **complete story** about why your product is of value to the prospective buyer. Pile on the benefits.

Use the **first person** in your copy. Speak directly to your reader. Use a warm, friendly "from me to you" style.

Once your copy test becomes a proven winner, you are ready to prepare a "conversion" to another media.

Without a successful "full blown" offer test, the odds are against creating a successful, limited copy test, especially in a card deck.

It's tougher to make a card deck work than a sales letter or space ad. Reason? In a card deck, you have less room to write sales copy to pull in orders. When you do create a card deck offer, the copy included needs to be the very strongest elements from the "long" offer.

Common mistakes to avoid with card decks

For years marketers have seen my successful card deck offers for $70 books and other products and services. These run over and over again. Attempts by other marketers to run successful ads inevitably result in bombs. Why? Here are mistakes I've observed:

1. Entirely new copy is prepared for the card deck, which is untested in any other form or media.
2. The copywriter hired to do the job is not the "big gun" usually retained for the longer sales letters and space ads.

It is assumed that because the card deck media is less costly than others, a relatively inexperienced low cost copywriter or someone on the house staff is asked to do the job.

This is a big mistake! Precisely because you have less room to tell your complete sales story, you need to distill the essence of the very best headline and benefits, which can be crafted for your product. Only a "big gun" can do this. You must use the very best copywriter for limited copy offers.

What about fractional page ads?

Fractional page ads are great for generating leads. Sometimes these ads can be converted into "cash with order" offers. Simply take the winning headline and expand the benefits and features into a "full blown" 7 × 10 space ad and/or multi-page sales letter. Then carefully test it. You'll often be able to come up with winning ads using this method. But remember this. It's a lot easier to get someone to reply to an offer for free information than to order your product.

Making catalogs pay

Less than 10% of catalogs are profitable. One of the biggest reasons is, once again, the failure to test copy before it's used in the catalog format.

The best and safest procedure is to take tested copy used in "solo" offers as the basis for inclusion in the catalog. Then you cut and modify the copy to fit the catalog format.

When you see a catalog from one of my companies, you can be certain that every major product and every word of copy, including price, has been pre-tested in "long copy" space ads or sales letters.

It's about getting more "mileage"

You will multiply by at least three or more times the sales results from successful ads when you learn and apply, what I call, **mileage strategy**.

The key is to do exactly what few marketers ever do. When a successful ad is working in any format: fractional page, full page, or sales letter, adapt it in other proven formats. You will multiply results many fold.

Here is an example of a successful sales letter converted into an even more successful space ad. I'll also show you how this was converted into card deck copy.

(Sales Letter)

What Will You Do When Your Personal Assets Are Seized to Satisfy a Judgment Against Your Corporation?

Your corporate shield is one of your biggest assets. It's especially valuable during any business catastrophe. But this legal "veil" could be pierced.

If this happened, your personal liability protection and all the tax benefits through owning a corporation could be wiped out overnight. This means you could be forced to sell your personal home, automobile, cash, etc. to justify the judgment.

Does this seem far-fetched? It's not. All the I.R.S. has to do is pay you a routine visit. When they examine your corporate records, they may discover deficiencies.

If you haven't kept complete and accurate minutes and other documents, your troubles could start almost immediately. Of course, if you are like most small corporate owners, your main concern is the operation of your business. That's understandable. Keeping records at first just doesn't seem like a good use of your time.

However, under the alter-ego doctrine developed by the courts, the personal assets of a shareholder may be seized for satisfaction of a judgment against the corporation. That occurs only if the affairs of the corporation have not been managed in such a way to keep its identity separate from you.

Formalities must be observed even in the small individually owned and run corporation.

If your corporation's corporate veil were pierced, you also risk losing the important tax benefits to which the law entitles you.

When you figure in this loss along with losing your personal liability protection, it's just not worth the risk.

No business action has become as important as documenting your corporate actions. You've heard it a million times. The importance of getting it in writing! Up until recently it's been a big hassle to do so.

Banks, insurance companies, and various state and federal agencies, besides the I.R.S., all require notarized authorization to grant loans, buy property and equipment, enter into leases and even to sell assets. And other problems can be equally devastating. The reason? The owner didn't document important transactions. The small business owner simply has to "Get It In Writing."

Here are some recent "horror stories" direct from actual court cases:

- Joseph P. obtained a loan from his corporation without the proper loan documents and corporate minutes. As a result, the court required him to pay additional taxes of $27,111.60. He narrowly escaped a penalty of $13,555.80.
- B.W.C. Inc. was forced to pay $106,358.61 of accumulated earnings tax because its corporate minutes were incomplete. They expressed "no specific, definite, or feasible plans" to justify accumulating earnings, according to the court.

Keeping records has always been a bother, and an expensive one, especially for small companies. Most entrepreneurs do not like to spend time keeping records—probably because no one ever became rich by keeping records.

In a small one-person business, it seems downright silly to keep records of stockholder meetings and board of director's meetings . . . keeping minutes . . . taking notes . . . adopting resolutions . . . isn't it all just a waste of time?

Not if you ask any of the thousands of entrepreneurs who have lost fortunes because they failed to keep records.

You should look at corporate record keeping chores this way: It's part of the price you pay to get the tax benefits and personal protection from having a corporation.

A corporation does not exist except on paper, through its charter, by-laws, stock certificates, resolutions, etc.

Anything you do as an officer or director has to be duly authorized and evidenced by a resolution of the stockholders or the board, or by both in some cases.

It makes no difference if there is only one stockholder or one million stockholders. The rules are basically the same.

You can hire a lawyer, like big companies do, and pay $100 or more just to prepare one form.

But you may need, at minimum, a dozen or more documents to keep your corporation alive and functioning for just one year.

This type of work is the bread and butter for many corporation lawyers. Most of the work can be done by their secretaries, yet they will charge you enormous sums because they know how important the forms are to you and your business.

Lawyers know that the I.R.S. will insist that you have the corporate records to prove that you are entitled to all the tax breaks from having a corporation.

There is now a way for you to solve your corporate record keeping problems—without a lawyer, without paying big fees, and without spending a lot of time.

THE COMPLETE BOOK OF CORPORATE FORMS was prepared by Ted Nicholas.

Nicholas is the author of the best-seller, HOW TO FORM YOUR OWN CORPORATION WITHOUT A LAWYER FOR UNDER $75. This book has become the largest single source of new corporations in America. It has revolutionized the business of forming new corporations by making the process simple, easy, and inexpensive.

But forming a corporation is only the first step toward building the "ultimate tax shelter."

Through carelessness or neglect, many people are denied their rightful benefits from their own corporation.

Ted Nicholas saw that many, many business owners need more help after they incorporate. They didn't know how to turn their corporation into the ultimate tax shelter.

And so, he prepared THE COMPLETE BOOK OF CORPORATE FORMS. Virtually all the forms you will ever need are all ready for you. Everything is simplified. Either you or your secretary can complete any form in minutes. All you do is fill in a few blanks and insert the completed forms in your record book.

When you own this new book, you are granted permission to reproduce every form.

If you are behind on keeping good corporate records, now you can catch up in no time. Just complete a few blanks for the things you've already done in the company. It's legal and it works.

Best of all, the price is less than you would pay a lawyer for one hour of counseling.

Here is just a sampling of what you'll receive:

- Minutes of Stockholder Meetings
- Minutes of Director's Meetings
- Minutes of Special Meetings
  (Any of the minutes can be used whether you are the only stockholder or director, or there are other shareholders.)
- Amendments to Articles of Incorporation
- Amendments to By-Laws
- Change in membership of the Board

You will also receive all the stockholder and directors resolutions you will need to take any major business action, including:

- Negotiation of contractors
- Authorizing of loans to corporation
- Approval of corporate loans to you
- Designation of purchasing agent
  (Some suppliers may want to know who is authorized to buy from them.)
- Setting your salary
- Authorizing your expense account
- Mergers
- Sale of corporate assets
- Dissolution
- Bankruptcy
- Declaring dividends
- Appointment of attorneys or accountant

Plus, you'll receive the forms needed to authorize any of these tax-saving fringe benefits:

- Pension or profit-sharing plans
- Medical and dental reimbursement plans
- Sick pay plans

- Split-dollar life insurance
- Educational loan program
- Stock options
- Group life insurance
- Financial counseling plan
- Group legal services
- Christmas bonus, special bonuses

Just one of the above forms can save you hundreds of dollars in legal fees . . .

This entire $8^{1}/_{2} \times 11$, loose leaf collection of simplified forms (over 150 pages of forms), clear instructions for their use, as well as samples of completed forms, sells for only $69.95 plus $4 for UPS shipping and handling. It comes in a luxurious gold embossed binder as well.

As with all Enterprise Publishing products, it sells under an iron-clad 30-day money-back guarantee.

After you examine the collection, if for any reason you are not pleased, return it for a prompt and courteous refund. Take a moment to place your order now, and immediately begin saving time and money.

Complete the enclosed free trial request and mail for rapid delivery.

Sincerely,

Nicholas Peterson

Nicholas Peterson
President

P.S. Your corporation shield is a valuable asset. Help protect yourself for a nominal tax deductible cost.

(Space Ad)

What Will You Do When Your Personal Assets Are Seized to Satisfy A Judgment Against Your Corporation?

All your many tax benefits of owning a corporation could be wiped out overnight. How? The I.R.S. could visit you and claim you have not kept proper corporate minutes. You could lose the very tax benefits to which the law entitles you.

Banks, insurance companies, and various state and federal agencies, besides the I.R.S., all require notarized authorizations to grant loans, buy property and equipment, enter into leases and even to sell assets. And other problems can be equally devastating. The reason? The owner didn't document important transactions. The small business owner simply has to "Get It In Writing."

Here are some recent "horror stories" direct from actual court cases.

Joseph P. obtained a loan from his corporation without the proper loan documents and corporate minutes. As a result, the court required him to pay additional taxes of $27,111.60. He narrowly escaped a penalty of $13,555.80.

B.W.C., Inc. was forced to pay $106,358.61 of accumulated earnings tax because its corporate minutes were incomplete. They expressed "no specific, definite, or feasible plans" to justify accumulating earnings, according to the court.

Keeping records has always been a bother, and an expensive one, especially for small companies. Most entrepreneurs do not like to spend time keeping records. Probably because no one ever became rich by keeping records. And in a small, one-person business, it seems downright silly to keep records of stockholder meetings and board of directors meetings . . . keeping minutes . . . taking votes . . . adopting resolutions . . . isn't it all just a waste of time?

Not if you ask any of the thousands of entrepreneurs who have lost fortunes because they failed to keep records. You should look at corporate record keeping chores this way: *It's part of the price you pay to get the tax benefits and personal protection from having a corporation.*

A corporation does not exist except on paper, through its charter, by-laws, stock certificates, resolutions, etc. Anything you do as an officer or director has to be duly authorized and evidenced by a resolution of the stockholders or the board, or by both in some cases. It makes no difference if there is only one stockholder or one million stockholders. The rules are basically the same.

You can hire a lawyer like the big companies do, and pay $100 or more just to prepare one form. But you may need, at minimum, a dozen or more documents to keep your corporation alive and functioning for just one year. This type of work is the bread and butter for many corporation lawyers. Most of the work can be done by their secretaries, yet they will charge you enormous sums because they know how important the forms are to you and your business. Lawyers know that the I.R.S. will insist that you have the corporate records to prove that you are entitled to all the tax breaks from having a corporation.

There is now a way for you to solve your corporate record keeping problems. Without a lawyer, without paying big fees, and without spending a lot of time. It is truly **The Complete Book of Corporate Forms**. It was prepared by Ted Nicholas, author of the best-seller, *How to Form Your Own Corporation Without a Lawyer for Under $75*. This book has become the largest single source of new corporations in America. His book has revolutionized the business of forming new corporations by making the process simple, easy, and inexpensive.

But forming a corporation is only the first step toward building "the ultimate tax shelter." Through carelessness or neglect, many people are denied their rightful benefits from owning their own corporation. Ted Nicholas saw that many business owners needed more help *after* they incorporated. They didn't know how to follow through, how to turn their corporation into the ultimate tax shelter.

And so, he prepared **The Complete Book of Corporate Forms**. Virtually all the forms you will ever need are all ready for you. Everything is simplified. Either you or your secretary can complete any form in minutes. All you do is fill in a few blanks and insert the completed form in your record book. When you own this book, you are granted permission to reproduce every form. If you are behind on keeping good corporate records, now you can catch up in no time. Just complete a few blanks for the things you've already done in the company. It's legal and it works. Best of all, the price is less than you would pay a lawyer for one hour of counseling.

Here is just a sampling of what you'll receive:

Minutes of Stockholder Meetings
Minutes of Director's Meetings
Minutes of Special Meetings
(Any of these can be used if you are the only stockholder and director.)
Amendments to Articles of Incorporation
Amendments to By-Laws
Changes in Membership of Board

You will also receive all the stockholder and director's resolutions you will need to take any major business actions, including:

• Negotiation of contracts • Authorizing loans to corporation • Approval of corporate loans to you • Designation of purchasing agent *(some suppliers may want to know who is authorized to buy from them)* • Setting your salary • Directors fees • Authorizing your expense account • Mergers • Sale of corporate assets • Dissolution • Bankruptcy • Declaring dividends • Appointment of attorney or accountant

Plus, you'll receive the forms needed to authorize any of these tax-saving fringe benefits:

• Pensions or profit sharing plans • Medical and dental reimbursement plans • Sick pay plans • Split dollar life insurance • Educational loan program • Scholarship aid program • Stock options • Group life insurance • Financial counseling plan • Group legal services • Christmas bonus, special bonuses

Just one of the above forms can cost you hundreds of dollars in legal fees...

This entire $8\frac{1}{2}$ x 11, loose leaf collection of simplified forms (over 150 pages of forms), clear instructions for their use, as well as samples of completed forms, sells for only $69.95. It comes in a luxurious gold embossed binder as well.

As with all Enterprise Publishing products, it sells under an iron-clad 30-day money-back guarantee. After you examine the collection, if for any reason you are not pleased, return it for a prompt and courteous refund. Take a moment to place your order now, and immediately begin saving time and money.

Complete coupon and mail.

THE COMPLETE BOOK OF
Corporate Forms
Ted Nicholas

Please rush me a copy of **The Complete Book of Corporate Forms** by Ted Nicholas at $69.95, under your 30-day money-back guarantee.

Enclosed is ☐ Check ☐ Money Order

Charge to my ☐ Visa ☐ MasterCard ☐ Diners Club ☐ Carte Blanche ☐ American Express

Account# ______________________

Initials ______________ Exp. Date ______________

Name ______________________

Address ______________________

City ______________ State ____ Zip ______

Mail to: Nicholas Direct, Inc., Dept. DMS-9, P.O. Box 877, Indian Rocks Beach, FL 34635

Card Deck

What Will You Do When Your Personal Assets Are Seized to Satisfy a Judgment Against Your Corporation?

Every single one of the many tax benefits you receive from owning a corporation could be wiped out overnight. How? The IRS could visit and claim you have not kept proper corporate records.

And banks, insurance companies, and various government agencies require notarized authorizations to grant loans, enter into leases, and even sell assets.

In a small, one person business, it seems silly to keep records. Isn't it just a waste of time? NO! Recordkeeping is part of the price you pay to receive all the advantages of incorporation.

You could hire a lawyer to keep your records — just like the big corporations do. And to have one form prepared, you'll pay $100 or more, even though your lawyer's secretary may complete the standard forms.

There is now a way for you to solve your corporate recordkeeping problems. Without a lawyer. Without the high fees. And without spending a lot of your valuable time. It's THE COMPLETE BOOK OF CORPORATE FORMS by Ted Nicholas, author of the bestselling book, HOW TO FORM YOUR OWN CORPORATION WITHOUT A LAWYER FOR UNDER $75.

SEE OTHER SIDE FOR MORE DETAILS

Virtually every form your corporation will ever need is prepared for you, and there are simple easy to follow instructions for each document. Each form can be complete in minutes. And you have permission to reproduce any form in the book.

Here is just a sampling of what you'll receive:

THE COMPLETE BOOK OF
Corporate Forms
Ted Nicholas

- Minutes of Stockholders' and Director's meeting.
- Minutes of Special Meetings.
- Forms authorizing your expenses and salary. And much more.

Even if you are behind in keeping accurate corporate records, this book will help you catch up. Just complete a few blanks to document your companies' activities. It's legal and it works. And best of all, if you use just one of the forms in the next year, you will more than justify your modest investment in it.

Please rush me__________copy (s) of THE COMPLETE BOOK OF CORPORATE FORMS by Ted Nicholas at $69.95 plus $4 for shipping and handling. I understand my purchase is covered under the Enterprise 30-Day Money Back Guarantee if not satisfied.

☐ Check enclosed.

☐ Visa ☐ MasterCard ☐ American Express

Account No. Exp. Date Initials

Name

Company

Address

City State Zip

Daytime phone (in case of questions about your order)

Mail to: Nicholas Direct, Inc. Dept. DMS-9
P.O. Box 877, Indian Rocks Beach, FL 34635

(Outside teaser copy appearing next to window on envelope)

**What Will You Do When
Your Personal Assets Are Seized
to Satisfy a Judgment
Against Your Corporation?**

Free Sample Form Enclosed Protects You.

A quick review

So while it's possible to make short copy work when written from scratch, as in a card deck or space ad, the safest procedure is to:

1. Write a complete "long copy" offer, including every possible benefit and feature your prospect could possibly derive from your product. Usually this will be in the form of a sales letter.
2. Test the long copy offer.
3. Determine whether or not you have a profitable offer based on your analysis of all costs versus sales.
4. Including the key elements of the long offer, adapt the copy to a space ad and test. Use the exact same headline or teaser and opening.
5. Adapt this copy to a card deck and test. Use the exact same headline or teaser and opening.
6. Adapt this copy to a catalog.

Of course, if your testing starts with a space ad, you can and should convert this into a sales letter. By using these procedures, you'll undoubtedly multiply the sales of your successful products and offers by a large multiple!

How to Write the Ideal Sales Letter

There is a great deal of misunderstanding in our society about sales letters.

The liberal press condemns so called "junk" mail. Yet the finest examples of writing excellence in America (or any country) are found in successful sales letters and ads.

Think about this. When archaeologists dig up the ruins of this century hundreds of years from now, sales letters will clearly represent the values of this century. A sales letter not only must communicate clearly, it also must persuade.

Anyone can learn to write a powerful sales letter.

Successful letters are those which pull in sales profitably. The only true test of whether a letter is profitable is whether it's repeated.

In order to improve, you need practice.

Suggestion: **Hand write** successful sales letters, while developing your own letter writing style. When you hand write someone else's work, a remarkable thing happens. You actually can experience the thought process and even the emotional state of the copywriter.

And you can model your own work to letters you like until you develop your own style.

A general formula

Any successful mailing must have these elements in **balance**. Each element is approximately 33⅓%.

1. **Product and offer**—has to be appealing.
2. **List**—the audience must be a carefully selected target.
3. **Copy**—has to sell.

There are five essential ingredients of a good letter:

a. clearness
b. flow
c. passion
d. believability
e. close

Shortcut to a successful letter

The best way I've found to determine whether a letter has all the ingredients of success is surprisingly simple. Yet, few people do it.

Just read it out loud!

Mistakes, confusing statements, and unclear sentences will pop right out.

You will thus avoid sending poorly crafted letters. Ask yourself—Does this sound as though I'm speaking? A good letter needs to sound like it's coming directly from your heart, as though you are talking to a close friend.

The letter needs to sound like you. You need to encourage the reader to get the product. You need to convince the reader he/she will be better off as a result. If your letter does not accomplish this, rewrite until it does.

You have just one goal in writing any sales letter. You want the prospect to do exactly what you ask. As you write the copy, think about your reader as you create each sentence. Imagine you are addressing a close friend or favorite relative, perhaps a brother or a sister.

Remember that your reader listens to that great radio station in the sky, WIIFM! Your reader is asking this question after each sentence: "What's in it for me?"

That's exactly what you must answer.

No one deep down really cares a whit about your problems, dreams, or goals. Only their own. You must appeal to the prospect's self-interest. Otherwise, they will stop reading and, of course, not order.

Prepare yourself to write

I'm often asked how I prepare myself to write copy. This is a good question. It's crucially important because I've never seen any marketer address this issue. I'll share with you my approach.

As you prepare yourself to write powerful and persuasive copy with lots of "juice" in it, you need to get into a **peak emotional state**.

Reason? Daily experiences can have a negative effect on your emotional state. Suppose today you learned of a forthcoming IRS audit, had a fight with your spouse, colleague, or neighbor which has upset you, do you feel the tone and power of your sales letter will be affected? Of course it will!

In order to write well, here are a few tips which can prepare you. Warning: Some of them at first may seem "off the wall." But if you try them, I know you'll be delighted with the result! Before you sit down to write anything important:

1. Be fully rested with a good night's sleep.
2. Eat sparingly before writing, as a heavy meal will affect your mental sharpness.
3. Exercise moderately on days you write, preferably **before** starting. Walking, swimming, or cycling are ideal, providing you have no physical problems which prevent these activities.
4. Do not accept telephone calls or other interruptions for the duration of your writing effort for it breaks your concentration. If appropriate, let your answering machine, spouse, or secretary answer calls. Or unplug the phone.
5. Count your blessings. Think about all the things that give you pleasure and write them down. Feed yourself as much positive "mental food" as you can.

Here is the most important part. Our emotional state is 54% derived from our physical actions. The rest is mental. Here are a few simple physical actions which will help put you in a terrific emotional state.

You must be excited and passionate about your product. Otherwise, your copy will commit the unpardonable sin. It will be boring. However, to feel passionate about your product, you must first feel passionate about yourself. There is no way to "fake it." It comes through in your copy. However, you can enhance your emotional state through simple physical actions.

Here are some tips:

6. Walk briskly outside your house or apartment for 5 minutes. Stand straight while you walk, as though someone had a string keeping your head straight. Smile as big a smile as you are capable during this whole 5 minutes.
7. Come inside, stand in front of the mirror and say **out loud** 3 times, "I (your name) am going to write a terrific and inspirational sales letter!" Repeat it. Say it out loud one more time. The fourth time, however, now look straight up at the sky when you say it.
8. Sit at your desk in front of your computer, typewriter, or with a yellow pad. Put yourself in a position with your back straight.

You are now ready to write a compelling letter.

Do you think you could be upset or down or depressed at this point? It's nearly impossible. For more elaboration and practice, there are numerous, helpful books on the techniques called "Neuro-Linguistic Programming," NLP. One good one is "Using Your Brain" by Richard Bandler.

Isolate your benefits

Begin your writing only after you have studied the product carefully. If, for example, it's a book or tape, re-read it or re-listen to it, even if you are the author!

Your goal should be to isolate as many **benefits** as you can from the product from the prospect's point of view.

Write the benefits down on 3 × 5 cards in short, telegraphic sentences. use short action words, which are exciting. Remember WIIFM. Answer this question as you write each benefit. "So what?"

The benefits written on these 3 × 5 cards will become the meat of your letter. The only reasons your prospect would ever be interested in your offer are the benefits gotten from your product. The benefits must be perceived as more valuable than the money you ask.

The most important benefit often can become your best headline. Or you can use it as the "teaser" copy on the envelope. Often this benefit pops out strongly at you, as though by magic. It's very exciting when the biggest newly discovered benefit seems obvious. But only after you've found it.

When you are finished writing down all the benefits anyone could possibly gain from your product, shuffle your 3 × 5 cards. Place the second strongest benefit next to the first strongest. The third strongest after the second strongest, etc.

Many people ask me: Shouldn't you save one or more strong benefits until later? Aren't you firing all your sales ammunition too soon? The answer is no! Your prospect will simply stop reading unless your very strongest benefits are up front at once. You will then lose the sale.

Sometimes you can write a successful sales letter with a single powerful opening sentence. Then you can proceed immediately to the benefits. For example, here is how you can open a letter:

> "Here is good news! You no longer have to depend on expensive, time-consuming lawyers every time you need a legal agreement. ***The Complete Guide to Business Agreements*** by Ted Nicholas, provides 117 ready-to-use legal forms for your convenience.
>
> Now you will be able to . . ."

At this point, you can begin the benefits from the 3 × 5 cards. Place a bullet in front of each benefit in your letter.

Or you can "weave in" the benefits in your letter without bullets in a more narrative style like this. (Use same opening and continue from just before the bullets.)

> "Now you will be able to immediately access carefully prepared forms for every important business purpose. Imagine, you are in discussion with a new employee prospect you feel could really be an asset to your business. You look at the table of contents to employment agreements and remove the one that fits your needs.
>
> No more time wasting meetings with a lawyer. No

more waiting for weeks until your document is prepared. You can have it in minutes.

Or suppose you want to simply raise your salary and have proper documentation for this action."

In the second letter above, the technique is to incorporate the benefit in a more conversational style.

The previous examples should make clear two of the strongest letter opening styles you can use. Of course, there are many other ways to open a letter.

Length of letter

How long should a sales letter be? There is no single length that is best for every sales letter. It depends on the product and the offer. Sometimes one or two pages is fine. Sometimes four. Sometimes eight. Sometimes as many as 16 or 24 or even more.

One good rule to follow is that a letter must be **complete**. It cannot be too long, with one condition. Every word must be **relevant** to the reader. Never write copy just for length.

When you've completed your letter, put it down. Let it cool for a day. The next day, go back and cross out any unnecessary words or phrases. Also, eliminate any words which cannot truthfully and honestly apply to your product. What copy remains will be more than adequate to describe and sell the reader on your product.

Your job is to build a picture in your prospect's mind's eye of your product—all the benefits and pleasures he/she will derive from it.

Do not exaggerate! If you do, your prospect will immediately sense the falsehood. Any feeling of a falsehood written in a single word of your letter and your prospect will toss out your message.

In fact, this is why most advertising is so ineffective. And it deserves to be condemned and ignored. There is so much exaggeration or puffery, it's just not believable. There is zero credibility in such advertising.

Unfortunately, over 90% of what comes out of advertising agencies does nothing to enhance sales of the product. Very often sales are reduced by the advertising that consumers find distasteful.

That's why as an entrepreneur, owner, or entrepreneurial manager within an organization where you are measured, you have bottom line responsibility, you are often a better copywriter than you can ever hire outside your company. You have the product knowledge **and** passion for it and a stake in the advertising results.

Closing the sale

Closing the sale is probably the weakest element in all of direct marketing. It's the area that needs and deserves the most work in all sales situations.

You must apply the selling rules that 90% of sales and marketing people never learn. It's simple. But for many tough to do. After you've effectively presented the benefits of your product:

Ask for the order!

The most hated part of all selling is the close.

There is nothing more pathetic than to watch a sales person work hard on giving a great sales presentation or a beautiful sales letter, which sells benefits of product convincingly, but with no close. When the close is not handled smoothly, sales will be lost.

However, once you understand and can apply the psychology of closing, it becomes infinitely easier. And more acceptable to the buyer.

One big factor is you must have a product and offer that is a true value for the buyer. And you must believe it yourself with every fiber of your being. If you don't, your lack of conviction shows through the copy.

How to ask for the order

There is a natural human inertia in all of us. We usually need some nudging. We appreciate being led to an action that is a benefit to us.

We also need a compelling reason to act now. As a copywriter, it is not enough to say "mail this card at once." You must give a compelling reason for immediate action.

In every closing situation, there must be a "hook," a reason to act right now. Why?

A delayed sale is almost always a lost sale. When you present your hook, it must be specific and definite. You must hold over the prospect's head the "Sword of Damocles." Describe what will happen if the action you're asking for is not taken at once. Here are some examples of effective hooks:

- **Limited quantity**. Avoid disappointment. Order now. When inventory of 197 sets is gone, this offer will expire and your order and check will be returned.
- **Price will rise**. Orders will be honored until November 30, after which the price will go up.
- **Limited opportunity**. For example, "There will be a limited number of distributorships sold in any area. When the territories are sold, there will be no further opportunities to be a licensee in your city."
- **Slightly damaged and irregular goods**. "When the quantity of 743 shirts and blouses that you can now have at the bargain price are sold, this offer will be immediately withdrawn."
- **Special combination offer**. "The special price for this combination offer will expire on (specific date)."
- **Pre-publication opportunity**. "If your order is received by December 31, you will receive a 20% discount on the book, only $39.95, normally $50. Place your order and payment in the mail now."

Say what you mean, and mean what you say. Tell your prospect there will be no last minute concessions. Be definite and be positive. You will lose a few orders, but more than make up for it in increased sales.

Add one or more free bonuses

Everyone likes to get free gifts. I sure do! Don't you?

Use free bonuses in every offer you make. There has never been an instance in my experience wherein sales have not been dramatically improved by using an appealing free bonus or premium, regardless of what you sell.

A good way to judge whether or not to use a particular bonus? The prospect wants it and would gladly pay for the bonus if it weren't free. If a dull and uninteresting bonus is used you will not enhance the offer.

Make sure you tie in the offer of the free bonus for acting now. One good way to increase sales with a free bonus is to limit the number of people who get it and to present your offer like this:

> "The first 100 people who order will get a beautiful Gold Mont Blanc Pen, normally $100, absolutely free. So pick up the telephone and call our toll-free number right now."

Guarantees

An unconditional money-back guarantee is almost essential in today's competitive world of direct marketing.

If your product is of superior quality and this is what you strive for, your returns should not exceed 5% on most offers.

As to the length of guarantee, generally the longer the period, the less returns. I use 30, 60, 90 days, or one year for most offers. Here is language I frequently use in guarantees:

> If for any reason, in your sole judgment, you are not delighted with the product, after you have examined it for 60 days, you may return it for a prompt and courteous refund.

Types of sales letters

There may appear to be many types of sales letters. However there are really only two primary ones.

Those mailed first class and those mailed third class. There are positives and negatives to both. Bottom line: You have to test to see which is most profitable.

Results in my tests have been mixed. Currently I mail first class more often than I ever have before as tests have shown performance is better on most offers.

Here is traditionally what you normally would include within a sales letter for best results:

- Sales letter
- Outer envelope
- Order form
- Return envelope or BRE (optional)
- Lift letter (optional)
- Flier or brochure (optional)

Regarding size, there are no fixed rules. As with all direct mail, you must test. However, I recommend #10 envelopes on most letter offer tests. Reasons? Prices are competitive, and prospects are used to them as most mail is sent in a #10 envelope so they are within the buyer's comfort zone.

On the envelope, you should use strong "teaser" copy. A bulk stamp usually outpulls metered mail.

Use a Courier typeface in all your sales letters. A typewritten look almost always outpulls a typeset look. For best results, tests show the signature on a letter must always be printed in reflex blue. For signatures don't use any other color, such as black, red, or green.

What about a P.S.? Never send out a letter without a P.S. Next to the headline it is the best read part of any letter. Completely restate the offer or biggest benefit in the P.S.

The logo. The only person who truly loves a company logo is the owner or employees. Your customers could care less, no matter how beautiful it is. The best place for a logo in a sales letter is at the end of the last page.

Of all the elements in any direct mail package, the most important is the letter. This is where you want to put your primary efforts. It's a good idea to keep an "idea file" of good openings, descriptions, bonuses, closes; not for the purpose of copying them. Instead, use them to inspire greater efforts.

How to Write the Ideal Sales Letter

Part II

The secrets revealed in this chapter apply to "killer" sales letters that ask the reader for one of these 5 responses.

1. Buy your product, or request more information.
2. Agree to be called by a salesperson.
3. Contribute to a fund raising effort.
4. Enter a sweepstakes or contest.
5. Come to a retail store.

In the previous chapter headlines and "teaser" copy were discussed.

What goes at the top of the letter?

What important elements should you include at the top of a sales letter?

Shouldn't your logo be the first thing a reader sees?

No, No, No, No! Contrary to common practice, **do not** put your logo anywhere on the first page of your sales letter! Why?

A logo is a "me" message. You love it. Every entrepreneur, including me, feels the same way about their logo. But alas, your prospect could care less. He/she only responds to the "what's in it for me" appeal.

If you include a logo at all in your sales letter, there is only one good place for it. At the very end of the letter.

Where to begin a letter?

Lead off with a **headline**.

There are several proven ways to present the headline. The headline can be **typeset** like this:

**Protect Your Corporation's Tax Shelter
Status Without a Lawyer**

Or typewritten like this:

Protect Your Corporation's Tax Shelter
Status Without a Lawyer

Or typewriter written and placed in a "Johnson Box" like this:

```
*******************************************
*                                         *
* Protect Your Corporation's Tax Shelter  *
*          Status Without a Lawyer        *
*                                         *
*******************************************
```

The next decision you need to make is the **salutation**.
Here are some that I've used:

Dear Bob Smith (Personalized to the addressee)
Dear Friend
Dear Beleaguered Taxpayer
Dear Overburdened Taxpayer
Dear Potential Victim
Dear Fellow American
Dear Fellow Citizen

I've also tried no salutation at all. Recently I've successfully tested a new one to my house list:

Dear Friend of Nicholas Direct;

I've found that including a salutation works better than not having one. There are no measurable differences in response as long as your salutation is related to the person you are addressing. And never forget, you are writing to a single individual. Never sound like you are addressing a group.

The personalized salutation pulls more response than any other. To all humans, reading or hearing their name is the sweetest sound. However, a computer generated letter usually costs more than one that is mass produced. In most cases, the costs do not justify a personalized letter.

Here is a general rule. It does not pay to personalize unless your product sells for $500 or more. But you could be the exception. That is why you may want to test a personalized letter against one that is mass produced.

Here are most ways to enhance the success of your sales letter

One highly effective strategy is to begin with an anecdote or two.

You then follow the anecdote(s) with a powerful statement, called a "billboard." Your billboards should be your unique selling proposition.

Next you follow the billboard with supportive statistics. These help give your position the most important element in any letter, credibility.

Then, ideally, you present all the benefits, offer a free bonus, describe your guarantee, give a compelling reason to close, and add a P.S. Your order information can be part of the last pages of the letter or on a separate order card.

Here is an example of an anecdotal opening:

anecdote

"In 1991 Pat McCallister went broke in the commodity business. A Chicago resident, he decided to try a new business. Pat started a computer cleaning company and operated from his home. After 3 years his sales soared to $500,000. This year he expects $1,000,000. His profits exceed $1,000 a day.

anecdote

In 1990 "Guerilla" Bill Myers lived in a remote cabin in the country without running water. He had no savings or capital. With a borrowed $600 he created a video, a low budget information marketer. It was a big hit. By 1993, after grossing a million dollars, he retired and moved to New Zealand.

billboard

Pat and Bill, along with thousands of others, had something in common. They mastered the secrets of direct marketing. These techniques are taught by a small but elite handful of master marketers. Direct marketing has the power to change anyone's life overnight.

statistics

There are over 20,000 direct marketing companies in the U.S. They are mostly small businesses. According to the Wall Street Journal, gross sales by direct marketing companies exceed 350 billion dollars.

You, too, can use the power of direct marketing to build a small business and achieve your financial goals."

Another letter opening style is to begin with a powerful short sentence or paragraph. Then you proceed straight to the benefits. Here is an example:

"I will reveal the shocking truth about the Clinton tax bill. Once you discover the secrets, you can survive and even prosper under the biggest tax increase in history. Learn how to:

- Limit your federal to just 15% of income. (See page 12).
- Put aside $30,000 each year in a lucrative pension plan (See page 77) that accumulates tax free so you can retire in style (See page 39).
- Set up tax deductible educational plans for your children (See page 18).
- Pay zero tax if you want to be really aggressive (See page 141) in ways that are perfectly legal (See page 173)."

Another example of a letter opening is to open with a compelling first sentence that supports the headline and sub-headline. Then your opening short paragraphs amplify the headline promise like this:

"How to Get Enthusiastic Applause—Even a Standing Ovation—Every Time You Speak!"

Leadership in all fields today requires you to be an outstanding public speaker.

Dear Friend:

Picture yourself enjoying the smiles and the pleased look of excitement on the faces of your audience.

When you finish speaking, you receive thunderous applause. Several in the audience stand. And then the audience rises spontaneously and gives you a standing ovation!

Suppose this response was typical of every speech you were to ever give from here on? Wouldn't you then look forward to future speaking engagements? Most likely you would enjoy every minute of it!

At times you may consider public speaking commitments an uncomfortable, or even a dreaded task. Many people feel this way when asked to or are obliged to speak.

Just imagine what a difference it would make to get only enthused, positive feedback from all your presentations. The personal satisfaction of a well-received speech is one of life's greatest pleasures.

There are an infinite variety of ways to begin a sales letter. But, I've shown you some of the best styles for big results.

The lift letter

A unique type of letter can be included in the same envelope with your main letter. It's called a "lift" letter. Why? Because as the name implies, it can increase response. The most successful lift letters have at least one or several of these characteristics:

- Has a different tone than the main letter
- Is signed by someone other than the sender of the main letter
- Includes a benefit which is not in the main letter
- Is printed on a different color paper
- Contains or is a testimonial
- Is from a celebrity
- Is brief, not more than one page
- The words "Please read only if you are still undecided" are printed on the reverse side.

Colors of ink and paper

The most important thing to remember about color use in a sales letter is to use it **sparingly**. The single most important place to use color is on the **signature**. Test after test have shown **reflex blue** is the most effective color to use. People associate a signature with blue ink. Do not ever use any other color than blue. If you do, response will drop.

Handwritten margin notes used sparingly can help draw attention. I also like the use of blue for **margin notes** like this:

Here is what
lawyers will not
tell you even
if they knew

The text of your letter should always be printed in black. Be sure the printer does a good job with ink coverage. Tests have shown that **darker type increases response** by as much as 15%. It surely is easier to read. Headlines should be in black, as should subheads.

For most products and services simple two color printing, black with blue signature and margin notes if any, is effective. And inexpensive. If you want to test a third color, use it on your subheads.

However, unless you are selling a colorful product such as jewelry or artwork, the added cost of a third and fourth color does not pay for most offers. Of course, you can always confirm this by doing your own test.

Remember, a sales letter is a personal medium. It should look and feel like it's from "you to me." The feeling you are striving for in a sales letter is that of a **personal** letter. Of course you would not print a message to a friend in multiple colors.

Paper colors

For both ease of reading and cost, you can't go wrong using white. However, off white, pale yellow, blue, green, or pink can also be used.

Paper weight should be heavy enough so you can't see through it and there is no "bleed through" if printing both sides. A 20 pound paper is inexpensive and usable for most offers.

The lift letter and order card should be printed on a different color stock than the main letter so they stand out.

Crossing out words or phrases for emphasis and readership

A useful technique for emphasis is to use a felt tip pen to cross out words or phrases. Readership and response go up markedly. Here is what it looks like:

The price is ~~$75~~. Special $49.99

What about the envelope?

The outside envelope plan and design is crucial to the success of a sales letter. Obviously, if the envelope is not opened you have a zero chance of response.

If you mail first class do not use teaser copy. There is one exception. When responding to a customer inquiry use a rubber stamp on the envelope imprinted with the words "Here is the information you requested."

Plan your envelope so that it has the personalized appearance of a private letter. Your corner card should be your **street address only**. By not including your company name you will get more envelopes opened. Use **a live first class stamp**, not a postage meter.

In addressing a first class letter, do not use a label. Instead, the address should be impact printed as would any typewritten letter.

While there are always exceptions, when mailing 3rd class, here are some guidelines to help decide what works best.

- Print powerful "teaser" copy enticing the reader to open the envelope.
- Apply either a live stamp or metered postage, as it doesn't seem to matter.
- Use a **window** envelope as opposed to close faced. In fact, **two windows** on an envelope work even better. Use one for address and one for the photo of the product, or a subhead.

Envelope sizes that produce highest response

Number 10 envelopes or number 9 work best to executives at business addresses.

Oversized 6 × 9 envelopes often work better than number 10 to home addresses.

How to increase orders from businesses

Executives change jobs, get fired or are laid off frequently. It is difficult to always send your letter to the correct person by name. Here is a simple but little used strategy that will get more people to read your letter even if the original address has gone.

Add routing information by **function** or **title** on the envelope. Tailor it to the industry you are addressing. Add a blank next to name where a check mark can be added. Here are a few examples:

- ☐ President
- ☐ Purchasing manager
- ☐ Marketing Manager
- ☐ Person in Charge of Hiring Lawyers
- ☐ Vice President
- ☐ Sales Manager
- ☐ Person in Charge of Publications

More low cost secrets that boost sales

If you simply **enclose a return envelope** in your mailings you will lift response by up to $33\frac{1}{3}\%$!

The return envelope makes it convenient and easy for your prospect to respond. He/she doesn't have to hunt for an envelope or go to the store to buy one.

You can pay the return postage by getting a postal permit enabling you to make such arrangements with your post office. However, my tests consistently show no difference in response when the customer pays the postage! You can print on the envelope a square the size of a stamp on the upper right corner of the envelope with the words "place stamp here" and you'll save big money on return postage as your volume grows.

Use two order cards

A simple and surprisingly effective strategy is to **include two order cards** when you're mailing. Some offers get as much as a 50% boost in sales by simply adding a second order card!

The recipient of your mail can then pass the order information on to interested friends or colleagues.

Try both of these low cost strategies. You'll be delighted with the results.

More little known secrets of super successful letters

I'm sure you agree most sales letters you get are not well written. Because they are so poorly prepared, people don't read them. And of course don't respond.

The letters **shout** or **scream** at their prospects. The prospect is not treated **with dignity and respect**. Your letters will not be successful if they contain either of these flaws. Why?

The number one reason any sales letter fails is lack of **credibility**.

None of us like to be shouted at. Do not scream that your offer is the greatest thing since sliced bread. Even if it truly is great, no one believes a screamer.

Your offer does not have to revolutionize mankind. To succeed, just make a **believable promise**. Then prove it with benefits, features, and testimonials.

The letter **tone** is also very important. Never plan to write a sales letter.

Instead, write a personal message in the same tone as when you speak to a close friend. Be warm. Be friendly. Be sincere.

If you'll study direct mail you'll find it often **lacks common courtesy**. Most direct mail is discourteous, even insulting. Never be even slightly discourteous. And don't try to be funny, as humor is easily misunderstood.

How to Get 1,000 People to Subscribe to a $100 Newsletter with Zero Marketing Cost

A newsletter may be the most ideal product in the world to market. Why? For four primary reasons:

1. **Cash flow**. You do not produce the product until **after** you sell it. Think of it! No money is tied up in advance production costs. No money is tied up in inventory. Can you conceive of another highly salable product where these dynamics apply? It's very rare indeed.
2. **Low cost**. Production costs are low while perceived value is high. Many monthly newsletters selling for up to $500 a year cost less than $1 per month or $12 per year to produce, print and mail. Remember, a subscriber wants the information. No one cares a whit about the cost of paper and ink.
3. **Recurring income**. A newsletter provides continuing cash flow. Once you have a subscriber who is happy, each year the subscription will be renewed. Good newsletters experience a 60% to 90% renewal rate. So, once you have a customer on board they can be an ever present source of revenue. Forever.
4. **Bonding**. You can develop a closer bond with a newsletter subscriber than with perhaps any other product. A solid product will earn your customer's trust over time. Subscribers will get to know you are "for real" and deliver as much or even more than you

promise. Then you will enjoy a high percentage response to future offers of products, especially if related in some way to your newsletter topic. These "back end" products can include books, tapes, seminars, equipment, etc. It's no wonder there are over 20,000 newsletters published in the U.S. A newsletter can become a valuable money-making machine just like an annuity.

The most successful newsletters serve their own special niche audience

One caveat.

Newsletter subscribers are the most intelligent of all information buyers. They are selective. And discriminating.

Therefore, if you do plan to publish a newsletter, make sure you are a flat out expert on the newsletter subject. Or hire a top expert who is to be your editor.

Anything less than useful information written in an exciting way from a true expert will not succeed.

What is the biggest problem with unsuccessful newsletters?

You guessed it!

For the most part they are . . .

BORING!

A typical, boring, typeset newsletter printed on slick paper with a corporate look has a predicable fate. It will die. How long it takes depends on how deep the publisher's pockets are. You've undoubtedly seen many like that.

The worst examples of newsletters I've seen are the ones produced by most lawyers, accountants and banks. I'm sure you too have gotten them. I suspect nobody reads them.

What do subscribers want in a newsletter?

A personality. An editor who has strong opinions about the subject the newsletter covers. Even when the views differ with subscribers, that's OK. Sometimes, in fact, a contrarian viewpoint really sells better.

Remember this. A middle of the road wimpy, wishy-washy publication that tries to please everyone doesn't have a chance in the marketplace.

Common myths exploded

To have a profitable newsletter you don't need fancy graphics and photography—slick paper stock or color printing. The most successful newsletters in the U.S. are set in **Courier** type. The printing can be done simply. Use one or two colors. The feeling you want to communicate is "from me to you." Hot off my typewriter or computer to your eyes. And that's the reality anyway.

One of my clients is Phillips Publishing International in Potomac, Maryland. The owner is my friend, Tom Phillips. They are the largest newsletter publishers (over 50 newsletters) in the U.S. Sales of $117,000,000. **All** of their newsletters have a typewritten personalized look. They really know how to package newsletter products. That's one of the reasons they are successful.

The foregoing is about producing the product.

What about selling it?

While editorial is crucial, over 90% of a successful newsletter publisher's time and budget is devoted to guess what?

Marketing!

Newsletter marketing can be done via direct mail (the most used method), space ads, TV, card decks, and Electronic Bulletin

Boards. Of course all these methods require an investment in marketing.

I want to share with you a method no one ever used before to launch a newsletter, to my knowledge. It involves no investment or risk whatsoever!

Are you interested?

OK. OK. Since I have your undivided attention:

Here is the secret.

A few years ago I published a book called "The Insider's Guide to Complete Asset Protection" by Brett K. Kates Esq.

The author is a knowledgeable attorney with excellent writing skills.

Kates and I agreed that a newsletter would be of benefit to the readers of the book. He would be the editor.

New information and legal decisions about the book's topic were constantly changing. Readers would benefit from updated information on a monthly basis.

So we came up with the idea for a newsletter. We would call it "LAWSUIT AND ASSET PROTECTION LETTER." It would be a monthly newsletter. The charter subscription rate would be $97 per year.

I wrote a sales letter. The marketing "secret" behind its launch was simple. The shipping department simply enclosed my letter inside the front cover of the outgoing books. There were no postage costs necessary. The letter rode along with the book free. The only cost was printing, which was minimal.

We put the sales letter in the next 20,000 books sold. Approximately 1,000 people (a 5% response) sent in $97 and became subscribers. That's approximately $100,000 in just a few weeks. Our total monthly investment aside from printing? Zero!

Does the idea of getting in $100,000 even before you launch a product appeal to you? I thought so!

This technique will surely trigger some ideas with regard to your products.

Many times the best low cost way to sell a new product or service is by "piggy backing" on another successful product. Try it and see. And remember where you learned this powerful strategy.

On the following pages is the actual letter I used. Pay close attention to the outer envelope. What you say on the face of it is key to the success of the offer. Also study the headline and subhead at the top of the letter. The one I created really attracted attention. Make sure yours does, too!

TED NICHOLAS
PUBLISHER

An urgent message from the publisher—
To be opened and read immediately

Standard #10 envelope
(reduced view)

TED NICHOLAS
PUBLISHER

Would You Invest $97 in a Newsletter If It Helped Protect Your Life Savings and Other Personal Assets While Keeping You Lawsuit and Judgment Proof? What if the Newsletter Came With an Unconditional Guarantee?

This lawsuit and liability explosion we're living in today can ruin you overnight. But now you can protect yourself and your business from judgments, creditors, lenders...even the IRS

Dear Concerned Reader:

It's tragic but true. Massive lawsuit...nasty divorce...business disaster...or whopping tax liability can bring instant financial ruin to you and your family. Nothing you own is safe. Your home...business...savings...investments...even your paycheck is on the line when trouble strikes. But by then it's too late.

Don't make the mistake of thinking that it could never happen to you. It definitely can. The answer to avoiding disaster is to take some surprisingly simple steps to protect yourself today.

There is an urgent need for information on asset protection now. For you, your family, and your business.

Executives, small business owners and their advisors owe it to their companies and themselves to keep up to date. Recent court decisions, as well as new laws and regulations, are constantly changing.

Here is your opportunity to take that first decisive step. Introducing an important monthly publication that will easily pay for itself over and over again with the hard-hitting, money-saving advice it provides.

Announcing the "LAWSUIT AND ASSET PROTECTION LETTER"

I publish a new newsletter you can't afford to be without. The information in it is indispensable to anyone with assets to protect. It's called the "LAWSUIT AND ASSET PROTECTION LETTER."

Our expert legal advisory panel pulls together the most profitable ways for you to protect assets month after month. Finally, you can discover easy-to-apply tips and strategies that will help you build and maintain a fortress of protection around all your assets.

Astute lawyers are constantly working on new "judgment-proofing" and "lawsuit immunity" techniques. As new approaches are developed almost daily, you should know about them.

Written in laymen's language, you'll also receive ready-to-use business/legal forms with instructions so you can apply them to your own personal situation. You'll even benefit from our "Action of the Month" that can quickly and easily be put to use.

The frightening trends and solutions:

There are many new situations which can put all your personal assets in jeopardy. The "LAWSUIT AND ASSET PROTECTION LETTER" will guide you in solving problems and protect your hard-earned assets by showing you:

- How to protect yourself personally if you have $1,000,000 in liability coverage and you are sued for $15,00,000 and lose.
- Specific ways to avoid loss of all your personal assets if your corporation is sued and you are held responsible as an officer or director.
- Proven methods of preventing creditors from seizing assets in children's and spouse's names for your business obligations.
- How to avoid personal bankruptcy if you or your spouse is secretary of a corporation.
- The easy way to protect your personal assets if your insurance company becomes insolvent.
- Realistic alternatives to skyrocketing malpractice and liability insurance premiums.
- How to avoid malpractice insurance claims after your retire for events which happened years ago.
- When it can be a disaster if property ownership has the designation of joint tenancy, tenancy by the entirety, or community property.
- How to insulate your assets once a suit has been filed or legal action is pending.
- Steps to take today to prevent creditors from seizing assets held in irrevocable and revocable trusts.

The "LAWSUIT AND ASSET PROTECTION LETTER" also shows you the latest developments on:

* maximizing the personal benefits to you of corporations and partnerships
* how to control all your investments so you get maximum benefits from them without any liability
* how to own real estate without personal liability
* how to safely buy distressed property and companies
* how to keep creditors happy and supplying you when you need to delay payment
* stopping the IRS from seizing assets when you owe them money
* settling debts amicably without bankruptcy
* which states are the best places to transfer assets
* latest developments in prenuptial and cohabitation agreements which give the most protection
* using banks and laws of other countries such as Canada, Austria and Switzerland to legally and ethically protect assets.

Who needs this unique Newsletter? Business owners, executives, accountants, corporate officers, CPAs, doctors and other professionals, lawyers, bankers, life insurance agents, financial advisors, and concerned households with assets to protect.

You've worked long and hard for your life's savings and other personal assets. If you are like most people your assets are far greater than you realize. When you add up your investments, cash, savings, home, furniture, cars, life insurance, jewelry, etc., the total can quickly rise from $200,000 to $500,000 or more. And if you own a business, your net worth is probably higher!

This is a litigation-happy society we live in with over 750,000 practicing lawyers. A single lawsuit can become a costly nightmare. Chances are someone is considering suing you right now! With all of today's legal hazards, doesn't it make sense to keep abreast of the latest news and developments to protect your assets?

Subscribe to the "LAWSUIT AND ASSET PROTECTION LETTER" now. Protect your life savings and other personal assets and learn the techniques to help your colleagues and associates do the same. There is absolutely no risk. The charter subscription price of $97 (normally $147) is tax deductible as a business expense.

100% Money-Back Guarantee

Subscribe to the Newsletter without risk of any kind. If you are not completely happy with your subscription after trying it for three months, you will receive a prompt and courteous refund.

To subscribe, call now at 1-813-596-4966 or complete the subscription request below.

Sincerely,

Ted Nicholas
Publisher

P.S. If your subscription is received within 30 days, you are guaranteed the special charter rate of $97, a full $50 off the regular rate, and it's entirely tax deductible as a business expense.

Detach Here

No-Risk Subscription Form

YES. Please enter my subscription to the "LAWSUIT AND ASSET PROTECTION LETTER." I understand that if it does not live up to my highest expectations, I may cancel anytime within three months and receive a refund of all my money.

[ ] One year: Special Charter Rate of $97—(I save $50 off the regular $147 rate)

[ ] Two years: $170—(I save $124 off the regular rate)

[ ] **Best Deal:** Three years $240—(I save over $200 off the regular rate)

[ ] Enclosed is my check.

[ ] Instead, charge my:

[ ] Visa

[ ] MasterCard

[ ] American Express

[ ] Diners Club/Carte Blanche

Card # Expires

Signature (credit card orders only)

Name

Company Name (if applicable)

Address

City State Zip

Daytime phone (If we have questions on your order)

Nicholas Direct, Inc., One Nicholas Square, PO Box 877, Indian Rocks Bch, FL 34635

More Sales for Your Buck

Every advertiser says: "I want more bang for my buck." But what does this really mean? In general advertising the real impact is tough to accurately measure. Not so when you are coding every order. The direct marketer can trace the source of each and every order including the publication or other specific media. In direct marketing a more accurate phrase is "More sales for your buck."

As a successful direct marketer, you constantly must seek a higher level of response and/or increased profitability from your advertising investment.

Two paths to greater profitability

1. Reduce costs (to be covered in a future chapter).
2. Produce higher response from your ads through better copy and strategy.

In this chapter I'll focus on copy and strategy.

Learning from real world examples is best accomplished through studying actual ads. I'll review a few ads and comment on them.

How to "model" successful ads

An important point to grasp is how to incorporate good ideas others are using into your own ads. This is known as "modeling."

I'm **not** referring to copying other advertisers' actual words and appearance in your ads.

If you copy, you can be charged with plagiarism. This is a serious crime. You can be held liable for damages and fines. So be very careful not to violate another's intellectual property. (Of course, if anyone copies your work you can lawfully block the further use of it and collect damages, etc.) Your goal should be to do better—rise above others' works!

Appeal to the emotions of your prospects or brag about yourself. Which do you think is better?

95% of all dollars spent in advertising are wasted in my opinion.

One big reason is so-called image ads. Results cannot be tracked. Experienced direct marketers know they don't produce sales.

Why? Image ads contain a "me" message.

For your advertising to be measured in the real world and to be profitable, it must offer a . . .

"You" message

You've seen plenty of "me" message ads. A few examples include most advertising for buying watches, automobiles, and even franchise lead generating ads. Examine the Thursday section of the Wall Street Journal Mart.

"Me" message ads are basically all the same. They contain the logo of the advertiser as large as possible. The copy states the following:

> **We** are the best. **We** have been in business since 1937. **We** have won awards. **We** employ the world famous designers. **We** have a long tradition of quality.

There is one problem with such ads. They do **not** produce sales.

You probably have a beautiful company logo ad. All the statements about your company may be accurate. But no one cares! Except you. If a prospect bothers to read your entire ad message—and a few will—an image ad violates two of the basic direct marketing success rules.

Your headline does not

1. **attract attention**
2. offer a **benefit** to the reader.

And you do not answer the all important question in everyone's mind and heart when any ad is read.

"So what's in it for me?"

Most ad agencies love creating "me" ads. They are quick and easy to prepare. They do not have to produce sales. And no one can measure their effectiveness.

Madison Avenue type ad agencies often quote surveys to support the power of their ads. The problem is marketing surveys have no relationship to reality in my experience.

The only objective reality-based measure of any ad is sales from and attributable to the ad.

An effective ad must appeal to the "you" in the heart and mind of a prospect.

AD#1—The first example of a **Before** and **After** ad is originally prepared by Ricoh. It is shown as it appeared in the Wall Street Journal.

A few comments about Ricoh's approach:

- The entire ad breaks my first rule as a "me" message. Who cares about a "Cannata Report" which virtually no one has ever heard of. Have you?
- The headline contains no clear benefit for the prospect who is being asked to read the ad.
- Body copy is mostly "me" message.

The "you" approach should be self-evident in the **After** ad I've written.

To which would you respond—Ad A or B?

AD#2—The **Before** ad was written by a client of mine, Leslie Brice, President of Gateways, a prominent tape publisher in Ojai, CA. The **After** ad was prepared by me.

These ads illustrate the marked contrast between a good basic ad and the more emotional editorial style ad approach which I favor.

BEFORE-AD#1

A LOT OF COMPANIES SAY THEY MAKE THE BEST FAX MACHINES

ONLY ONE CAN BE RIGHT

Which fax to buy. The selection is staggering. The claims, impressive.

Well, the latest Cannata Report did your homework for you. In a recent survey of office equipment dealers—the experts, Ricoh was named fax manufacturer of the year. For the second straight year. Second to none. The best.

This surprised some people. Not us. The fact is, Ricoh makes more fax machines than anyone else in the world. Everything from a super compact portable fax to super productive plain paper laser models.

So now you have a clear choice for your office. One of the best fax machines in the world. Or someone else's.

THE NAME TO KNOW

RICOH®

1-800-63-RICOH

Extension 1457

AFTER—AD#1

Before you buy your next fax machine. . .

"Free Report Reveals the Fax Machine Chosen by Experts as the Very Best"

Which fax is best for your needs?

The selection is staggering. For a fax machine is one of today's most relied upon pieces of office equipment. But there is a problem. When you are in the market for one, unless you do some research, how can you be sure you made a wise decision?

Well, the latest Cannata Report, a respected industry publishing, did your homework for you. In a recent survey of office equipment dealers—the experts revealed all their trade secrets. Free report available without obligation. Recorded message gives details. Call anytime 24 hours a day 1-800-000-0000.

BEFORE—AD#2

Bring your batteries BACK FROM THE DEAD!

- **Make Your New Batteries Last for Life!**
- **Charge Your Batteries 3 to 4 Times Faster!** (Ni-Cds & Gel-Cells)
- **Wipe out Ni-Cd Memory!**

There's No Better Charging System in the World!

PANA-CHARGE can save you hundreds, even thousands, of dollars on camcorder, cellular phone, laptop computer batteries, etc.

Do you have battery problems?

Is your battery only giving you 5 to 15 minutes of operating time when it used to give you an hour or more?

Are you tired of spending money on replacement batteries just to have them end up in the same condition?

We have the solution!

Your Batteries Can Last for Life!

Nickel-cadmium batteries have the potential to last for the life of the product they were designed to power. But why don't they? The problem lies in the way **they have been charged.** If batteries are to last for life, two requirements must be met: (1) they must be correctly discharged before being recharged (2) they must be **properly charged** to their absolute **full potential.** Factory-supplied and other chargers don't do this.

Why You Should Never Use a Factory-supplied Charger

As you repeatedly use your charger, you repeatedly add a barrier called "memory," which continuously shortens your running time — each and every time you use it. The reason? Factory-supplied chargers **do not properly charge** a battery to its full potential, as required by Ni-Cd chemistry. It gets worse when your charger doesn't correctly discharge your battery. This creates a **double memory barrier.** Each time you charge your battery with a factory-supplied charger, you perpetuate a vicious cycle that shortens its running time and eventually leads to its premature death.

The New Breakthrough Battery Manufacturers Don't Want You to Know About

Now there is a new technology developed right here in America that will make your Ni-Cds last for life: *PANA-CHARGE.* It precisely delivers a power burst of current that breaks through the memory barrier and properly charges the battery to its full potential. This reconditions your battery to a brand-new state and gives you the **full running time you had when the battery was brand new.** *PANA-CHARGE* not only wipes out destructive memory in old batteries, it also prevents memory from ever forming in new batteries.

Compare PANA-CHARGE to factory-supplied and other chargers:

Factory-supplied charger:

- drastically depletes times you can recharge your batteries
- never fully charges batteries
- damages cells by overheating
- doesn't correctly discharge batteries
- creates disabling "memory," which shortens running time by 50% to 90%
- charges very slowly — in most cases takes overnight
- limited to specific battery design
- limited to a specific voltage & current capacity
- provides very limited or no battery protection

PANA-CHARGE:

- makes new batteries **last for life**
- charges Ni-Cds to their **absolute full potential**
- has tapering-down charge to **eliminate thermal overload**
- correctly discharges batteries to their **safe level**
- completely **wipes out destructive memory** and restores batteries to brand-new condition
- fast-charges most camcorder batteries in **1 to 2 hours**
- charges almost any **type of battery**
- **automatically adjusts** to voltage & amp-hour of battery
- reverse-voltage, overcharge, and short-circuit **protection**

PANA-CHARGE will charge any voltage up to 14.2 and can even operate from your car's cigarette-lighter plug, so you can charge your batteries while driving! Adaptors available for almost **every conceivable battery, including video camera, camcorder, cellular phone, laptop computer, power tool, photo flash, and remote-control hobby batteries.** Note: When ordering, have your brand & model no. ready.

Don't Throw Your Old Batteries Away — Bring Them Back to Life with *PANA-CHARGE*

Start saving your batteries and your money! Order *PANA-CHARGE* now at the **special introductory price** of only $159[00]. Call 1-800-477-8908, Dept. 59, or send check or money order to: **LogicTronix**, Box 1706, Ojai, CA 93024.

Please include $5 for shipping.
CA residents add 7.25% sales tax.

Customer support and factory guarantee directly from the manufacturer: Cool-Lux — the best video light and accessory manufacturer in the U.S.

30-DAY GUARANTEE
Pana-Charge is guaranteed to restore your batteries to new condition* or your MONEY BACK.

© 1993 LogicTronix MADE IN USA *unless batteries were destroyed by reverse polarity.

To order: Call 1-800-477-8908, Dept. 59

"When the Battery Failed, It Broke My Heart... I Could Not Recapture That Special Moment"

At last, an astonishing new breakthrough in battery chargers makes premature battery failure virtually impossible. Plus it saves a small fortune on new batteries.

When a battery fails at the wrong moment, your special occasion can be ruined. Here is what happened to me.

Competing against several strong soloists, my son Steve was chosen to sing the class song at his high school graduation. He practiced singing the moving ballad, "The Long and Winding Road," for weeks.

To record this special moment, I planned to use one of the highest rated camcorders. And several days before the event, I made sure my battery was fully charged by leaving it on my charger overnight.

Finally, graduation day came. It was beautiful and sunny, perfect for the occasion. Over 2,000 people attended the ceremony in the outdoor football stadium. My goal was to capture this moment for grandparents, relatives and friends who couldn't come. And for Steve to have as a lifelong memory. For his friends. And eventually his wife and children.

The heart-breaking moment

Just as the announcer introduced Steve, my camcorder shut down—the battery failed! While Steve sang beautifully, there was no video record. And I couldn't do a thing about it. It just broke my heart.

Every one of us has special events we want to cherish and record. A birthday party, a friend's wedding, a special vacation, a son's little league game, your parents' wedding anniversary. Those rare moments to preserve and remember.

To avoid anything like this from ever happening again, I embarked on a quest for reliable batteries. No doubt you know what it's like to have a battery fail. The failure of your power supply, cellular phone, or power tool can be a major frustration—sometimes even a catastrophe.

A friend recommended what has proven to be a foolproof solution. A new product called Pana-Charge.

Pana-Charge is the result of a new breakthrough technology developed right here in America. It will revolutionize the battery industry. Now it's possible for your batteries to last for life. What I would have given to have had this miracle product on graduation day!

Here is the best part

Think of it. You'll never have to replace your old batteries again. Not only will you avoid serious problems, you will also save hundreds of dollars by not having to buy new replacement batteries.

Bring your old batteries, the ones you gave up for dead, back to life!

You no longer need a closet full of batteries for all your important equipment needs.

Pana-Charge is the only way to keep your batteries alive for the life of the product. And it's surprisingly affordable.

There is no better charging system in the world! A Pana-Charge can save you hundreds, even thousands of dollars on batteries you would normally throw away.

But how does it work?

Nickel-Cadmium (NiCad) batteries *should* last for the life of the product they are designed to power. Why don't they?

The problem lies in the way NiCads have been charged in the first place. If any battery is to last for life, two things must happen:

1. They must be correctly discharged before being recharged.
2. They must be properly charged to their absolute full potential.

Why you should never use a regular charger

The "memory" in batteries is the key. When you repeatedly use your regular charger, you are constantly adding a barrier called "memory" to the battery. This continuously shortens your running time each time you use it to charge your battery.

Yes! Each time you charge a battery with a regular charger, you shorten the battery's running time, eventually causing its premature death.

Unlike any other charger available anywhere

Pana-Charge is different. It's the perfect battery charger, created by engineers who understand Ni-Cad chemistry. And it has the potential to last for at least 3000 charges or the lifetime of the product.

Using a special computer chip, Pana-Charge discharges a battery to its safe level and then charges it to full potential. In the process, destructive memory is wiped out, restoring batteries to brand new condition.

This means your batteries last. You can depend on them to give a full hour's worth (or more) of shooting time on your camcorder or video camera. Your cellular phone won't suddenly go dead in the middle of an important call. Your laptop computer won't shut down on you, losing all the precious work you hadn't yet saved.

Astonishingly fast

You'll be delighted to know Pana-Charge is fast. It takes one to two hours to fully recharge batteries. Compare this with a regular charger, which takes overnight and still doesn't do the job properly.

Pana-Charge is also *environmentally friendly*. Because you recycle your batteries, landfills are not used up unnecessarily. You'll be getting your money's worth and contributing to saving our environment.

How much would you expect to pay for a product like Pana-Charge? $250? $300? $400? At that price it would still be a cost-effective investment. But you don't need to invest anywhere near that amount. Under our special introductory offer, good only for 30 days, we'll rush you Pana-Charge for only $159 for 6, 7.2 or 9.6 volt models. Or $189 for 12 or 14.4 volts. (Orders received after the introductory period will not be accepted at this price.)

Money Back Guarantee

We are so confident that you'll find your charger indispensable you can order at our risk, not yours. Try Pana-Charge in your home or business for 90 days, a full three months. If for any reason, or for no reason at all, you'd like to return it, we'll send you a prompt and courteous refund.

To order now call **1-800-477-8908 Dept. 63** toll free, fax to 805-646-0980, or complete the coupon and mail.

Yes! Please rush me Pana-Charge. I understand I have 90 days—3 full months—to try the product and that I may return it for any reason during the guaranteed period for a prompt and courteous refund.

Check one. I would like the:

__6, __7.2, or __9.6 Volt at $159 + $5 S&H.

__12 or __14.4 Volt at $189 + $5 S&H.

(California residents add 7.25% sales tax.)

❑ Enclosed is my check for ________.

Bill my: ❑ MC ❑ VISA ❑ AMEX

CC# ________________ Exp. ________

Signature ________________

Name ________________

Address ________________

City/State/Zip ________________

Daytime Phone ________________

(In case of questions on your order)

LogicTronix, Dept. 63
Box 1706 Ojai, CA 93024
1-800-477-8908 1-805-646-0980 fax

AD#3—Before version is a highly successful ad written by me. This ad breaks all the advertising rules, including my own!

But nevertheless, it was a huge success. What rules does it break?

1. The ad draws attention to itself. Normally a good ad only draws attention to the product being offered.
2. Uses a kind of "Archie Bunkerish" language normally used by men after a few drinks.
3. Uses slang and profanity.

But gosh was it fun to write! The reason it worked? As with all good advertising every word is true.

The **After** version was prepared by one of my newsletter subscribers, James Anderson, who modeled his ad after mine! The client reports this ad beat his former control ad by 381%.

However, notice the ad contains some of the same words and phrases as exist in the original ad. Had I not specifically given permission for this ad to run when the client submitted it to me, I could have stopped its further use. If its use continued, I could have sued and probably collected damages.

Modeling an ad can be a very good idea

But make enough changes to avoid possible disputes. Remember this. When you model an ad too closely you are in the danger zone. Therefore, always get permission to run it from the original marketer or change the words and appearance so it does not resemble the original ad too closely; or you could have legal problems. If you have doubts, it's a good idea to get a legal opinion before running the ad.

Only Way Left For Little Guy to Get Rich...

Here is the uncensored message my wife asked me not to write

"I love my wife. And I understand why she wants me to keep my mouth shut. She just wants to protect me from the IRS.

But I can't be quiet any longer. I'm angry. We are really getting jerked around. And I'm tired of it.

The government says one thing. Then does the opposite. Especially Bush. And I even voted for him. One of my biggest mistakes.

First the Feds talk tax cuts. Then they increase taxes. Remember the "read my lips" promise? Who are they kidding?

Average taxpayers, you and I, are getting screwed.

The new law doesn't bother the rich fat cats much. They still have loopholes galore. Let's face it. They always will.

But recently I ran across a workable angle. It's cheap. And it's legal. It's meant for the rich. But it's perfect for us little guys. You don't need any money. And we can get the same breaks the rich get.

I can hardly believe it. Catch this. I formed a corporation. Of my own. For peanuts.

It's my way of fighting back.

Now I have a small, one-man corporation. I operate out of my apartment. My work? I'm a commercial designer, Freelance. Brochures, fliers—stuff like that. On my income I didn't think I could save much. But I'm paying almost zero taxes. And it's legit. Just like big business does it. I have no guilt. Uncle Sam already gets plenty. Too much from all of us.

One thing the Feds didn't bother much under the new tax laws—corporate tax goodies. I guess they figured it would burden business too much. And with what result? No jobs for anybody. Including them. But not to worry. They're not that stupid.

From a buddy, I heard about this unusual book. It's called HOW TO FORM YOUR OWN CORPORATION WITHOUT A LAWYER FOR UNDER $75, by Ted Nicholas. Damnedest book I've ever seen. Has the forms right in it. Pages are perforated. You just fill in some blanks and rip 'em out and mail them in.

A couple days later you've got a corporation. No wonder it's a best seller. (They tell me over 900,000 copies have been sold.)

No need to bring in other people. You can be President, Vice-President, Secretary, Treasurer all by yourself. Just like me.

You know lawyers charge $300 to $2,500 for incorporation. Talk about ripoffs! And their secretary fills in the form—a single page with two blanks. Now you don't need a lawyer. And there is no hassle at all. It's simple No wonder lawyers like you to think everything is so complicated.

You don't have to employ anyone either. Just by your lonesome. And I always thought corporations had to have lots of employees.

Oh well, Now I know.

Let me tell you something. I'm a skeptic. It's easy and convenient to shop by mail. But I've been ripped off in mail order. So, before I sent my check, I checked out the company. Called consumer and business bureaus. Found out the publisher has a good record. And the book is guaranteed. So, what the hell. I spend that much on a few beers.

Damned if it didn't come in a couple of weeks.

I expected a shlocky-type mail order book. What a shock. Instead the book was typeset. Has a shiny red, white, and blue cover. And it's big, 8 1/2" x 11".

I've had it for only three months. Already I've given myself all kinds of fringe benefits. Kind employer I am! Put in a medical reimbursement plan. A one-page form did it. Makes all my doctor, dentist and medical bills tax deductible—for me, my wife, and my kids.

Now my wife has been seeing a shrink. Guess living with me is no picnic. We deducted over $600 in the last two months alone. Also just got myself new teeth. Caps, I should say. Cost me $2,500. My son's braces I figure will cost $2,000 next year. And I can deduct it all. Right off the top.

Savings have been scarce for me. I've always had a helluva time saving money. But with this little corporation, I'm really socking it away. How? First, I tax deduct any extra cash I don't need in the business. A corporation makes this easy to do. And then I sock it away in stocks, bonds, etc. Interest and dividends are completely tax-deferred until I retire. In the meantime, I can even borrow the money back. So I don't lose the use of it like in an IRA or Keogh. This gimmick is called a Pension/Profit Sharing Plan. Again, I just filled in a couple of blanks on a standard form.

Now, I'm no financial genius. But I'll tell you this. I'll be a fat cat myself soon at this rate. It may not be as tough as I once thought. Incorporation is the only way left. Now little guys like me have a shot at the big money.

This little corporation even covers my rear end. I could get sued. Everybody likes to sue these days. Something for nothing. And some judge might not like me. But you know what? They only thing anyone can get is what's in my little corporation. Big deal. A drafting table. A desk. And a little paper. Nobody can touch the real bucks. My home, cash, cars—even benefit plan monies are protected.

Maybe you've got some little business deal going. Or maybe you can get something started. Even a part-time business. This book can help. It can make the difference between just making it or operating just like the big boys. Even better, since you don't have their expenses.

For a real shot at big bucks, isn't it time you looked into a corporation?

It worked for me. So well that I wrote a fan letter to the company. They asked me to write this message. In my own words. But I did ask them not to print my name. Who knows? Maybe my wife is right. You can't be too careful. The IRS might want to hassle me. Even though everything is 100% legal. They may not like my message.

If you order now, the publisher will throw in a free bonus. A report called *The Income Plan*. Worth 20 bucks by itself. Shows you how to turn most jobs into a corporation. Outlines how to operate as an independent contractor instead of an employee. You can increase your take home pay up to 40%. Taxes will no longer be withheld before you get your hands on the money.

Here is how to get your copy of HOW TO FORM YOUR OWN CORPORATION WITHOUT A LAWYER FOR UNDER $75. And remember. Get the book. Look it over for 30 days. It will give you ideas. Lots of them. If you don't want to keep it for any reason, return it for a full refund. And keep the bonus. No questions asked."

Please rush me a copy of HOW TO FORM YOUR OWN CORPORATION WITHOUT A LAWYER FOR UNDER $75, by Ted Nicholas, at $19.95, plus $2.95 for postage and handling. I have up to 30 days to look it over. If, for any reason, I don't feel it's for me, I can return it for a fast refund. And the bonus *Income Plan* is mine to keep, regardless.

❒ Enclosed is my check.
Charge my: ❒ MC ❒ Visa ❒ AmEx

Card Number ______ Expires ______

Signature ______

Name ______

Address ______

City/State/Zip ______

Send to:
Nicholas Direct, Inc., 1000 Oakfield Lane
Wilmington, DE 19810

The Only Way Left for "Genetically-Average" Bodybuilders to Get Huge.

Here is the Uncensored Message My Training Partner Asked Me Not to Write.

My training partner is a great guy. And I understand why he wants me to keep my mouth shut. He just wants to keep our "get huge" secrets—secret. But I can't keep quiet anymore. I'm angry because most bodybuilders are really getting jerked around. And I'm tired of it.

The champs say one thing in the magazines. Then they do the opposite. I even used to believe what they said at one time—swallowed it hook, line and sinker. Biggest mistake I ever made.

First they say they never use drugs, then they get busted at the airport trying to smuggle stuff in from Europe. Who are they kidding? The "genetically-average" bodybuilder like you and me is getting screwed.

Why? I'll tell you. All the fancy routines the champs claim to follow work great, if you're taking a bunch of drugs. Couple that with studly parents, and no wonder they have 23 inch arms.

But here's the deceit. Most guys today don't have access to the majorly potent drugs. Or the genetics. The result? The "champ" routines they follow are worthless. Totally void. Non-applicable to genetically-average guys like you and me.

But recently, I stumbled across a workable system. You can still get huge. I promise.

The method? It's easy. No gimmicky stuff. No Bulgarian this or Czechoslovakian that. Basic stuff—with a few new twists. So, secretive training partner or not, I'm going to reveal everything. Nothing held back. By the way, you don't need a training partner to get huge with this new system. You can train all by your lonesome. And, don't expect some crummy training course designed for the masses. Actually, what you'll get is a collection of little-known, almost-secret training techniques specially designed for the genetically average bodybuilder. Guys like you and me.

Here's just a small sample of what you'll learn:

- **Why you should** never imitate the training methods of genetically-gifted bodybuilders. If you do, your progress will come to a screeching halt.
- **How 2 exercises,** if done properly, can juice your system, flooding it with muscle building testosterone.
- **The best way** to develop one body part 90% of all bodybuilders neglect. It's not the calves. Once you learn this secret, your overall muscle growth will accelerate like crazy.
- **How an ancient** bodybuilding device can blast your muscular growth into orbit. This device is inexpensive—and almost never advertised in any bodybuilding magazine. Use it for 21 days and grow like mad!
- **Learn how** to super-set 2 exercises and put 3½ inches on your chest. It's not benches and flys!
- **How to work** a body part 6 times a day. Yeah, 6 times a day (and cause a 13% increase in permanent muscle size).
- **Why nutrition is not** 80% of the genetically-average guy's success formula.
- **The one food** genetically-average bodybuilders should always eat. Always. And you don't have to buy it from a health-food store.

Let me tell you something. My training partner wants me to see a shrink. He thinks I'm a bona-fide nut for revealing all these inside secrets. You see, he's a genetic wimp. But he doesn't look like it. His arms are 17 and ¾'s on the hang. All 3 heads of the tri's sticking out. 25 and ¼ thighs. Separated to the max. The truth is, he gets off when people accuse him of using drugs. It's an ego thing. He loves to let them think he might be. But he isn't. He just follows the secrets I'll reveal—and he grows like mad. I suspect he loves the attention. And doesn't want anyone else to steal his show. That's really why he wants me committed. Listen, I've been cheated, lied to and ripped off for all my younger years, before I wised up. I like bodybuilders, especially average ones. And I. want to spare you from being cheated like I was.

These secrets work for me. Here's more...

- **Overtraining**. How to instantly tell if you are. And why it will halt your progress faster than eating nothing but Twinkies and Ding Dongs.
- **Exercises** you should never do if you want to continue training past the age of 30.
- **How you can** grow the fastest way known to man, while never picking up a weight. This inside tip will make you grow beyond comprehension.
- **How to quickly** recover from your workouts and make sure you get strength increase of at least 1.5% a week! Remember, you get strong first, big second.
- **6 ways to properly** construct a training cycle that will cater to your specific needs. This is something all the magazines never tell you.

Will these secrets work for you? Who knows? But I'll bet it's worth the investment. Maybe my training partner's right. Maybe most guys who get the new 231 page book, *Brawn,* won't follow its advice. Too bad for them. But for the really smart guys who do follow its advice. LOOKOUT. Get ready to spend a few bucks on some new clothes because you'll be growing out of the ones you have on now. Real fast. Guaranteed.

If you order *Brawn* now, I'll throw in a special report valued at $12.50 on 10 foods that you can buy at any grocery store that work better than practically any supplement on the market. You must hurry. This special report is available to only the first 100 people who order.

To get your copy of *Brawn,* fill out the coupon below and send it back today with a check or money order for $19.95 plus $2 postage and handling. To order by credit card, call 1-800-637-1572. (Ask for Dept. A932.) Once you get *Brawn,* look it over for 30 days. It will give you ideas. Lots of them. If you don't want to keep it for any reason, return it for a full refund. No questions asked.

Yours for muscle,

James Anderson

James Anderson

CLIP AND MAIL TODAY

YES! Please rush me a copy of Brawn. I understand I have up to 30 days to look it over. If, for any reason I don't feel it's for me, I can return it for a fast refund. And the bonus special report valued at $12.50 is mine to keep, regardless.

☐ Enclosed is my check ☐ Money Order (Make checks payable to Mile High Publishing. Personal check orders are held for 14 days. For faster service please use your credit card or money order.)

☐ Charge my credit card:

☐ MasterCard ☐ Visa ☐ American Express ☐ Discover Card

Card Number__________ Exp. Date__________

Signature__________ Phone__________

Name__________

Address__________

City__________ State__________ Zip__________

Send. to: **Mile High Publishing**, P.O. Box 277, Dept. A932, Golden, CO 80402

How to Create More Profitable Mailings by Knowing How to Test

You've heard it a million times. The secret of super direct marketing success is to constantly test.

But what are the most important mail elements to test? How do you decide to implement an effective testing strategy? Testing is the subject of this important chapter.

The twelve most important elements in any mailing are:

1. Teaser copy on envelope
2. Headline on letter
3. Letter
4. Offer
5. Bonuses
6. Price
7. Guarantee
8. Lift Letter
9. Brochure
10. List
11. Order Card
12. Graphics

The biggest mistake made by direct mailers is testing too many elements at the same time. Reason? You cannot be certain what affected your test.

Unless the information you gain from a test is valid, you obviously can't make good decisions. The only way to assure an accurate reading of any test element is . . .

Test one at a time!

The only variation to this principle might be your mail list selection. More on this in a moment.

Before we move further, remember the three basics of a successful offer.

I. Product and offer
II. Mailing list
III. Copy

Any test affecting one of the elements can make a huge difference in response. Let's now break a mailing down further and look more closely at 12 major elements which can be tested.

1. Teaser copy on envelope

Has the same function as does a headline on a space ad. You can help get your prospect to take the first step toward responding to your offer by opening the envelope. Because it's so very important, exercise great care in creating a powerful benefit-oriented teaser.

The easiest to change as well as the lowest cost element in a mailing is the teaser copy on an envelope. I've seen differences in results of over 200%—that's over two times the response in mailing results. The only change was a different teaser!

On every mailing that you do, test at least one new teaser against your control. Here is an example of two mailings I did with all elements being the same (identical letter, offer, etc.) except for envelope teaser:

**"Discover Today's Best
Business Turnaround Strategies"**
(Envelope A)

**"How To Get Very, Very Rich
Turning Around A Business"**
(Envelope B)

Which pulled best? Envelope B by 271%.

TIP

Because the task of teaser copy is to get the envelope opened, here are a few tips to help induce your prospect to open the envelope. Add these words after the teaser copy.

. . . See inside for details
. . . Open at once and read immediately
. . . Free gift inside
. . . Open at once for free sample form
. . . See sample form inside
. . . An urgent message from Ted Nicholas (or you)

A word of caution. Don't be cute or use any tricks or gimmicks. When you offer a free gift make certain you give something of **real value to the prospect**. Otherwise, while you may get many people to open the envelope, you will alienate the prospect. An upset prospect, of course, will not buy your product.

2. Headline on letter

Can be as simple as repeating the teaser copy from the envelope. Or, you can create an entirely new headline. Of course a new headline must be congruent with the teaser and the entire offer.

There is no hard and fast rule on this. I often repeat the teaser copy. However, on many mailings my headline on the letter is different from the teaser copy. A mailing currently being done for a client for a speaker's product uses a headline successfully pretested in a space ad as teaser on the envelope. Here it is.

"How To Get Enthusiastic Applause, Even A Standing Ovation—Every Time You Speak."

The headline on the sales letter is the subhead used in the original space ad as follows:

"Leadership Today Requires That You Are An Outstanding Public Speaker"

Notice that in the above example the original subhead is strong enough to be a headline. And your subheads should be as well.

3. Sales letter

Establishing credibility is the challenge on writing your letter (as well as all advertising copy). It must be written with honest conviction. And passion. You must persuade and practically compel the prospect to take the action you request.

4. Offer

The product must be perceived to be worth more to the prospect than the price you ask. Answer this question in the mind of all prospects clearly and distinctly. What is the offer and of what benefit is it to me?

Too many offers are overly complicated. Simplify as much as possible.

You need to show that compared to the money involved in the purchase, the value to the prospect is many times greater.

TIP

You can markedly strengthen your offer by comparing its investment with others with which your prospect is familiar. For example, when you carefully compare the cost of your product with a weekend at a resort, a night on the town, a new car, or a new suit, the price will undoubtedly be perceived as a terrific bargain!

Here is an example of copy that makes a valid comparison. "What would you expect to pay for such a product? About $75?, or $60?, or $50?, or the cost of a special evening for two at your favorite restaurant? No, it won't even cost you 50% of this. You can have XXX product for less than half a night on the town, only $29.97!"

5. Bonuses

Perhaps the least understood, and therefore underused, of all the elements of a mailing is the use of bonuses. I have **always** increased response to my offer by including one or more free bonuses! But here is the key to a successful bonus.

It must be so appealing the prospect would want to buy it if it weren't free.

When I first started in business I thought I was being clever. I offered a free bonus of a special report that wasn't selling successfully by itself. Result? Sales actually decreased when I added the bonus to the offer versus no bonus at all!

So I came up with a valuable rule that I'll share with you.

If you can't sell it, you can't give it away!

Never break this rule.

However, highly saleable free bonuses will increase response. You must constantly search for powerful products you can use as free bonuses to be a super successful direct marketer.

Your bonus can be nearly anything which appeals to your prospect. Just a few bonus ideas that are proven to work effectively in direct mail offers include:

- Special reports
- Books
- Flashlights
- Mugs
- Pens
- T-shirts
- Video tapes
- Audio tapes
- Pocket knives
- Business cards
- Hats
- Calculators (one of the hottest bonuses today)

Bonus ideas are limited only by your imagination. One of the most unusual and fun bonuses I used a few years ago was a new Rolls Royce!

The headline offering rentals of my mailing list to direct marketers was "How To Get A New Rolls Royce Free Just For Testing A Hot Mailing List."

The copy described that we would deliver a beautiful Rolls Royce replica to the customer's office. Everyone loved it and the offer was highly successful. Our cost was over $100 per unit but well worth it.

Use bonuses properly and your mail results will soar.

6. Price

The ideal price can never be decided by the marketer. Your customers, not you, are best qualified at setting the price. I see most direct marketers making this classic error.

They do little or no price testing.

Pricing is really a fascinating art. Depending on the product, the way it's presented and the audience, sometimes a higher price actually pulls more total sales as well as units than a lower price! Other times a product produces a higher profit at a lower price.

Sometimes, the profitability of a product is about equal at a higher price or a lower price. In this instance you need to clarify your strategy. If you want more customers to whom you offer other "back end" products, you would go with the lower price. If you accept less front end response to produce the same profitability handling less units, you would go with the higher price.

The safest thing to do as previously mentioned is:

Let your customers set the correct price for you!

This is a typical pricing scenario for a product such as a piece of quality costume jewelry, a handbag, book, exercise device, or special report that might sell for a price less than $100. You could offer the product at four price points. The prices need to be different enough from each other so that the "read" you make of results is meaningful.

Your prices might be $29.97, $47.97, $77.97 and $97.77. Remember the appeal of prices which end in the digit 7!

Keep everything else in your mailing exactly the same. Then include of course your letter, order form, offer, bonuses, lift letter and brochure.

Now if you were to send your offer to a list of 20,000 names broken down into 4 segments and your letter pulled at least 30 responses from each segment, price test results would be statistically significant. You could then "roll-out" the most profitable price.

Someone always asks this question at my seminars. "Suppose a customer were to discover that they paid more than someone else for the product?" Answer. This rarely happens. In 21 years and hundreds of tests, it's happened perhaps a dozen times. If and when it does, here is a low-cost way to handle the matter. Simply send a letter with an explanation of the truth. Namely that we were price testing. We apologize for any confusion and then send a full refund of the purchase price paid, allowing the customer to keep the product with our compliments. If the product is a subscription, we refund the difference of what has been paid at the higher price.

7. Guarantee

You will **always** improve response with an unconditional money-back guarantee. The longer the guarantee period is, the more orders and fewer returns you will get.

Here is a powerful guarantee style and wording you can use with any product:

Money-Back Guarantee

After you have the product for a full year, if for any reason you are not completely delighted, return it to us and receive a prompt and courteous refund.

The words "prompt and courteous" are extremely important as they help build credibility.

Other effective titles for your guarantee are:

- Iron-Clad Guarantee
- No-Risk Guarantee
- Better Than Money-Back Guarantee

You can also offer a **conditional guarantee**. This might result in fewer orders but more qualified long-term clients. Here is an example of a conditional guarantee:

Money-Back Guarantee

If, after trying out our program for up to one year (12 months) you have not achieved at least the minimum results described in our advertising, upon proof of completing the steps described in your manual, simply return the program for a prompt and courteous full refund of every penny you've invested.

Changing the wording of a guarantee can improve response to your offer.

8. Lift Letter

An extra letter included in your mail package. Properly done you can "lift" the level of sales from your offer, hence the name.

Here is how to prepare a lift letter.

- Present a benefit not found in the main letter.
- Write in the voice of someone other than the signer of the main letter, i.e., a customer testimonial, an officer in your company other than yourself, or an industry expert.
- Keep it short; no more than approximately 150 words.
- Print it on another color paper stock, such as primrose, yellow, peach, or blue.
- On the outside fold of the letter say: "Please read only if you are still undecided."

Replacing a weak lift letter with a stronger one can materially improve mail results.

9. Brochures and fliers

Can sometimes add substantial sales power to a mailing. This is particularly true when photographs of your product enhance the appeal as with jewelry, leather goods, cosmetics, watches, pens, scarves and other luxury products. Also, products such as automobiles, appliances, tools and clothing are often enhanced by good photography printed on quality paper.

In marketing information products, my tests show that there is no hard and fast rule. Sometimes a brochure adds sales. Sometimes, surprisingly, results can even be less than without a brochure. And obviously it's more expensive to include a brochure. A valid test for any product is to mail your offer to different list segments with and without a brochure.

Here is how to prepare a brochure or flier with real sales power:

- Use powerful headlines and subheads.
- Include features of your product as well as benefits. Specify its size, weight, color, how it's made and any other unique aspects of the product. This helps build credibility by displaying your expertise. Features indicate you really know what you are doing.
- Print on white stock.
- Do not use screens behind any blocks of copy as you will decrease readership. Use screens only outside copy areas, unless you don't want the prospect to read the copy.
- Use first class photography. Don't forget to caption each photo.
- Include people enjoying the product in some photographs, as well as the product by itself.
- Print in at least 2 colors, and if the product is greatly enhanced, as with jewelry, use full color.
- All words should be printed in black ink. Never use another color. Black is easiest to read.
- Print on glossy stock.
- For a flier, use 81/2 × 11 printed both sides. For a brochure make sure no matter how many pages you use (4 pages makes an excellent size) the first page should unfold to 81/2 × 11.

TIP

Always include the price, address and toll-free order information on brochures. Most people neglect to do this and miss extra sales from people who keep just the brochure from the mailing, or who give the brochure to a friend.

10. List Selection

Obviously a major key to your mailing success. Your mailing will not succeed if you send your offer to an uninterested or unqualified prospect, no matter how good the product offer or copy.

The very best prospects for your offer next to those who have already raised their hand by answering an inquiry ad or otherwise inquired of your company are:

> People who have in the last 3 months bought a similar product in the same price range by mail. A good list broker can help you locate such buyers from hundreds of mailing lists available on the market.

You must constantly be on the lookout for prospects for your product.

Two experienced mail list brokers who can help are:

> **Lee Kroll**, Kroll Direct Marketing Inc., 666 Plainsboro Road, Suite 340, Plainsboro, NJ 08536; Telephone (609) 275–2900; and

> **Eric Weinstein**, the Listworks Corp., 2151 West Hillsboro Boulevard, Suite 203, Deerfield Beach, FL 33442; Telephone (305) 481–9400.

TIP

Look at incoming orders and if, for example, you are receiving a high percentage of orders from medical doctors or CPAs or other professionals, you might find a bonanza of new lists to test, i.e., CPAs who buy similar products to yours by mail. We have struck gold many times through this simple process.

On every roll-out mailing that you do it's important to test 5% to 20% of new lists as you need to constantly seek new prospects for your product. But don't become "test crazy." It's vitally important to test new lists. But, if you use too heavy a proportion of new untested lists your profitability may drop. So keep your test lists as a small percentage of your overall mailing unless, of course, your percentage of response is huge and you can afford a larger percentage.

11. Order Card

A huge weakness on the part of most mailers is a poorly prepared order card. The main reason is that order cards are often prepared as an afterthought. Typically most of the creative effort is expended on the letter, teaser and brochure. And there may be a built-in aversion by entrepreneurs and writers, as with most people, to ask for the order.

But the order card is where the sale is finally closed. It is crucially important. Yet most order cards have no passion, zest or sales power. It's as though the creative engine is "out of gas."

Here is how to prepare an order card that increases mail results.

1. The sequence of when you prepare the order card is vitally important. Write the order card copy right after you write the envelope teaser copy, headline, subhead and opening letter paragraph. But before you begin the sales letter!

2. Assume your prospect will look at the order card first. Many prospects do just this. Or perhaps he/she only reads the mail element and not your beautiful letter, brochure, or lift letter. Ask yourself, "Does my order card alone excite the prospect enough to close the sale?"
3. Repeat your headline, subhead and a few of the most important benefits derived from your product.
4. Repeat your guarantee. Perforate order card so customer may keep guarantee for his/her records, thus further building credibility.
5. Include a photo of your product on the order card.
6. Use an attractive border. For an executive prospect a "certificate border" can be very effective.
7. Use an appealing title for your order card, such as:
   "Free Trial Request"
   "Charter Subscription Offer"
   "Limited Edition Certificate"
   "Seminar Reservation Request"
   "Special Investment Application Certificate"
8. Print in at least 2 colors on a different paper stock than the letter.

There is no more important element within your mailing to test than the order card. Add vitality (all sales of products and services depend on vitality) and benefits and watch your sales explode.

12. Graphics

Can make the difference of profit or loss in a mailing.

Don't misunderstand. I'm not suggesting that a mail "bomb" which pulls almost no orders can be turned into a winner by changing the graphics.

However, when you are in that tough area where your mailing is close to break-even, improved graphics can improve the mailing to break-even or better and save the day.

Graphic designers who can help improve direct mail results are rare. The best graphic designers in the U.S. for direct marketers realize their proper role. They know this important truth.

Copy—the words—are the most crucial part of an offer.

The proper role of graphics is to enhance the feel and power of the copy. This can often be done simply by careful selection of typefaces and arrangement of copy. Or, by using photos and other graphic images which can enhance the offer.

Two graphic designers I can highly recommend are:

Sandy Taccone, 16 Vane Court, New Castle, DE 19720, Telephone: (302) 323–0343, Fax: (302) 323–0518.

Terry Finder, The Terry Group, 4356 Bonney Rd., Bldg. 3, Virginia Beach, VA 23452, Telephone: (804) 431–0600, Fax: (804) 431–1416.

Another world-class graphic designer who does great work for people with a somewhat higher budget is:

Ted Kikoler, Ted Kokoler Design, 43 Beveridge Dr., Donn Mills, ONT Canada M34A 1P1, Telephone: (416) 444–6631, Fax: (416) 444–6632.

Now that you have the 12 major secrets of testing effectively as well as other tips to enhance results, I look forward to more success stories about dramatically improved mailings!

How to Market Yourself

How you market yourself is at least as important as marketing your product. Why? Because you deal with business people on a personal basis daily. That's why this chapter is devoted to personal marketing.

I was inspired to write about marketing yourself because I see avoidable mistakes constantly being made by entrepreneurs. For example, here is what happened recently.

John D., one of my newsletter subscribers, was lamenting his recent experience a couple of months ago. He was turned down by his bank for a merchant account. His fledgling mail order business could not process credit card orders. Of course, without this capacity it's difficult, if not impossible, to operate a direct marketing company today. Yet, banks are leery of mail order businesses. Banks have experienced credit card losses with a few mail order marketers. Large losses are rare, but nonetheless, many applicants are being turned down these days.

After asking John a few questions, it became clear to me that he made some mistakes. In fact, the way he handled things he probably wouldn't have succeeded in any negotiation.

To get the desired outcome with another business person you must . . .

Market yourself effectively.

What I will cover in this chapter may come across as a form of manipulation. Let me assure you that it is! But, the issue needs clarification.

There is mass confusion throughout the world on the proper role of advertising and marketing in a society. Indeed, as part of persuasion all marketing is designed to manipulate people to take a certain action. Critics of advertising are quick to condemn business people for precisely this reason. However, criticism is undeserved. Why?

Manipulation—it is good or bad?

There is a major difference between **positive** and **negative manipulation**.

Negative manipulation in any business situation occurs when a seller gets one or more people to purchase something or take an action that benefits only the seller. Buyers **lose** money or time or something else of value to them without gaining an equal value. The outcome is a win/lose proposition.

Positive manipulation is when the seller gets others to do exactly what the seller wants. But here is the important point. The benefit derived by the buyer is at least equal to the seller's. Indeed, it can be many times greater than the seller's. It's a win/win proposition. My writings always stress positive manipulation. The benefits derived by the buyer of my products are at least equal to and up to 10 times or more those of the seller.

Vive la difference

While there are similarities between marketing on a one-to-one basis or in print, the most important difference is this.

In print you must **anticipate objections** and answer all of them satisfactorily. **What** you say and **how** you say it is the key in print. Be **pro-active**.

In personal one-on-one marketing, **asking questions** in a certain way **combined with active listening skills** is the key to success. Be **reactive**.

When communicating verbally your business prospect seldom listens to and really hears all your benefits or sales points. He/she simply stops listening somewhere during your presentation.

If the prospect were reading a well-written letter from you, the likelihood of your getting across your complete message is much higher.

It's human nature that most people prefer to hear themselves speak rather than listen to you or anyone. Therefore, because you will not be fully heard, to sell a person on an idea **your job is not to tell**.

Instead, **listen more and speak less**. But active listening is a very rare skill practiced by only a select few super marketers. You will be far more successful if you give prospects what they rarely get from anyone but really want from you:

To speak and be heard!

Make it easy for prospects to communicate. Ask questions which encourage them to speak. Listen carefully to them, which is the want of all humans. You will be thought of as a great friend as well as conversationalist!

Don't make the common mistake made by entrepreneurs. They talk too much. Prospects get turned off. The marketer does not make the sale.

Another underused marketing strategy is whenever you speak to someone about a proposed business transaction . . .

Assume Consent

Ask questions the nature of which **assume** the end result you seek. For example, with a banker you might ask these questions:

1. "How long does it normally take for a credit card charge to be credited to my account?"
2. "What discount or percentage of credit card sales will the bank charge us for your service?"
3. "How long would it take to get the service in place?"
4. "What equipment do we need to buy to make it easier for your bank to process our orders?"

Let's look at some of the biggest mistakes John made. How could he have handled the matter so as to markedly increase the chance of a favorable outcome?

Note how John approached the bank. He dropped by. Without an appointment. He was dressed in a typical outfit worn by many home-based business owners—jeans, open-collared shirt, windbreaker and running shoes.

He asked his favorite teller Fred, "How can I get a merchant account for my new information-based mail order business?" Fred, who didn't have decision-making power, said he'd look into it. He would call John by the end of the week. Fred did call with the answer. Not surprisingly it was . . .

No!

Here is how you, in similar circumstances, might handle a potentially important business relationship.

First, remember what you have often heard but can easily forget—the power of the all important . . .

First Impression.

Let's back up to the beginning. We first have to choose **who** we'd like to impress. In any business relationship the logical person on whom to focus is the individual who is authorized to say yes or no.

The best way to locate the person of authority is simple. Call the bank and ask for the name of the person in charge of merchant accounts. Call and make an appointment directly with the responsible person or his/her secretary. On the telephone, do not go into any details of the forthcoming meeting if possible. Save them for the meeting.

On the phone just say that "I am a good customer of your bank and would like to make an appointment to discuss a possible way to increase the business I do with the bank. Would Tuesday or Thursday at 11:00 a.m. be possible?"

Make sure you're on time for the appointment.

On the day of the appointment be prepared. Also make sure you are dressed appropriately. Your attire has enormous impact in any business encounter.

Dress for the occasion

John Molloy, author of *Dress for Success*, says: "The man who wants to succeed in business should make a habit of wearing suits, not slacks and sport jackets. Dark blue, dark gray, and pin-striped suits carry the strongest success message. Don't wear brown—it alienates some people.

"A woman should wear at least a two-piece or ideally a three-piece suit and dress fashionably, although conservatively, and as expensively as she possibly can."

You should look on your wardrobe as a blue chip investment that will pay huge dividends.

I once made a mistake about my choice in clothing on an important occasion that taught me a lot. After successfully direct marketing my books and other products for 5 years I was fortunate to have numerous favorable articles written about me. Frankly, I was more than a little cocky.

One day the local Wilmington, Delaware, paper called to set up an appointment to interview me for a newspaper article. On the day of the interview instead of wearing a suit I dressed casually, the way I often do when writing and not seeing clients—in jeans and a T-shirt. What a mistake!

The reporter "roasted" me in the article. He focused not on my business, but on my non-businesslike attire. And the paintings hanging on my walls. He used negative words such as "irreverent," "eccentric" and "rebellious" all because of the way I chose to dress and decorate my own private office! This came through more strongly in the article than the nature of my work. The article did little or nothing to enhance my business. An important opportunity was wasted! But what a learning experience.

The lesson that I derived from that experience was this. Always dress carefully—deliberately—for all important business meetings. Don't dress above or below the level of those with whom you are meeting.

Clothes are not everything

Just as important as your choice of clothing is your physical appearance. Pay attention to:

- The way you hold yourself.
- The way you walk.
- The way you smile.

Several important studies show we all tend to believe attractive people have virtues they may not possess. We think good-looking people are more sensitive, more intelligent, more exciting than those who are physically mediocre. Hold yourself confidently with your back straight and chest forward. Smile warmly. Look the person straight in the eye when you speak. Be well-groomed.

You will undoubtedly be considered attractive and possessing many good qualities.

How to build rapport

When you arrive at a business meeting your first task is to establish rapport.

One of the best ways to establish rapport is to ask relevant questions. As previously mentioned, contrary to popular belief, it is far **better to be a good question asker and listener than an articulate communicator**.

Everyone enjoys talking about themselves, their family or their job. Observe the desk and other surroundings for evidence of a hobby such as golf, tennis or bowling, which you may relate to. Ask questions like:

- How long have you been with the bank?
- Are you a native of the town or city?
- Is it as interesting as it appears to hold a responsible job in banking?
- Is this a good area in which to play golf?

Answer any questions you are asked promptly and honestly. Be brief with your answer to questions. Resist the nervous temptation everyone has to over talk.

Listen carefully to the voice pace of your prospect—a very important element of building rapport. What is the **pattern** of speaking? If your banker talks slowly, you speak slowly. Match the pace.

If he/she speaks rapidly, you speak rapidly. Everyone naturally feels more in their comfort zone when those business contacts with whom they speak have approximately the same timing.

Type your prospects

Another good way to build rapport can be put into action once you identify your prospect's favorite style or type of communication. Everyone prefers a particular style of communication unique to them.

Neuro-linguistic programming (NLP) teaches that we all are more comfortable communicating in one of three basic styles. Putting this in a marketing context the three types are:

1. Audio—Prospect likes to verbally hear the benefits. Prospect might give signals such as saying, "I'd love to **hear** more about this aspect of your product."
2. Kinesthetic—Prospect likes to physically experience the benefits. Prospect may give a signal such as picking up or wanting to **touch** the product or asking for a demonstration.
3. Visual—Prospect likes to be **shown** the benefits visually. Prospect may respond to a photo, chart or other visual aid you may be using.

Look for signals such as these from your prospects and business contacts. Once revealed to you, simply give your prospect more of what their style indicates they want.

When do you present the nature of your business? Ideally after you have a chance to establish some rapport, perhaps in five to ten minutes.

Be careful with your choice of words. If you are in the information business do not say you are in mail order! Instead say: "I'm in the **publishing** business and would like to better serve my customer. Therefore I'm interested in applying for a merchant account. What steps are necessary for me to complete an application?"

Then, shut up!

Whenever you ask a question. Don't say another word. Whenever you ask any type of closing question, wait for your banker or prospect to speak first. Sometimes this wait can seem like an eternity. But it's very important not to speak before he/she does.

At that point if the merchant account seems like a "go," your banker will probably explain the procedure involving completing some forms and ask you a few questions. You simply listen and take notes. Politely end the meeting as quickly as you can. And leave. Don't dally. You would be wasting the most valuable commodity the banker, you, everyone has—time. Your prospects appreciate you more if you respect their time.

Use testimonials

Take the application form home with you. After completion, call and make another appointment to deliver the application. On your return visit bring at least three letters from people who have done business with you for a few years, regardless of whether the bank asks for references.

These letters, of course, serve the same purpose as does a testimonial in a sales letter. They help build your credibility.

Of course, even if you follow the foregoing steps, there is no guarantee you will get a merchant account or make any business deal favorable to you. However, unless there is a bank policy precluding merchant accounts, I submit you will markedly increase the chances of your getting a favorable result.

There is a happy ending to the story of John D. He followed my recommendations. At the second bank he approached they agreed to give his merchant status. Today he is happily processing MasterCard, Visa and American Express orders!

Please note. In this issue, I'm deliberately using a very tough example in getting a merchant account. Acquiring a merchant account is difficult for any direct marketer today. And even some very large and established companies have lost their accounts through no fault of their own but simply because of changes in bank policy.

However, here is the point. Regardless of what you are seeking from a supplier or sales prospect, you will be more successful if you handle it properly.

As to getting a merchant credit account, you may be interested to know of my experience. After I sold my two former companies in 1991 I moved to Florida. There I reapplied for a merchant account through a local Florida bank for my new company, Nicholas Direct. I was told the bank had not opened a new merchant account for any direct marketing organization for the last two years!

I applied nevertheless using the foregoing procedures. Frankly, I was pleasantly surprised when the bank approved my application. Knowing that the bank policy was stringent, I was fully prepared to get at least one no before I got someone to say yes. Of course, I was helped by a successful track record in my former business.

In summary, let's note the main differences in John D.'s successful approach to a bank over his first. He . . .

1. **Found** the person who could make the decision.
2. **Made** an appointment with the decision maker.
3. **Dressed** appropriately and made a favorable impression.
4. **Built** rapport.
5. **Listened** more than he spoke.
6. **Positioned** his business as a publishing company, not a "mail order business."

Important point. Don't make this common error in referring to your business. There is really no such thing as a mail order business. Mail order, although the phrase is commonly used to describe a business, is not a business. It is a method of distribution!

The words you use to describe your business are very important. It positions you in the mind of the prospect. Unfortunately, the phrase "mail order" has a negative aura about it in many circles, probably because of the poor reputation of "junk mail," along with the reputation of a few shady operators who garner unfavorable stories in the media.

Here is my most profitable no-cost marketing secret:

TIP

It always pays to hand out a professionally done business card every time you see a prospect or business contact.

Here is a simple idea you can use to make money with your business card as well as add impact to your first impression . . .

Print on both sides of your business card.

For years while traveling on airplanes and trains, on request I'd write the names of one of my books on the back of my business card. Then I'd say, "If you have any problem getting any of my books in a bookstore, you can call my office which has a supply of them for immediate shipment. Tell them you spoke with me and I suggested you call."

I always got calls and orders.

One day this idea occurred to me. If I had the most popular titles printed on the back of the card, more copy would fit than I could hand write, thus more orders. That's exactly what happened. And, of course, I love getting book sales with zero marketing costs.

Your business card is a very powerful marketing tool. It gets looked at three times. This is perhaps more than any form of print advertising. Those three times are:

- When you hand out the business card
- When the recipient takes it out of their pocket or bag.
- When it gets tossed.

Some cards are looked at even more than three times. Nearly everyone looks at business cards several times trying to decide whether to file or toss.

On the next page is a sample of my business card. Notice a line is left on the back. If a conversation with a prospect reflects an interest in a product not listed, like a tape or a newsletter, it can be written there!

Attendees of my seminars have created many variations of business cards with products and services featured on the back. You should offer your most appealing products that you'd like prospects to remember. And order!

Others have effectively described the U.S.P. (unique selling proposition) of their business.

Bottom line. Print a powerful sales message on the back of your card and increase sales.

Look upon any personal meeting as an opportunity to market yourself, which you must do before you can effectively market your product. As a national direct marketer, unfortunately you cannot meet each and every one of your customers personally. Of course, while having some downside this factor also has many positive aspects. For example, you're able to service tens of thousands, even millions of customers with few or even no employees.

However, customers are not the only people important in your activities. Vendors, banks, the media and many other contacts are all extremely important to building a successful business. When we have occasion to talk business with anyone who can help us, we need to focus on personal marketing strategies that are proven to work.

Master the strategies presented here and you will market yourself as never before.

NICHOLAS DIRECT, INC.

Ted Nicholas
President

1 Nicholas Square
P.O. Box 877
Indian Rocks Beach, FL 34635
(813) 596-4966
(813) 596-6900 Fax

Front side

Books Include:

How to Form Your Own Corporation Without a Lawyer for Under $75 .... **$19.97**

Secrets of Entrepreneurial Leadership **$19.97**

Golden Mailbox **$39.97**

How to Publish a Book and Sell a Million Copies
Special Price **$87.00**

Other: ____________________

Back side

How to Uncover the Most Important Secrets of a Successful Sales Letter

Part I

What makes a sales letter work?

The biggest shortcut to preparing an effective sales letter is to study real life examples of those that are successful. Then when you prepare an offer you can "model" your letters using these winning strategies. You will greatly improve results.

This chapter will analyze in depth a recent sales letter I prepared for a client. It is a big winner.

To model direct marketing success, the best way to do it is to know how the mind of the creator of a campaign works. But very seldom does a copywriter "spill the beans." Few pros go along with having their brain picked.

I'm going to reveal the secrets to a successful letter. I'm going to share my thought processes. So now I will invite you into my head. Come and join me on a special journey. A creative one. Are you ready? Let's go!

First, before the letter was written let's look at the creative goal. The client and I mutually decided to:

> Prepare a direct mail "package." This would include a sales letter, flier, and order card. The product? A health book entitled *How to Fight Cancer and Win*. The author, William Fischer. To enhance the offer I would select bonuses or develop new ones from scratch. I would review past offers and suggest a new offer. Retail price target between \$19.95 and \$29.95. Client would supply

numerous testimonials from consumers, doctors and other health professionals.

How long did it take to complete?

I worked on the project on and off for 2 weeks. The final package consisted of these elements:

- 16-page sales letter
- Two page flier
- Bonus reply envelope
- Order card
- Outer envelope—size 6 × 9
- Business reply envelope

The mailing would be sent via third class mail.

Step-by-step to success

The very first thing I did was to read and study the book. Then I examined the credentials of the author as well as medical experts described in the book. Since the book had been sold for about a year, I also reviewed previously used sales materials. Both successful and unsuccessful.

Using 3 × 5 cards while reading the book I captured the benefits. I wrote a single benefit on each card. From some pages I found one benefit; other pages two or three, some pages none, and so forth. I write each benefit as a headline, as dramatically as possible.

I found the book absolutely loaded with benefits. I was able to capture 153 benefits which could also be used as "bullets" in the sales letter.

TIP

Very important when capturing benefits. Note the page number in the book where the benefit is found on each 3 × 5 card. Credibility, drama and curiosity are all increased when you cite the page number in the copy.

As I isolate the benefits on the cards, I'm on the lookout for what I can use as the all important "teaser copy" for the envelope and/or sales letter. As mentioned many times before in this book, teaser copy is as important as the headline in an ad.

I wrote over 100 benefits **before** I found the one that was the most compelling.

How did I choose the premier benefit?

When I discovered the section that described how a famous doctor found a natural cure for cancer that was scientifically proven by incorporating two natural foods in your diet, I knew I had the "grabber." I then wrote several headlines centered on this theme. I felt this was the strongest:

**"You can Prevent and Cure Cancer Simply
By Eating Two Natural Foods"**

Now I had the most important element in any direct mail offer. The lead—the theme—the unique selling proposition—the marquee—the teaser copy, the all important . . .

Headline!

The scene was set to pave the way for the headline. I wrote a **preheadline:**

World renowned doctor says . . .

Reason? Credibility. I felt such a powerful, startling, controversial headline needed lots of proof.

TIP

It should never be forgotten that establishing credibility is ***always*** *the biggest challenge facing any copywriter.*

I became very excited about the teaser copy. I felt everyone getting the mailing would surely be compelled to want to tear open the envelope to know more.

The next task. Create a subheadline good enough to be a headline by itself. It ideally should tie into the headline.

Since Dr. Budwig, who is featured in the book, is a world renowned doctor with impressive credentials, here is what I wrote:

> **"Seven time Nobel award nominated doctor shows how certain natural foods and nutrients actually *prevent and cure cancer.***
> **Leading medical doctors endorse her breakthrough findings."**

Do you see how this subhead helps build still more credibility?

As a second subhead I quoted Hippocrates, perhaps the best known doctor in history (you may be aware that all U.S. doctors must recite the Hippocratic oath before they can practice medicine):

"Let food be your medicine,
let medicine be your food."

Why? Again, for even more credibility and to support the concept that the right foods are critical to your health.

Then I added a copy element containing the most powerful word in the arsenal of any copywriter—Free. The subhead reads:

5 Free Reports

TIP

Sequence of copywriting. When you write each part of the offer is critical. I always begin with the ***envelope****.*

Most copywriters begin their effort with the letter. The ***envelope*** *should always be the first thing you do. Reason? No one will ever read your letter, no matter how powerful, unless they first are intrigued enough to take the first step to a successful offer:*

Open the envelope!

Next I selected 12 benefits for the back of the envelope. These, of course, are taken form those all important 3 × 5 cards. I felt the ones I chose were the most likely to arouse enough curiosity and practically compel the recipient of the letter to open it. I felt satisfied at this point that opening the envelope was nearly irresistible. The envelope would be opened!

TIP

Exception. On most offers, especially if the weight is less than one ounce, I test a segment of the mailing using an envelope with these elements:

1. *No teaser copy.*
2. *No company name, just a return address.*
3. *Typewritten address.*
4. *Live first class stamp. (Or you can test a variation using a metered indicia. This looks like first class mail.)*

Sometimes this works more profitably than a third class mailing with a teaser.

In the "cancer book" offer, because the mailing is quite heavy in weight, to reduce expense a first class test was not done in the initial test.

The order card is crucial

The second element I always prepare in a mailing is the **order card**.

TIP

Prepare order card right after the envelope. Most copywriters make the mistake of preparing the order card last in a direct mail package. Don't you do it! Avoid the fate that awaits most order cards. Indifference. They are boring, lifeless, and confusing. Such an order card will not capture sales effectively, if at all.

The reasons you are more likely to create an exciting, powerful, clear, easy to follow order card if you do it right after the envelope include:

1. You'll communicate more excitement and passion because you are still fresh. You are not "out of gas."
2. You'll clarify the offer in your mind. Thus, order instructions will be easier to follow.
3. The letter will be stronger and easier to write as a result.
4. You will be in a better position to select or create bonuses that will improve the offer.

Bonuses increase sales

I have **never** made a direct mail offer wherein results did not substantially improve when I offered one or more exciting and saleable bonuses.

In the cancer book the products available in the client's catalogue, particularly their titles, were not compelling enough to be bonuses in my opinion.

Develop new bonuses

So I suggested using the contents of a very fine book from the catalogue. From it I created not one but 5 separate bonuses! Then I created these 5 titles:

1. The Truth About a More Exciting Sex Life
2. How to Take Off the Pounds and the Years
3. Nutritional Secrets to More Youthful Skin
4. How to Improve Brain Capacity Naturally
5. How to Increase Your Energy and Enjoy Living Longer

Aren't these the health benefits all adults want? Don't you? Of course! These are the same wants that people had 50 years ago. And they will still want them 50 years from now! And they really enhance the order card, don't you agree?

TIP

Ask yourself. Is your order card exciting, complete and compelling enough to sell the product all by itself? If not, it needs more work.

I included the elements listed below on the order card to enhance its power. And if someone didn't read my letter or if the order card is passed along to someone else, it must be strong enough to sell the book even without a sales letter!

1. Photo of the book
2. Featured doctor
3. Guarantee
4. Order information
5. Price
6. Two testimonials

As with all direct mail elements, an effective order card always is stronger with a **headline!** Look carefully at your mail. Many order cards are prepared without a headline. This is a wasted opportunity.

A headline I often use on order cards is:

Free Trial Request

The cancer book order card copy reads:

Mail This FREE Trial Request Today!

Notice that the word **Free** is emphasized.

The order instructions are to **Please Rush** copies of the book.

The titles of four of the free reports are repeated.

The fifth report was chosen as an "early order" benefit. In this way you add more excitement and urgency to the offer. And you give the prospect an additional reason to buy now.

F.P.C., One Fischer Square
Box 368, Canfield, OH 44406

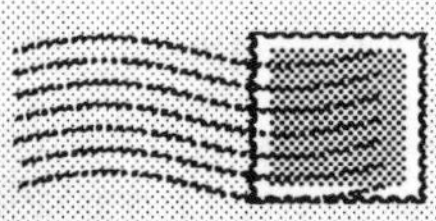

World renowned doctor says...

"You Can Prevent and Cure Cancer Simply by Eating Two Natural Foods!"

7 Time Nobel Award nominated doctor, "Dr. Johanna Budwig discovers natural cancer cure"

See Inside for Details...

Envelope—Front

"Seven time Nobel Award nominated doctor shows how certain natural foods and nutrients actually prevent and cure cancer. Leading medical doctors endorse her breakthrough findings."

***"Let food be your medicine, let medicine be your food"* --Hippocrates**

- Why do people in northern and eastern states have much higher incidence of colorectal cancer than people who live in western and southern states? Page 62
- What vegetable does new research indicate may have preventative, even curative powers over cancer, particularly of the lungs? Page 191
- Laboratory studies indicate that cancer rates can be reduced by up to 79% by simply adding this important supplement found in the soil to our diet. Page 63
- Why the death rate is 5 to 10 times higher in America than in Japan. Page 64
- What important trace mineral in butter and cream actually helps your body prevent cancer? Page 191
- Why drinking bottled or filtered water can help prevent premature aging and cancer. Page 204
- These lifestyles choices such as diet over which you have control represent 72% of the causes of cancer. Page 12
- Which vitamin helps protect smokers from lung cancer? Page 60
- How Nobel Prize winner Linus Pauling uses vitamin C to keep advanced cancer patients alive for as long as 12 years. Page 61
- 7 Nutritional secrets used by the Chinese to keep cancer rates down. Page 76
- What common cooking method is as carcinogenic as smoking 600 cigarettes consecutively? Page 70
- Avoid having problems with prostate, including cancer. One out of three men over 50 develop prostate problems serious enough to require medical attention. Page 7

Envelope—Back

Mail This FREE Trial Request Today!

7 Time Nobel Award nominee, Dr. Johanna Budwig

Please rush me __ copies of HOW TO FIGHT CANCER AND WIN by William L. Fischer.

Also send me the following free reports:

1. *The Truth About a More Exciting Sex Life*
2. *How to Take Off the Pounds and the Years*
3. *Nutritional Secrets to More Youthful Skin*
4. *How to Improve Brain Capacity Naturally*

☐ Also send the FREE report for my prompt response: *How to Increase Your Energy and Enjoy Living Longer.*

I enclose not the original price of ~~$50~~, but only $29.97 (plus $3.00 shipping & handling. Ohio residents please add 6% sales tax). I understand I may examine this revolutionary new book for one full year, since I am fully protected by your 100% No-Risk Double Guarantee as stated on the reverse of this card.

Fischer Publishing Corporation
One Fischer Square, Box 368, Canfield OH 44406
Phone: (216) 533-1232 Fax: (216) 533-9860

HOW TO FIGHT CANCER AND WIN
$29.97
Plus $3 shipping & handling

☐ Enclosed is check or money order (U.S. currency only) payable to Fischer Publishing Corporation in the amount of:_________.

☐ Charge my: ☐ Visa ☐ M/C ☐ AmEx

Card #

Expires

Signature

Jason Brown
2018 Malvern Ave.
Clearwater, FL 34601

Are your name and address correct? If not, please make the necessary revisions to this label

Order Form—Front

What Readers Are Telling Us:

"I have prostate cancer. My urologist is interested in the book... I'm going to follow Dr. Budwig's methods."

—John Repasy, OK

"Your book is fascinating. I have followed some of your instructions faithfully, and can't explain how good I feel already. God Bless."

—Susie Steel, NY

Fischer Publishing Corporation, One Fischer Square, Box 368, Canfield OH 44406

DOUBLE GUARANTEE

You are protected by this 100% No-Risk Guarantee:

1. If you don't like this amazing new book when it arrives, return it for a full refund, no questions asked, and keep the bonus reports regardless.
2. Or, keep and use it for one full year. You are still protected. You must get all we promised, or send it back anytime during the entire year. You still get every penny of your purchase price back.

Order Form—Front

HOW TO FIGHT CANCER AND WIN

INSIDE:

Highlights of Featured Topics

HOW TO FIGHT CANCER AND WIN
Hardcover
$29.97 plus shipping and handling

Cancer Explained

I) Brief explanation of the disease
II) Causes of Cancer: brief overview
- A. Lifestyle Choices
  - 1. Tobacco Use
    Lung, Esophageal, Throat Cancers, Contributes to others as well
- B. Dietary Choices
  As many as 35 percent of the cancers many experts now say, are a result of the food we eat.

Eminent Doctors and Alternative Cancer Treatments Today

I) Natural Cancer Killers
II) Nutritional Metabolic Treatments
- A. A 500-page study of cancer patients was hailed as "the finest case review ever conducted concerning Alternative Cancer Therapy."
- B. Promising medical doctors have given us convincing evidence that diet and nutrition produce long-term remission in cancer patients, almost all of whom were beyond conventional help.
- C. Much research has been done in recent years, not only on the part nutrients play in preventing cancer, but how specific foods help to deter cancer.

Orthodox Medical Treatment

I) Importance of Early Detection
- A. Regular Physical Exams
- B. Early Detection

Use what modern science has available. Evidence that early detection improves your chances. Examples from three types of cancer. Statistics show that finding it early helps:
1. Breast Cancer
2. Cervical Cancer
3. Colorectal Cancer

II) Conventional Treatment: An Overview
- A. Surgery
- B. Radiation
- C. Chemotherapy

The Importance of Dietary Fats

I) Fat and Oils
II) Destructive "Industrial Strength" fats
III) The refining process explained
IV) Margarine vs. butter
V) The Good Fats
- A. Fish Oil
  - 1. Its contribution to good health and the possible prevention of the following diseases:
    - a. Cancer
    - b. Arthritis
    - c. Psoriasis
- B. Essential Fatty Acids
  - 1. Definition of linoleic acids.
  - 2. Signs of deficiency
  - 3. Minimum needed for good health
  - 4. Food Sources of EFA

Dr. Budwig's Research Findings

I) Results of her work with cancer patients
- A. Budwig's thoughts on cancer and other diseases
- B. How Linoleic and Linolenic Acids Affect the Body
  - 1. How they may help cancer and heart problems
  - 2. What foods contain these EFAs

Flier—Front

HOW TO FIGHT CANCER AND WIN

Highlights of Featured Topics– cont.

3. Danger of "processed" fats

II) Use of a certain oil in the fight against cancer— Research from around the world:

Brief review of the scientific studies being performed all over the world including the following countries: Poland, Great Britain, Germany, India, Australia, France and Austria.

III) Successes with various cancers including: malignant osteoma, basal cell carcinoma, Hodgkin's Disease, stomach cancer, osteosclerotic sarcoma, and brain tumors.

Also reports of several other degenerative diseases which have improved, including: hypertension, atherosclerosis, and faulty metabolism.

The Dietary Delights of Certain Oils

I) The Basic Formula
II) Muesli Breakfast
III) Dressings for Salad Greens and Raw Vegetables
IV) Spreads
  A. Butter
  B. Mayonnaise

The Magic Food Provides Real "Health Insurance"

I) Potent Cancer Prevention— And Much More
II) Benefits of this miraculous food
  A. Storehouse of nutrients
  B. Heart health
  C. Prostate protection

Oriental Secret Diet

I) Introduction to the philosophy behind the diet
II) The Secret Oriental Concept
  A. Relationship between diet and disease
  B. The Diet Itself
  C. Oriental Food Preparation
III) Stories of Success
  A. Prostate cancer
  B. Cervical cancer
  C. Ovarian cancer
  D. Other cancers

Mind Power Therapy

I) The Therapy Explained Briefly
II) The Power of Positive Imagery
III) How to Practice Mind Power Therapy

Some Little Known Avoidable Carcinogens

I) Electromagnetic Fields (EMF)
  Also ELF, Extremely Low Frequency radiation, as emitted by computers.
II) Geopathogenic Zones
  Among the proponents of this theory are Hans Nieper, M.D., and Dr. Ernst Hartmann, of Eberbach, Germany, who say that there may be certain zones on the planet that foster the formation of cancer cells in people.
III) Air Pollution
IV) Water Pollution
V) Fluoride

Defeating Cancer

I) Recommendations on how to keep cancer out of your life
II) Regular visits to doctors; avail yourself to diagnostic techniques
III) Healthy Diet
  A. Follow the Food Pyramid
  B. Follow diets as outlined by National Cancer Institute, the American Cancer Society, and the American Heart Association
  C. Avoid all refined sugar
  D. Avoid using aspartame
    1. Review of research on the problems of this artificial sweetener, also known as NutraSweet
  E. Other factors

How to Enjoy the Miracle Fat

Four weeks worth of menus that incorporate a certain oil, and nutritionally sound butter and mayonnaise to provide a variety of healthy meals for successful cancer treatment.

Fischer Publishing Corporation
One Fischer Square, P.O. Box 368
Canfield, OH 44406
Phone: (216) 533-1232 Fax: (216) 533-9860

Flier—Back

The title *How to Increase Your Energy and Enjoy Living Longer* was selected for two reasons.

1. The number one complaint people have when visiting a doctor is **lack of energy**.
2. Everyone wants to live longer according to many health studies.

Establishing a price

Remember, three elements must be in balance for any direct mail to succeed:

A. Offer and price
B. Copy
C. List

The price is a vital part of any offer. The book has been sold in the past for prices ranging from $19.95 up to $50.00. The lower price range was the most profitable.

The goal of the mail list was primarily to test the copy. We settled on a price of $29.97. The ending digit 7 has proven to have more sales appeal on a variety of direct mailings—minc and others.

To help build perceived value, I used this phrase in the copy:

"I enclose not the original price of $50.00, but only $29.97."

The all important guarantee

Direct mail **always** pulls more orders with a strong guarantee. Study carefully the **double guarantee** especially created for this mailing.

A good product with a strong guarantee will experience refund requests of less than 5% if the product lives up to the copy. This is acceptable on most offers. And the longer the guarantee the less refunds. In this case I used a year.

The back of the order card

On some offers I use both the back and front of the card, and others just the front. Having tested both ways the conclusions to what works best is:

It depends!

The nature of the product and offer help determine the layout of the order card.

On the "cancer" card with the **large author and book photos** on the front **and** two strong testimonials besides, the layout simply worked better using front and back. To get all the elements on one side would have resulted in a huge order card or copy with so small a point size it would be tough to read.

Use of the company logo

Every entrepreneur wants to have at the very top of page one of their letter and on the outside of their envelope their company logo. But guess who loves the logo? Your customer? No! You, the company owner. However, it serves no marketing purpose. It's a "me" message. Not a "you" message. Only "you" messages sell. Your prospect wants to know the answer to one question.

What's in it for me?

Forget what you may have learned in business school about logos and proper letter style. Unless you are writing to your best customers who already know and trust you, it's best **not** to have a logo on the top of your letterhead. Or on the outside of your envelope.

If you must have a logo somewhere just to make you happy, place it on the **order card**. And/or last page of your letter. And/or on fliers and brochures.

Notice how the logo is used sparingly on the order card.

The flier or brochure

Sales results from many mailings can be improved with a descriptive flier or brochure. Product offers in the luxury goods category, such as jewelry, leather goods, clothing, watches, and accessories, are clearly enhanced by attractive photography combined with powerful copy.

Information products and services can also benefit from a brochure or flier. In the cancer book I felt the table of contents was both complete and strong. So I used it as the basis of a flier. I rewrote many of the sections to strengthen them.

Prepare fliers and brochures third in the copywriting sequence. To build more credibility, combine features of the product in the flier along with benefits. Describe the color, size, finish, pages, contents, etc.

Up to this point we haven't written word one of the letter! So far we have prepared these elements:

1. Envelope
2. Order card
3. Flier

Follow the "E.O.F." sequence and you will create more effective mailings!

TIP

To maximize orders from all your mailings, here is a technique rarely used even by experienced mailers. Always include the price of your product and your name, address and telephone number on each and every major element within your mailing! This includes the flier, brochure, and letter. And, of course, the order card. Reason? Many prospects toss out your letter and keep the flier. Prospects may want to order later, long after they've forgotten the price. And, of course, they wouldn't have your number, address or telephone number. Or they will pass along information to an interested friend. This no-cost technique accomplishes an important task. It makes it easy for anyone to order from you! Use it and watch sales increase!

How to Uncover the Most Important Secrets of a Successful Sales Letter

Part II

In this chapter I'll reveal my thought process in preparing a "killer" sales letter.

Continuing from the last chapter, to refresh your memory, we used the E.O.F. sequence.

1. Envelope
2. Order Card
3. Flier

For best results, follow this sequence every time you create a direct mail package.

The fourth element then in the package is the sales letter. A sales letter is the real "workhorse" in any direct marketer's arsenal of sales tools. It is the most carefully read part of your sales package. So let's look at one closely.

Important point. Readers often ask me this. "How long should a sales letter be?" The answer is long enough to do the job. My experience has shown a 2-page letter outpulls a 1 pager, a 4 page outpulls a 2, 8 pages outpull 4, 16 pages outpull 8, etc. The key is that all copy must be **relevant**. If it's not relevant, your prospect won't read even 3 sentences! As to length, when you write copy your job is this. Simply tell a complete story. Include every benefit from use of the product. You never know what will motivate the sale. Obviously, people vary in what turns them on. By including all the benefits you can, this increases your chances to sell.

First page of the letter

If you've done a good job on the teaser copy and envelope, the important top portion of the letter is easy. Simply repeat the major envelope elements: headline, subhead and graphics.

TIP

Effectively use the space available on the first page of the letter. Don't start the narrative of the letter until sufficient space is given to dramatically presenting all the elements. Notice that the letter narrative in the cancer book example starts 2/3 of the way down the page.

Typeface

Always use **Courier** in your letter for the "feeling" most conducive to a sale. Courier is personal. From me the writer to you the reader. Do not use a typeset look. Sales will not be as good.

You begin the letter with surprise, surprise the . . .

Salutation

If you begin a sales letter with the salutation "Dear Friend" you simply can't go wrong. This is the one I and other successful letter writers most often use.

Others I could have used are: *Dear Friend of Fischer Publishing, Dear Natural Health Enthusiast,* or *Dear Friend of Natural Healing.*

How you start a sales letter is crucial, so we need to focus on the:

First sentence

The goal is to immediately capture the interest of the prospect. Why? Yes! So they keep reading.

Therefore, your first sentence must be captivating. Compelling. It sets the tone for the rest of the letter. Its purpose is to motivate you to read what? That's right! The second sentence.

TIP

A good learning exercise. Make a habit of studying the first sentence of a successful ad, sales letter, book or article. The best ones are very powerful.

As an example of a strong opening, here is the best ever written for a fiction book, in my opinion. Remember how *The Tale of Two Cities* by Charles Dickens began?

**"It was the best of times.
It was the worst of times."**

Wow! Does that set the tone for the rest of the entire book, or not?

After writing many drafts, my opening sentence in the sales letter is:

"At last, there is an answer to cancer!"

Why did I go with it? For several reasons. It . . .

1. Supports the headline.
2. Offers immediate relief and solution—hope to anyone worried about cancer.
3. Short and punchy.
4. Brought to my mind a recollection of a book written by Dr. William Kelly about 20 years ago based on nutrition. I always like the title, *One Answer to Cancer*. So I modeled my opening on this long remembered title.

Second paragraph

This reads: "A major medical breakthrough has shown you can now actually prevent and cure cancer. It's based on the oldest known form of 'medicine'—natural foods."

There are three reasons for the second sentence. Guess what they are: Right!

1. Further expands and supports the promise in the headline.
2. Builds credibility.
3. Motivates you to keep reading the third paragraph.

Third paragraph

Further expands and proves the advertising promise fundamentally in this idea. Every day more evidence supports the thesis that natural foods are the answer as evidenced by the research.

Use of anecdotes

While often I start a letter with a powerful anecdote, in this case I presented a dramatic story after three short paragraphs but while still on page one of the letter.

Subheads are important

Why? They break up large blocks of copy. And they intrigue you into reading more.

In the middle of page two see the first subhead:

"Many Have Been Cured"

Why this subhead?

That's right! For still more support for the great promise contained in the headline. My headline, while completely true, is still hard to believe without proof. Plus, everyone likes to read about humans overcoming obstacles, being cured of disease. It offers everyone hope.

TIP

For any claim to be believed, it must not only be true. It must also ***seem*** *true. When a headline claim is extremely strong, you must use several facts to support it.*

After the first subhead, the copy strategy is to add still more support to the promise of the headline. I proved that a natural solution does indeed exist to combat and cure cancer, the most dreaded of all diseases.

In the second paragraph after the first subhead, I introduce the real "hero" of the ad, Dr. Johanna Budwig.

TIP

Making real people the central focus of an ad is a very effective copywriting strategy.

On top of page three I describe Dr. Budwig's medical breakthrough and discovery. Notice how I dramatize her work.

Next in the letter sequence comes the real meat and reward of reading the letter, the . . .

Solution!

The next subhead reads . . .

"Nature Provides Answer"

My goal here is to show power of the enormous value of the natural discovery. And like all great identifications, at its core it's really simple.

So where is the product? So far the copy contains a lot of excitement and information. But no product is yet offered.

In this letter, I wait to introduce the book near the end of page three. By this time the reader is (hopefully) practically begging to be sold. At this point I also describe the full year no risk guarantee. Reason? I want the reader to focus on how great it will be to have the product and not worry one bit about risking a penny.

On page four I start dramatizing the benefits of the book.

The check marks are in front of 15 diseases (count 'em) the book's natural formulas prevents or cures.

Then comes the subhead:

"Get These Important Answers"

Here are the bulleted benefits taken from the 3 × 5 cards. (Remember how to prepare a 3 × 5 card for each benefit.) Checking a page number on which the benefit is found makes the benefit more "real" to the reader.

TIP

Look at the actual sales letter. At the top of the page is an effective graphic technique. A powerful benefit is taken from the 3 × 5 card and placed at the top of the page. Result? A powerful headline before each page!

Look at the bottom of each page of the sales letter. See how no sentence ends with a period? If you break the sentence rather than end it, there is a greater tendency of the prospect to turn the page and keep reading.

After nearly five pages of bulleted copy, see the subhead:

"What Medical Experts Say"

Reason? Why do you think? Yes, you are right! To support and lend credibility to both the promise of the headline and the bullets.

Testimonials add power

Do you have any doubt about the value of testimonials?

After the doctors' testimonials, I use a full 3 pages of testimonials from readers. There is no substitute for the actual words of satisfied users of any product.

TIP

It's a good idea to edit, hone down and edit testimonials. Of course, use the actual words—just trim them down. Also, make sure you get permission to use them. 99% of the time customers are happy to permit this use.

After the testimonials the subhead reads:

"More Thrilling Case Histories"

Everyone enjoys human drama. Especially with a happy ending! So I included short anecdotes taken from the client's files of readers who have experienced wonderful results from the book.

The ultimate purpose of any sales letter is to get the prospect to take a specific action. Therefore, you must ask the prospect to do exactly what you want in your close.

The next subhead begins the "call to action."

"Free Bonus Reports"

Each bonus has a few sentences of copy describing the benefits derived from using it. The copy here is very important, as often benefits contained in the bonuses really drive the sale. If the bonuses are strong, many people buy the product just because they want the bonuses!

The next subhead:

"Free For Promptness"

(Observe the use of the word free in the last two bonuses. Free is the most powerful word in sales copy.)

As part of the call to action right now, I reserved one of the five bonuses I created and offered it as an inducement to respond immediately. It was sent to the first 1,000 people who responded. Why? This added inducement. A delayed sale is nearly always a lost sale. So any technique you can use to enhance the sale now increases overall response.

The final subhead:

"Money-Back Guarantee"

Here I dramatize a one year guarantee.

World renowned doctor says...

"You Can Prevent and Cure Cancer Simply by Eating Two Natural Foods!"

5 FREE REPORTS!

"Seven time Nobel award nominated doctor shows how certain natural foods and nutrients actually <u>prevent and cure cancer</u>: Leading medical doctors endorse her breakthrough findings."

"Let food be your medicine, let medicine be your food"
—Hippocrates

Dear Friend,

At last, there is an answer to cancer!

A major medical breakthrough has shown you can now actually prevent and cure cancer. It's based on the oldest known form of "medicine"--natural foods.

The encouraging evidence which continues to pour in from around the world confirms the research findings. The results suggest this new discovery could supplement, if not replace, tumor treatments like radiation and chemotherapy.

Here are the actual words of a 33 year-old cancer survivor.

"I was horrified. My expert doctors gave me this diagnosis. I would have to be operated on to cut out the cancerous tumor that

The four most important zones of the body which need special attention during a physical exam. Page 39

was causing a swelling under my eye."

"Because the tumor size was greater inside there was serious bone involvement. The malignancy was far too advanced to respond to radiation. The doctors planned to remove considerable facial tissue and bone. I was afraid for my life. Being a young woman, I couldn't bear the thought of such disfigurement."

"Then I learned about Dr. Budwig's diet. I was skeptical, but desperate for help. After four months on the regimen the swelling completely disappeared."

"The doctors at University Hospital gave me exhaustive tests. One told me, 'If I didn't have your previous X-rays and medical history in front of me, I wouldn't believe you even had cancer. There is hardly any indication of a tumor remaining.'"

I never thought that using Dr. Budwig's formula would be so successful. My whole family and I are very grateful." says Magda W.

Many Have Been Cured

A similar human drama has been experienced by cancer patients who were not being helped through conventional therapies. Many people from around the world who were given just a few months to live are now living normal healthy lives. These people have cured serious cancer of all types.

All of them were taught a simple but effective diet by 7 time Nobel Award nominated physician, Dr. Johanna Budwig. They made a single major change in their lifestyle--their diet.

Cancer is the second leading cause of death in the U.S. In 1993 cancer claimed 482,000 Americans. The National Cancer Institute (NCI) estimates that at least 35% of these deaths (160,700) are believed to be due to dietary factors. NCI says "cancer is an avoidable disease when adequate preventative measures are taken."

The staggering medical costs of treating cancer annually is $104 billion dollars. This terrible toll exceeds the cost of any other disease. Family members of cancer victims are often impoverished as a result.

2

Avoid this one food and virtually eliminate the chance of cancers of the esophagus and stomach. Page 62

After doing research for 30 years, Dr. Budwig made an extremely important discovery. The blood of seriously ill cancer patients was always without exception deficient in certain important essential ingredients. These included substances called phosphatides and lipoproteins.

(The blood of healthy people always contains sufficient quantities of those ingredients. However without them, cancer cells grow and multiply out of control.)

Nature Provides Answer

Dr. Budwig then discovered an all natural way for people to replace these essential ingredients their bodies so desperately needed in their daily diet. By simply eating a combination of just two natural and delicious foods, not only can cancer be prevented, but in case after case it was actually cured. (These two natural foods must be eaten together to be effective as one triggers the properties of the other to be released.)

Cancer touches nearly every family. The likelihood of you or a loved one dying from it are one in five. Far too high to take any chances when you can take some simple preventative steps now.

One of the two foods in Dr. Budwig's formula is available in grocery stores. The other, however, comes primarily from Europe and can only be found in health food stores throughout the United States.

By simply mixing these two delicious foods together and eating them, you will be providing yourself and your family with the optimal preventative nutritional protection against cancer and —r disease.

u will learn about Dr. Budwig's formulas and how to protect .self in the latest edition of our book HOW TO FIGHT CANCER AND WIN. You will discover many surprising things that could easily save your life-- as well as the lives of your loved ones.

And the book comes with a money back guarantee for one full year. There can only be one reason for such an offer. I'm betting ɔu will never want to part with it once you add up all the ealthy benefits. After more than 10 years of solid clinical application, Dr. Budwig's natural formula has proven successful

3

Continued...

How to activate the immune system to devour diseased malignant cancer cells. Page 26

where many orthodox remedies have failed. Dr. Budwig's formula is now in use therapeutically in Europe for the prevention of:

- ✓ Cancer
- ✓ Arteriosclerosis
- ✓ Strokes
- ✓ Cardiac Infarction
- ✓ Heartbeat (irregular)
- ✓ Liver (fatty degeneration)
- ✓ Lungs (reduces bronchial spasms)
- ✓ Intestines (regulates activity)
- ✓ Stomach Ulcers (normalizes gastric juices)
- ✓ Prostate (hyper tropic)
- ✓ Arthritis (exerts a favorable influence)
- ✓ Eczema (assists all skin diseases)
- ✓ Old age (improves many common afflictions)
- ✓ Brain (strengthens activity)
- ✓ Immune Deficiency Syndromes (cancer, multiple sclerosis, auto-immune illnesses)

Get These Important Answers:

- Why do people in westernized nations have much higher incidences of colorectal cancer than people who live in uncivilized countries? Page 236
- What vegetable does new research indicate may have preventative, even curative powers over cancer, particularly of the lungs and why? Page 215
- Scientists at highly respected Nippon Dental College in Japan have determined that this minute amount of commonly known ingredient in our water supply is capable of transforming cells into cancer cells. Page 230
- Why the death rate is 5 to 10 times higher in America than in Japan. Page 57
- Did you know that contrary to popular belief, eating the right amount of butter, eggs, milk, cheese and well marbled beef can actually lower cholesterol? Page 60
- What important trace mineral in butter and cream actually

4

How to increase the body's ability to repair cellular damage from carcinogens faced daily. Page 4

helps your body prevent cancer? Page 215

- What often shunned herb, used by healers for over 5000 years, has shown amazing cancer fighting properties? Regular use also improves the immune system, promotes high energy levels and normalizes the metabolic rate, thereby assisting in weight loss. Page 217
- A 10-year German study has shown that people taking this common mineral for heart disease have 20% less incidence of cancer than occurs in the general population. Page 218
- What percentage of people are at risk of developing some form of cancer purely from a hereditary gene? What can you do about it? Page 228
- Why drinking bottled or filtered water can help prevent premature aging and cancer. Page 228
- In countries where this natural food is consumed in much larger amounts than the U.S., conditions such as colcn cancer are uncommon. Page 236
- People who chew tobacco rather than smoke it run twice the risk of developing oral cancer. Page 259
- These lifestyle choices, such as diet, over which you have control, represent 65% of the causes of cancer. Page 12
- 9 most common reasons people die of cancer. Page 12
- 9 factors which increase cancer risk and 7 factors which decrease cancer risk. Page 214
- Use these 6 early detection diagnostic techniques which could save your life. Pages 13-15
- National Cancer Institute list of both suspect and healthy foods. Page 214
- Discover NCI report which shows how 30,000 lives could be saved by the year 2000 if Americans modify dietary habits. Page 16
- Prevent the main cause of cancer treatment failure and metastasis (spreading). Page 2
- Avoid becoming a person whose cancers are spreading (metastasizing) as 5 year survival rate is just 1.2%. Page 12

5

Continued...

Learn the best sources of high fiber foods that prevent colon cancer. Page 265

- Why most fish oil supplements sold in health food stores are of little value and where to find the very best one. Page 10
- How to make a delicious and healthy home-made "butter" using 4 common ingredients. Page 161
- The best vegetarian source of some fatty acids. Page 111
- How the centuries old Hindu system of natural medicine (Ayiurveda) recognizes the importance of this oil to ext human life. Page 123
- How life energy is restored and symptoms of anemia cancer, liver dysfunction and diabetes are completely alleviated naturally. Page 127
- How to gain the amazing preventative benefits of a startling natural food discovery. Page 176
- How Dr. William Robinson of U.S.D.A. concluded that this surprisingly powerful nutrient is a powerful cancer fighter. Page 180
- A Dutch study conducted by Dr. Kromhout shows that a diet rich in these two foods reduces arteriosclerosis. Page 104
- Why margarine is bad for you and butter is better. Page 98-99

What Medical Experts Say

"HOW TO FIGHT CANCER AND WIN may be one of the most important books written on cancer and the degenerative diseases. In my 50 years as a country family physician I have never read a more down to earth, practical resume of cancer prevention and treatment."

- Edward F. Steichen, M.D.
Kansas

"I favor preventative medicine as the only viable approach to conquering this killer disease forever. HOW TO FIGHT CANCER AND WIN is the first comprehensive book for the lay person covering the entire scope of the cancer problem."

- Amar Makheja, Ph.D.
Doctor of Biochemistry
George Washington University School of Medicine, Washington, D.C.

8

Why most cold processed oils, even those sold in health food stores, have no vitamins or minerals whatsoever. Pages 93-94

"I commend you on your splendid book."
-Dr. J. Rinse
Biochemist, Vermont

"A 4 1/2 year old girl with five blood tumors on the back of her eye destroying her vision, was cured with the techniques described in your books including visualization, natural foods, and an immense amount of love."
-Leslie H. Salov, M.D.
Director
The Jeanne Patterson
Vision & Health Center, Wisconsin

What Readers Say

"Your book is fascinating. I have followed some of your instructions faithfully, and can't explain how good I feel already. God bless."
-Susie Steele, NY

"Your book was recommended to me by my dentist."
-Shirley A. Miller, MI

"I followed your instructions and after four months, I feel alive again and much stronger. I will be sharing all of this great information with my family and friends."
-Cathy Wheelock, NY

"I'm not surprised by overwhelming response to this fantastic and important book that spells it all out for you."
-Kim Sifert, AZ

"Best book I ever read or expect to read...had outstanding results...my whole life improved drastically...information goes far beyond health thinking of today."
-Hugh McMunn, NJ

"I have been using the information in your book and can feel a big difference in my health. My doctor is amazed how well I now feel. I think your book is just wonderful. Thank you."
-Joanne Maare, NY

9

Continued...

Tapping into the miracle of Mother Nature that keeps cholesterol in the healthy zone. Page 60

Dr. Budwig's formula. No more bleeding and friends tell me I'm looking younger. I'm 83."
-Clara Carr, CA

"Was exposed to asbestos 8 hours a day for years. I take Dr. Budwig's formula daily. I'm in excellent health. I'll be 95 next September. Enclosed is an order for 3 more books. Maybe someday I'll save somebody's life."
-Martin Tremp, OH

"HOW TO FIGHT CANCER AND WIN is a great book."
-Ralph LaPoint, NY

"Best book I have used in a long time. I truly believe it could be instrumental in promoting a wonderfully healthy body."
-Marion Layman, OK

"I'm 78 and feel this is the best book I ever read. I can't tell you how much pleasure it's given me."
Lori Barton, MI

"I have given away several copies of this book to friends who have cancer and are still alive."
-Mildred Schuler, KS

"Most up to date book I ever read on preventative medicine."
-Dick Porter, SC

"I have prostate cancer. My urologist is interested in the book...I'm going to follow Dr. Budwig's methods."
-John Repasy, OK

"Thank you for writing such a wonderful book. I wish everyone in the world had a copy."
-Dalton Sparr, AL

More Thrilling Case Histories

Thousands flock to hear Dr. Budwig lecture all over Europe. The many people Dr. Budwig and her formula has helped testify to the benefits of her remarkable discovery. The following are just a few examples:

11

Continued...

The secret of cooking meat in a special way that is not carcinogenic. Page 64

BRAIN TUMOR- Scotty A. experienced blurred vision, loss of balance, plus a complete shutdown of his bladder resulting in the pain and pressure of suppressed urine. Tests at a medical research center showed arachoroidal bleeding due to a brain tumor. He was promptly admitted to a hospital. Because of the location of the tumor doctors felt an operation would leave him both paralyzed and ...out his mental faculties. During the course of treatment, ...y's condition worsened and his health deteriorated rapidly. ...doctors informed Scotty he was beyond medical help. At his expressed wish, Scotty was discharged from the hospital and sent home to die in peace.

A friend came hurrying to his bedside bringing both comfort and hope in the form of Dr. Budwig's formula. Scotty was surprised to find that the few mouthfuls of the formula he was able to take stayed down. He writes: "Since I went on the Budwig regimen, the paralysis of my eyes, arms, and legs has receded daily. After only a short period of time, I was able to urinate normally."

"After eight weeks on the diet, I was able to walk unaided for the first time in months. My health improved so rapidly that I was soon able to return to my work part-time. Shortly after that, I was again examined at the Research Center and my reflexes were completely normal. The Budwig diet saved my life! Ten years later, I was given a thorough examination at the Center as a follow up. My incredible recovery has been written up in many medical journals and I have become what they call a 'textbook case,' and all because of Dr. Budwig's simple diet."

HODGKIN'S DISEASE- Seven year old Tommy G. was diagnosed as having Hodgkin's Disease. The child was operated on and underwent 24 radiation treatments, plus additional experimental therapies that the experts hoped would be of some small help. When Tommy failed to respond favorably to these heroic measures, he was discharged as incurable and sent home. His sorrowing parents were told his life expectancy was less than six months. After only a few weeks this unfortunate youngster lost his ability to speak entirely as his vocal cords had been severely burned by the radiation treatments. He was admitted to the hospital again, this time to die.

12

Which blood types place people at particularly high risk for developing cancer some time in life. Page 223

The desperate parents contacted specialists all over the world. A famous newspaper took up Tommy's cause and ran editorials pleading for someone to come forth who could offer hope for the life of a child. All the specialists who replied confirmed the cruel prognosis: There was no hope or help for Tommy. At this dark hour, the miracle the family had prayed for happened. Tommy's mother told her story to the press.

"A friend sent me a printed piece about one of Dr. Budwig's speeches. This material gave us hope and I contacted Dr. Budwig. I wanted to give my boy her diet in the hospital clinic, but the doctors told me they didn't have time for this special attention. We took Tommy home and started him on the diet ourselves. I kept in close touch with Dr. Budwig.

In just five days, Tommy's breathing became normal for the first time in almost two years. Three weeks later, his voice came back. From this day on, Tommy began to feel good again. He went back to school, started swimming and by winter he was doing craft work. He will soon be twelve years old and is now a healthy happy boy. Everyone who knows him says how well he looks."

The story doesn't end there. At age 18, Tommy is showing great promise in his university work. He knows he owes his life to Dr. Budwig and thanks her daily in his prayers.

CARCINOMA OF THE STOMACH- When Mr. William Y. (42 years of age, husband and father of three) began suffering from chronic indigestion, he chalked it up to the stress of his job as a prominent officer of the local bank. He took over-the-counter antacid compounds to relieve his distress and ignored the problem. The condition persisted and his wife began urging him to see a doctor, but he stubbornly refused. He soon began vomiting half-digested food after eating and noticed streaks of blood in his stool after a bowel movement. Frightened and worried by these developments, Mr. Y. visited his doctor, who immediately rushed him to the hospital for tests. His worst fears were realized when his doctor informed him that it appeared he had a malignant tumor growing in his digestive tract. Fortunately for Mr. Y., there was as yet no involvement of the lymph glands. (Because the lymph travels swiftly through the body, any involvement of the lymph nodes means that the malignancy can spread very quickly to other

13

Continued...

4 good sources of foods rich in essential fatty acids the body hungers for. Page 134

sites. In the case of lymph cancer, prognosis is extremely poor.)

Mr. Y. underwent an operation to surgically remove (excise) the cancerous growth, which appeared to be totally enclosed within its outer membrane. However, because of the possible danger of the blood stream carrying minute cancer cells to other parts of the body, Mr. Y. was placed on a program of advanced chemotherapy on an out-patient basis. He suffered all the classic side-effects of this toxic treatment, including violent vomiting and retching, progressive physical weakness, and almost complete loss of hair. The exhausted and nauseated Mr. Y. complained that the 'cure' was almost too terrible to bear.

Finally, a sympathetic friend brought Mrs. Y. some printed material which told in detail of the success of Dr. Budwig's formula in cases similar to that of her husband. The desperate wife and mother purchased these two foods and coaxed Mr. Y. to have it with lunch every day. Beginning by choking down just a few small spoonfuls daily, Mr. Y. progressed to the point where he was able to enjoy the entire amount. At this writing, Mr. Y. has returned to his employment as a bank officer and is once again able to support his family. He has completely regained his former robust health. As a preventative measure, the entire family now uses Dr. Budwig's formula daily.

Free Bonus Report

If you order now we will send you four special reports absolutely free:

E TRUTH ABOUT A MORE EXCITING SEX LIFE-- Everyone wants more .ement and passion in their sex life. Now you can have it!

Medical secrets that vastly improve the sex life of both men and women are contained in this special report. One big key to sexual pleasures is to fully activate our senses and one in particular. Little known techniques will be revealed to you in his writing that will result in a more satisfactory sex life for ıy mature adult. Enhance the pleasure of your most intimate ıoments with this important report.

HOW TO TAKE OFF THE POUNDS AND THE YEARS-- This special report offers an easy to follow diet along with special

14

The best preventative medicine in the world to ward off degenerative diseases. Page 158

nutritional supplements. As if by magic the fat will dissolve off your body hour by hour! Reach your dream weight without even resorting to dangerous drugs and prescriptions.

The work of Dr. Roy Walford, best-selling author of "Maximum Life Span", and recent participant in the Biosphere project in Arizona is featured in this report. Walford feels that his well documented program could increase your life expectancy up to 120 years!

NUTRITIONAL SECRETS TO MORE YOUTHFUL SKIN-- People judge your age, your level of self confidence, even your outlook on life by what they see on your face. Now you can have that skin that reflects your inner glow for as long as you live. This special report reveals amazing new methods that produce dramatic results. Have smoother skin and fabulous hair. Look up to 15 years younger. Discover how to use certain special supplements and enzymes that produce a more youthful, healthier looking skin in just a few weeks.

HOW TO IMPROVE BRAIN CAPACITY NATURALLY-- It's extremely exciting that our mental capacity can be improved naturally. Our entire thought process is dependent on two little known B-vitamins. Learn about the best sources in this special report. In addition you will discover the only amino acid that the brain is able to metabolize. The newest brain breakthroughs are responsible for IQ gains of up to 17 points in some people.

Free for promptness

If you are among the first 1,000 people to respond to the offer, you will also receive the following free report:

HOW TO INCREASE YOUR ENERGY AND ENJOY LIVING LONGER-- The number one complaint people bring to doctors' offices today is lack of energy. This report shows you exactly which foods, vitamins, and minerals are the best dietary components for maximum human energy. Your increase in energy could make you feel like a teenager! Learn about the foods to avoid which are energy killers. And discover the single remarkable foodstuff that enhances your energy more than anything yet found.

Money Back Guarantee

Take us up on our one year money back guarantee. You have

15

Continued...

nothing to lose except some powerful nutritional tips, the latest doctors home remedies and common misconceptions about preventing and treating cancer.

Send for HOW TO FIGHT CANCER AND WIN by William L. Fischer at our risk. All we ask is that you consult it regularly and add up the health benefits it provides you.

If you don't agree that it's worth hundreds of times its low purchase price, return it for a prompt, courteous refund. Even a year from now. And keep the bonus reports, regardless!

What could be fairer? Are you tired of the failure of conventional medicine to help you? If so, why not try these natural remedies-- without risking a penny? Mail the Free Trial request today. And many thanks.

Sincerely,

Wilhelm Longview

Wilhelm Longview
Vice President, General Manager

P.S. "HOW TO FIGHT CANCER AND WIN" will make a huge difference in the quality of your life. You risk nothing. The book is not the original price of $50.00, but only $29.97 and comes with a one year money back guarantee. And it comes with up to 5 free bonus reports which you may keep regardless. Order at once.

Fischer Publishing Corporation
One Fischer Square, P.O. Box 368, Canfield, OH 44406 Phone: (216) 533-1232 Fax: (216) 533-9860
Member Youngstown Area Chamber of Commerce

TIP

*Key words in my guarantee are **prompt and courteous refund**. Another credibility builder is: **And keep these bonus reports regardless**. Use these phrases on your guarantees and watch sales increase.*

The all important P.S.

The most read part of any letter next to the headline is the P.S.

TIP

Never send out a letter to anyone without a P.S. unless you want to waste a sales opportunity. To write a strong P.S., summarize the offer as well as guarantee as dramatically as possible.

See how I handled the P.S.:

"'HOW TO FIGHT CANCER AND WIN' will make a huge difference in the quality of your life. You risk nothing. The book is not the original price of $50.00, but only $29.97 and comes with a one year money back guarantee. And it comes with up to 5 free bonus reports which you may keep regardless. Order at once."

Use these tips and strategies in writing your sales letters and watch your sales explode. And all you need to send me is a mere 25% of increased profits.

OK, OK. While a percentage of profits would be fair under certain circumstances, I'm only kidding! As a reader of this book you get to pick my brain for no more than the cost of a single copy.

Unless, of course, you become a marketing or copywriting client. What are my fees? For clients my current fee for consulting, positioning and copy services is $15,000 plus 5% of sales. In some cases I accept 25% of the client company in lieu of upfront fees.

How to Use a 2-Step Marketing Plan to Increase Your Chance of Success

This chapter focuses on a powerful and underused marketing technique.

Perhaps the most cost-effective way to market a relatively expensive product (over $100 retail price) today is via a 2-step sale.

The 2-step concept works like this. Step 1 is an ad designed to generate inquiries. You first get a prospect to respond to the ad. They in effect raise their hand by requesting more information. In the ad, you sell the idea of learning more about the product. Unlike a 1-step ad, you do not disclose price. The ad can be any size, from a fractional to a full page.

Step 2 is a follow-up series of letters mailed to the prospect. In these letters you present all the exciting benefits of the product and discuss the price. ***Your goal is to close the sale.***

As with all sales situations, repetition is critical to closing the sale. In personal selling, on average a sale is not completed until the fifth sales call.

Some direct marketers think they can be successful in sending a single letter to an inquiry. Big success is rare with just one attempt to close the sale. In my opinion, direct marketers tend to give up too easily once they have captured the name of a lead who has responded to an inquiry ad.

Currently, my company, Nicholas Direct, sells a set of seminar tapes worldwide for $317. Tests have been run offering the product 1-step for sale versus the 2-step inquiry approach. In every case the 2-step inquiry approach works better than a 1-step cash-up-front offer.

On the following page is the full-page lead-generating ad which currently runs in publications such as the Economist,

"You, A Millionaire Writer?"

Bestseller, HOW TO PUBLISH A BOOK AND SELL A MILLION COPIES, shows you all the secrets. Thousands sold at $89, it can be yours **absolutely free**.

Ted Nicholas published 53 books, including million-copy seller, *How to Form Your Own Corporation Without a Lawyer for Under $75*. No one else ever had his self-publishing success with sales of over 2½ million books.

How would you like to earn at least $1,000 a day—every day?

Picture yourself making more money in a day than most people do in a week. You can do it! (You'll even earn profits while you sleep.)

Cash in on the most profitable field in the modern world.

How? By publishing books and other information.

What about you?

Work from home, start part-time or full time. Keep your current job. It doesn't matter if you are young or old. Black or white. Rich or poor. Learn how to make more money in one day than most people make in a week!

I've written a complete manual entitled HOW TO PUBLISH A BOOK AND SELL A MILLION COPIES, which shows you exactly what to do every step of the way. Plus, it's guaranteed, or it costs you nothing!

Today, we are truly living in the information age, wherein lie the biggest opportunities. I'll show you how to succeed at publishing information products. You'll create a lifestyle for yourself others only dream of.

Publishing is also the most fun and prestigious field you can possibly enter.

It's really simple to make a personal fortune. All you have to do is sell books, Special Reports, software, newsletters, or video or audio recordings people really need and want. For example, 30,000 copies of a product at $35 each equals a cool million dollars in your mailbox!

Exciting profit potential

The markups and profits are huge! Of course, people don't buy the paper and ink, disk, or video tape; the value is in the information itself. You can sell a Special Report for $15 when the cost is only 87 cents or a video program for $85 to $175 when the cost is as little as $2!

Does this kind of success excite you? Then you should definitely be selling information products of your own.

It's the kind of opportunity that will free you up to quit the 9-to-5 rat race. And you don't need an expensive office. Operate from home. Avoid commuting hassles. Live anywhere in the world, in a smaller town if you like. Work when you want to. Reside in a more desirable community (should you want to relocate) better suited for you and your family.

As a publisher of "how-to" information, you don't need writing skills. You'll know where to locate all the authors, copywriters, artists—all the creative people you will ever need, complete with names, addresses and telephone numbers.

Set up a low-budget publishing business

I'm a college dropout. While attending school, I was a pretty average student. I didn't have any contacts. Nor did I have any money so I borrowed $800 initially. I started with a $90 ad in a leading publication.

Today, I live in a beautiful penthouse on the beach in Florida. I drive a Mercedes convertible. I don't even have to work any longer, and now work only on projects I enjoy.

You can be of average intelligence (like me), starting with little or no money, and still earn a fortune. Publishing is, perhaps, the best opportunity for building a big income from small beginnings that's available to the little guy.

You don't need special attributes either. Once you know exactly what path to follow, you need only one quality! The willingness to take action and follow through with your plans.

Nothing could be easier. You can start part-time. You can keep your current job. And eventually quit when you start making big money. Or you can start full-time.

Discover how to:

- Write or have prepared for you a salable book, video, or other information product.
- Set up a low-cost corporation of your own and maximize personal and family benefits.
- Determine the profit potential of an information product *before* any time and money are spent in development, writing or production.
- Write killer magazine ads for your product.
- Acquire the rights to any product with a track record of success.
- License the valuable rights you own to others at a huge profit.
- Prepare a sales letter for your product that is so powerful it's almost irresistible.
- Learn ad copywriting, the highest paid form of writing in the world.
- Price your product for maximum returns.
- Manufacture your product at low cost. I provide a complete list of resources.
- Raise all the capital you need.
- Protect yourself legally.
- Copyright and trademark all your materials simply and easily.
- Get orders processed on a 24-hour, toll-free number.
- Get radio and TV stations to plug your books and other products absolutely free.
- Write powerful headlines, which is 90% of the task of writing a successful ad.
- Reduce your advertising costs by up to 80% by learning the secrets of buying ads at low cost in national publications.
- Completely avoid vanity and subsidy publishers, who often take your money without giving value.
- Use bookstores, libraries, and other retail stores as profitable sales outlets.
- Get started for as little as $600.
- And much, much more.

What well-known authors say:

"Your tips on writing and self-publishing led me to my bestsellers."—Doug Casey, Author, *Crisis Investing*

"You helped me publish my first book, which became a 'bestseller'. Thanks."—William Donoghue, *The Complete Money Market Guide*

"Sharing failures as well as achievements has steered me away from repeating these errors."—John A. Pugsley, *The Alpha Strategy*

Special Offer

I conduct special seminars on marketing and self-publishing for up to $7,500 per attendee.

I'm making available, for a limited time only, a complete set of tapes from my three-day nationally acclaimed self-publishing seminar at a bargain price.

It's most often referred to by both world-class marketers and beginners in marketing as the SEMINAR OF THE CENTURY. The 20 hours of tapes contain material on every concept of self-publishing. All the attendees' questions, all the valuable answers. Guest speakers and attendees include Gary Halbert, Pat McAllister, John Schaub, Frank Cawood, and many others.

The former marketing director of Entrepreneur magazine says . . .

"Your self-publishing seminar reveals the most valuable information for writers and entrepreneurs in the world today! Top secret—worth millions of dollars in the right hands."—Blade Thomas, Malibu, CA

Free information

Here is the fairest offer I can make. I'll send you complete information about the SEMINAR OF THE CENTURY tapes. Plus how to get a FREE copy of the 217 page book, HOW TO PUBLISH A BOOK AND SELL A MILLION COPIES, without cost or obligation.

Call now at **1-813-596-4966** (9-5 M-F, EST) or fax to **1-813-596-6900**, 24 hours a day. Or clip the coupon and mail today.

YES! Please send me complete information, without cost or obligation, regarding the TED NICHOLAS SELF-PUBLISHING SEMINAR ON TAPE and how I can get a copy of HOW TO PUBLISH A BOOK AND SELL A MILLION COPIES absolutely free.

Name______________________

Address______________________

City/State/Zip______________________

Daytime Phone______________________

Mail to: Nicholas Direct, Inc., Dept.
PO Box 877, Indian Rocks Beach, FL 34635

Lead Generating ad

National Review, Reason, Investor's Business Daily and Income Opportunity.

At present we send a series of 4 follow-up letters. Approximately 50% of the sales occur on letter #1. The other 50% is derived from letters #2, #3 and #4.

TIP

In responding to an inquiry, use a follow-up series of letters. The minimum number of letters you send should be three.

I've run inquiry ads often with as many as nine follow-ups. For super success, after the third letter just keep sending more follow-ups until the cost exceeds profit from the effort.

All four letters closely resemble each other except for a few important factors. The copy on the first page is somewhat different on each. And the paper color and texture varies.

Letter #1 is printed on white paper. Letter #2 on goldenrod. Letter #3 on pink. Letter #4 on copy paper.

On the following pages is the complete text of letter #1 and the first page of letters #2, #3 and #4.

A final word

I urge you to develop and test a 2-step sales approach as featured in this chapter for your product. Do it as soon as possible and watch your sales and profits grow.

Few U.S. direct marketers have seized the opportunities available with the 2-step marketing technique.

In my observation, a few European direct marketers who have attended my European seminars have mastered 2-step marketing. Europeans really appreciate this technique. Unlike in the U.S. their markets are much smaller, so they really enhance their bottom line when they refine their sales program.

Here is another great strength of 2-step selling. You can test and use many magazines and newspapers in which you would not be able to profitably run on a 1-step basis. With my self-publishing tapes, for example, we are not able to run profitable 1-step ads for products over $100 in opportunity magazines such as Income Opportunities as the subscribers tend to earn a lower income than our larger target audience. Yet, on a 2-step basis these publications are very profitable.

"You, a Millionaire Writer?"

Best seller, HOW TO PUBLISH A BOOK AND SELL A MILLION COPIES, shows you all the secrets. Thousands sold at $89, it can be yours **absolutely free.**

Ted Nicholas published 53 books, including the million-copy seller, HOW TO FORM YOUR OWN CORPORATION WITHOUT A LAWYER FOR UNDER $75. No one else ever had his self-publishing success with sales of over 2 1/2 million books.

Dear Friend,

How would you like to earn at least $1,000 a day—every day?

Imagine! Making more money in a day than most people do in a week. You can do it!

Cash in on the most profitable field in the modern world.

How? By publishing books and other information.

I've taken all my years of experience as a writer and publisher and written a complete manual entitled HOW TO PUBLISH A BOOK AND SELL A MILLION COPIES, which shows you exactly what to do every step of the way. You'll save years of trial and error and thousands of dollars in unnecessary costs.

Today, we are truly living in the information age, wherein lie the biggest opportunities. I'll show you how to succeed at publishing information products. Create a lifestyle for yourself others only dream of!

Publishing is also the most fun and prestigious field you can possibly enter.

It's really simple to make a personal fortune. All you have to do is sell books, Special Reports, floppy disks, newsletters, videos, or audio recordings that people really need and want.

The markups and profits are huge! Of course, people don't buy the paper and ink, disk, or video tape; the value is in the information itself. You can sell a Special Report for $15 when the cost is only 87 cents or a video program for $85 to $175 when the cost is as little as $2!

It's the kind of profit that will free you up to quit the 9-to-5 rat race. And you don't need an expensive office. Operate from home. Avoid commuting hassles. Live anywhere in the world, in a smaller town if you like. Work when you want to. Reside in a more desirable community (should you want to relocate) better suited for you and your family.

Want to make a million dollars?

It's not as tough as most people think. All you need to do

(please go to page 2)

Letter #1

is produce a "how-to" book, Special Report, video or audio tape set and sell 30,000 copies at $35 each.

That may seem like a lot of units. But not when you consider the market for information. In the U.S. there are over 200 million consumers, including 40 million small business owners. They are all hungry for useful information. It's a starving market!

The need for information is insatiable. You can create products to help people make or save money, cut taxes and increase personal safety. Or become fitter, thinner, sexier, improve skin care or in any way improve the quality of life. You can do it. Many million-dollar-a-year products are produced by people just like you.

If you sell just 25 units a day at $35 through classified ads, card decks, space ads or direct mail, you can earn over $183,750! And if you have several products on the market and have modest success with them, your income will soar to between a half million and a million dollars!

The opportunities for profit from "how-to" information are virtually unlimited.

Does this kind of success excite you? Then you should definitely be selling information products of your own.

As a publisher of "how-to" information, you don't need writing skills. I'll show you where to locate all the authors, copywriters, artists... all the creative people you will ever need, complete with names, addresses and telephone numbers.

As a publisher, you will also maximize your personal power.

In the days of early man, personal power arose from physical strength. Later, power came from the influence of kings and other royalty. During the industrial revolution, power came from capital.

Today, personal power comes from the control of information. Used correctly, this power can build unlimited wealth.

Here is the key to all wealth. You must completely control the rights to your products. Learn how to get people all over the world to stand in line with huge royalty deals and large cash advances for the right to reprint your material under license. You can make a fortune even before you incur any costs.

You can also sell your products anywhere on the planet. "How-to" information is the most needed commodity in the U.S. and throughout the whole world. Especially in all the Eastern Block countries where communism is collapsing and economies are switching to a free-market system.

I've spent 20 years developing my techniques. I can help you **avoid all the costly mistakes** I made. You will be able to get started immediately.

Many entrepreneurs are getting rich selling information prod-

2 (please go to page 3)

Letter #1—Continued

ucts. You don't need to be a genius or have special talents. If you have common sense, a desire to succeed, and follow my step-by-step plan, you will succeed. You don't need to have exotic, complicated products to make a lot of money. In fact, the simpler and more basic, the more salable!

Here are just a few people who are enormously successful selling products people really want.

Bill Myers from Little Rock, Arkansas, started a "Guerrilla" video newsletter, which shows ordinary people how to make money producing and selling videos for profit. He began with a borrowed $500 just three years ago. Today his company, Group M Productions, is one of the fastest growing small companies in America, according to Inc. magazine. Bill came to my $7,500 seminar this past summer and learned my secrets to increasing his mailing profit.

Pat McAllister was a commodity broker in Chicago. He started a profitable computer cleaning business on the side. He produced a video which sells for $89, and ran classified ads with the headline, "How to Make $25,000 a Year Cleaning Computers." He now is doing so well he quit his job and runs his profitable mail order business from home.

Bud Weckesser was a professor at Purdue. He started his company, Green Tree Press, part-time in Erie, Pennsylvania, by selling a recipe, How to Make Beer at Home, in a classified ad for $3. Today, his company is a multi-million dollar mail order success.

Leslie Brice sells huge quantities of high-quality audio tapes via full-color catalogs. The subjects deal with weight loss, self-improvement, etc. Her company is Gateways, located in Ojai, California. A few years ago, she wrote and produced a 30-minute TV infomercial for a self-improvement program which produced 24 million dollars in sales! Recently, she attended my marketing seminar to learn how to publish other types of information and to use space advertising more effectively.

Set up a low-budget publishing business

I'm a college dropout. While attending school, I was a pretty average student. I didn't have any money to start with nor did I have any contacts. I borrowed $800 initially and started with a $90 ad in a leading publication.

Today, I live in a beautiful penthouse on the beach in Florida and drive a Mercedes convertible. I don't have to work any longer, and now work only on projects I enjoy.

You can be of average intelligence, starting with little or no money, and still earn a fortune. Publishing is, perhaps, the best opportunity that's available to the little guy for building a big income from small beginnings.

3 (please go to page 4)

Letter #1—Continued

You don't need special attributes either. Once you know exactly what path to follow, you need only one quality! The willingness to take action and follow through with your plans.

Nothing could be easier. You can start part-time. You can keep your current job. And eventually quit when you start making big money. Or you can start full-time.

Discover how to:

- Write a salable book, video or other information product.
- Set up a low-cost corporation of your own and maximize personal and family benefits.
- Determine the profit potential of an information product before any time and money are spent in development, writing or production.
- Write killer magazine ads for your product.
- Acquire the rights to books and products with a track record of success.
- License the valuable rights you own to others at a huge profit.
- Prepare an irresistible sales letter.
- Learn ad copywriting, the highest paid form of writing in the world. (I charge $15,000 + 5% of sales for an ad and have a waiting list of clients. You can do the same when you know my secrets.)
- Price your product for maximum returns.
- Manufacture your product at low cost. You get a complete list of resources.
- Copyright and trademark your materials simply and easily.
- Get orders processed on a 24-hour toll-free number.
- Get radio and TV stations to plug your books and other products absolutely free.
- Write powerful headlines, which is 90% of the task of writing a successful ad.
- Reduce your advertising costs by up to 80% by learning thesecrets of buying ads at low cost in national publications.
- Avoid vanity and subsidy publishers.
- Use bookstores, libraries and other retail stores as profitable sales outlets.
- Get started for as little as a $600.

Nothing you get is based on theory. I've lived every single technique. And tested and proven every tip I share with you. My ideas have succeeded in the marketplace for 20 years and continue to do so today. Find the shortcut to your dreams of success.

Here is what a partial list of people who publish information products have to say about my work:

"Thanks for the guidance and suggestions during my writing of several best sellers."

Doug Casey, Author
Crisis Investing

4 (please go to page 5)

Letter #1—Continued

"Your book on publishing inspired me to get started. Since then, I've written two books on the New York Times best seller list."

William Donoghue, Author
The Complete Money Market Guide

"One of the real winners in direct marketing business. Generously shares his inside secrets of success in marketing that should help us all reach our goals."

Bill Myers, Publisher
Myer's Direct

"You don't know me, but I used your book on self-publishing to write my first successful book. That first book is now in its 12th printing. I have made money and a great reputation because of it."

Dr. John LaTourette, Author
The Way to Power

"Your willingness to share failures as well as achievements has steered me away from repeating these errors."

John Pugsley, Author
The Alpha Strategy

"With thanks for your support over all these years."

Richard Restak, MD, Author
The Brain Has A Mind Of Its Own

"Ted really gives all the secrets of his fabulous success."

Jerry Buchanan, Publisher
TOWERS Club Newsletter

"Ted, your name should be on the front cover of this book with mine. You were with me all the way."

George Tansill, Author
Why People Do Not Get Well

"No human alive knows more about making magazine advertising pay off than Ted Nicholas."

Gary Halbert, Author
Maximum Money In Minimum Time

Why publishing is the ideal business

I started 18 companies before getting into publishing. The fields included confectionery, real estate, building design, franchising, and cosmetics. I've also long studied business opportunities, searching for the perfect business.

Then I found it in publishing. The most ideal business in the world is selling information products. These include "paper and ink" products, books, newsletters, Special Reports, audios or videos.

Here are the main reasons why selling information is ideal:

- Products are easy to "manufacture." You can get products produced in almost any city in America.

5 (please go to page 6)

Letter #1—Continued

- There is a high perceived value for information. You have substantial markups. Profit margins can be high, from ten to as high as thirty times cost is not uncommon. It's not the paper or the video tape people buy, it's the information.
- The trends all point to growing opportunities in the future in our "information age."
- You have no competition. Your products are copyrighted. They are proprietary, cannot be copied and belong to you alone.
- You can live and operate from anywhere in the world. This business is completely portable.
- Your market is the entire planet.
- The business is not capital intensive. You can start with as little as $600.
- You have fewer hassles with government regulation in publishing than probably any other business, due mostly to freedom of the press, a constitutional guarantee.
- And if you sell the business, it's one of the most attractive to prospective buyers.

If you aspire to be a writer but are as yet unpublished, it's almost impossible to get a large publisher to take you on. The unknown author has less than one chance in one hundred to get published today.

But throughout history, it was never easy. And authors are often not happy with their publishers.

Some of the famous authors of the past and present who published their own work include Percy Bysshe Shelley, Walt Whitman, William Blake, Benjamin Franklin, Zane Grey, Gertrude Stein, D.H. Lawrence, Mark Twain, Upton Sinclair, Carl Sandburg, Ezra Pound, James Joyce and Robert Ringer. If you publish your own work, you not only ensure you will get into print, you keep 100% of the sales and the profits.

I conduct special seminars on marketing and self-publishing for up to $7,500 per attendee.

I'm making available, for a limited time only, a complete set of tapes from my three-day nationally acclaimed self-publishing seminar at a bargain price.

It's most often referred to by both world-class marketers and beginners in marketing as the "Seminar of the Century." The 20 hours of tapes contain material on every concept of self-publishing. All the attendees' questions, all the valuable answers. Guest speakers and attendees include Gary Halbert, Pat McAllister, John Schaub, Frank Cawood, and many others.

The former marketing director of Entrepreneur magazine says...

6 (please go to page 7)

Letter #1—Continued

"Your self-publishing seminar reveals the most valuable information for writers and entrepreneurs in the world today! Top secret—worth millions of dollars in the right hands."

Blade Thomas
Malibu, CA

Big money secrets revealed

Imagine owning the seminar tapes where you hear—live—the never before revealed inside secrets.

- Make it virtually impossible to ever again fail at any business endeavor.
- Acquire the valuable direct marketing rights to best selling books, tapes, software, and other products for as little as $250.
- Today's best no-cost/low-cost marketing methods to explode your sales.
- Write the most powerful headline possible for your product using the secrets of the **"hidden benefit."**
- Take your mailings of sales material to the post office on a certain day of the week and up your response by 20%.
- Avoid the all too common and costly mistakes made by most self-publishers.
- Get enough cash-up-front orders for your book or other information product before it's finished to pay costs and make a profit.

You Risk Nothing

If my tapes and manual are not everything I describe and much more, after reviewing them for 21 days—don't worry one bit—I'll buy them back from you.

Make a better life for yourself. Have a much freer, more profitable lifestyle.

Master the art of selling information. Make a great deal of money publishing and selling information products.

Help make the world a better place. You profit; so do your readers, viewers and listeners. It's a win/win lifestyle all the way!

I'm fortunate to be friends with some of the world's best authors and other wealthy information sellers. The thing that separates them from those who desire success but do not achieve it is just one thing. And it's not intelligence. It's not desire. It's not belief. **It is the willingness to take action.**

If you really want to make money and really be successful in publishing, my materials will help make that happen for you. And I fully guarantee it.

Unprecedented Guarantee

Here is the fairest offer I can make. I'll send you the tapes of the SEMINAR OF THE CENTURY, workbook, and all handout material for only $317. Plus a FREE copy of the 217 page book,

7 (please go to page 8)

Letter #1—Continued

HOW TO PUBLISH A BOOK AND SELL A MILLION COPIES. If you are not absolutely delighted after having the tapes for 21 days, return the tapes and keep the book for your trouble. Fair enough?

Just pick up the phone and order now. Your first step is always the most important one on the road to greater financial success.

For fastest service, call **1-813-596-4966** (9-5 M-F, EST) or fax to **1-813-596-6900**, 24 hours a day. Or clip the coupon below and mail today.

Sincerely,

Ted Nicholas

P.S. I'll show you how to get very, very rich publishing books and information products. Your small investment is fully guaranteed.

No Risk Order Coupon

Yes! Please send me:

❑ BEST DEAL. Ted Nicholas' Self-Publishing SEMINAR OF THE CENTURY on tape, 20 hours, at $317*, plus S&H, under your 21-day money back guarantee. If I'm not delighted I may return them and keep the book HOW TO PUBLISH A BOOK AND SELL A MILLION COPIES regardless.

❑ Send the book only for $89* (plus $5 S&H)

Enclosed is my check for $________ payable to Nicholas Direct

Bill my ❑ Visa ❑ MC ❑ AMEX (*Florida residents add 7% sales tax)

CC#________________________________Exp__________

Signature________________________________

Name________________________________

Company________________________________

Address________________________________

City/State/Zip________________________________

Daytime Phone__________________ (in case of questions about your order)

Mail to: Nicholas Direct, Inc. Dept.
PO Box 877
Indian Rocks Beach, FL 34635

Letter #1—Continued

SECOND NOTICE

"You, a Millionaire Writer?"

Free $89 book, HOW TO PUBLISH A BOOK & SELL A MILLION COPIES, reveals the secrets.

Ted Nicholas, author of the million-copy seller, HOW TO FORM YOUR OWN CORPORATION WITHOUT A LAWYER FOR UNDER $75, shows you how.

Dear Friend,

Perhaps you misplaced the last letter I sent you?

Does the concept of earning at least $1,000 a day in your spare time appeal to you?

Imagine! Making more money in a day than most people do in a week. You can do it!

Cash in on the most profitable field in the modern world.

How? By publishing books and other information.

I've taken all my years of experience as a writer and publisher and written a complete manual entitled HOW TO PUBLISH A BOOK AND SELL A MILLION COPIES, which shows you exactly what to do every step of the way. You'll save years of trial and error and thousands of dollars in unnecessary costs.

Today, we are truly living in the information age, wherein lie the biggest opportunities. I'll show you how to succeed at publishing information products. Create a lifestyle for yourself others only dream of!

Publishing is also the most fun and prestigious field you can possibly enter.

It's really simple to make a personal fortune. All you have to do is sell books, Special Reports, floppy disks, newsletters, videos, or audio recordings that people really need and want.

The markups and profits are huge! Of course, people don't buy the paper and ink, disk, or video tape; the value is in the information itself. You can sell a Special Report for $15 when the cost is only 87 cents or a video program for $85 to $175 when the cost is as little as $2!

It's the kind of profit that will free you up to quit the 9-to-5 rat race. And you don't need an expensive office. Operate from home. Avoid commuting hassles. Live anywhere in the world, in a smaller town if you like. Work when you want to. Reside in a more desirable community (should you want to relocate) better suited for you and your family.

Want to make a million dollars?

It's not as tough as most people think. All you need to do

First page of follow-up letter, #2

"You, a Millionaire Writer?"

Free copy of HOW TO PUBLISH A BOOK AND SELL A MILLION COPIES by Ted Nicholas, shows you all the secrets.

Last Chance/Reduced Price

Dear Friend,

I want you to have a final opportunity to own my book and tapes. So I'm offering you a one-time only special reduced price. Surely, you'd like to earn at least $1,000 a day in your spare time?

Imagine! Making more money in a day than most people do in a week. You can do it!

Cash in on the most profitable field in the modern world.

How? By publishing books and other information.

I've taken all my years of experience as a writer and publisher and written a complete manual entitled HOW TO PUBLISH A BOOK AND SELL A MILLION COPIES, which shows you exactly what to do every step of the way. You'll save years of trial and error and thousands of dollars in unnecessary costs.

Today, we are truly living in the information age, wherein lie the biggest opportunities. I'll show you how to succeed at publishing information products. Create a lifestyle for yourself others only dream of!

Publishing is also the most fun and prestigious field you can possibly enter.

It's really simple to make a personal fortune. All you have to do is sell books, Special Reports, floppy disks, newsletters, videos, or audio recordings that people really need and want.

The markups and profits are huge! Of course, people don't buy the paper and ink, disk, or video tape; the value is in the information itself. You can sell a Special Report for $15 when the cost is only 87 cents or a video program for $85 to $175 when the cost is as little as $2!

It's the kind of profit that will free you up to quit the 9-to-5 rat race. And you don't need an expensive office. Operate from home. Avoid commuting hassles. Live anywhere in the world, in a smaller town if you like. Work when you want to. Reside in a more desirable community (should you want to relocate) better suited for you and your family.

Want to make a million dollars?

It's not as tough as most people think. All you need to do

First page of follow-up letter, #3

"You, a Millionaire Writer?"

Free copy of HOW TO PUBLISH A BOOK AND SELL A MILLION COPIES by Ted Nicholas, shows you all the secrets.

Last Chance/Reduced Price

Dear Friend,

I want you to have a final opportunity to own my book and tapes. So I'm offering you a one-time only special reduced price. Surely, you'd like to earn at least $1,000 a day in your spare time?

Imagine! Making more money in a day than most people do in a week. You can do it!

Cash in on the most profitable field in the modern world.

How? By publishing books and other information.

I've taken all my years of experience as a writer and publisher and written a complete manual entitled HOW TO PUBLISH A BOOK AND SELL A MILLION COPIES, which shows you exactly what to do every step of the way. You'll save years of trial and error and thousands of dollars in unnecessary costs.

Today, we are truly living in the information age, wherein lie the biggest opportunities. I'll show you how to succeed at publishing information products. Create a lifestyle for yourself others only dream of!

Publishing is also the most fun and prestigious field you can possibly enter.

It's really simple to make a personal fortune. All you have to do is sell books, Special Reports, floppy disks, newsletters, videos, or audio recordings that people really need and want.

The markups and profits are huge! Of course, people don't buy the paper and ink, disk, or video tape; the value is in the information itself. You can sell a Special Report for $15 when the cost is only 87 cents or a video program for $85 to $175 when the cost is as little as $2!

It's the kind of profit that will free you up to quit the 9-to-5 rat race. And you don't need an expensive office. Operate from home. Avoid commuting hassles. Live anywhere in the world, in a smaller town if you like. Work when you want to. Reside in a more desirable community (should you want to relocate) better suited for you and your family.

Want to make a million dollars?

It's not as tough as most people think. All you need to do

First page of follow-up letter, #4

Secrets Reveal how P.S. can Increase Sales by 300%

Yes, it's true! My mail tests as well as those of other marketers have provided proof positive. With a well-crafted P.S. you can as much as *triple response* to your offers!

To my knowledge no direct mail professional previously has identified the important P.S. types in sales letters. This chapter is devoted to the 7 most powerful P.S. types I've found.

Why is the often neglected P.S. so important to the pulling power of your letter?

The P.S. is the *best read* part of any letter next to the headline. Yet, if you examine your mail carefully you will notice many direct mail letters do not include a P.S. Senders of such letters are missing a terrific opportunity.

To fully appreciate the impact of the P.S., first you need to make a distinction. What you would like to see happen and what actually happens in the real world are entirely different.

Wouldn't you like the prospect to sit down and read your every word? Sequentially? From beginning to end? Concentrating intently on every word of your offer? Isn't that what you want? Of course!

But, alas, this is not what happens. Here is what prospects actually do in most cases. They glance at the headline. Then turn to the end of the letter. They look at the signature, and then . . . *read the P.S.* So think of the P.S. this way—as your letter's

Bottom line

If you have ever mailed a letter without a P.S. don't fret. You are not alone.

Recently I was having lunch with Christian Godefroy, one of Europe's most successful direct marketers. He admitted for the first 5 years in direct marketing he never used a P.S. on his offers.

When he added a P.S. to an already profitable sales letter offer, the response increased 300%! Today, he wonders how much richer he would now be had he always used P.S.'s.

Early in my direct marketing career I also sent out sales letters without a P.S. I just didn't know any better.

But you don't have to go through the expensive learning curve. Now that you have been informed, you can avoid making the same mistake. One of the reasons you are reading these words is to avoid repeating my mistakes! So always, always, always add a P.S.

The 7 most used P.S. types in successful sales letters are those which:

1. *Motivate the prospect to take action.*
   This is the most important of all 7 P.S. types. Why? It compels action—placing an order now. Everyone tends to procrastinate, so you must do all that is possible to overcome buyers' inertia. Remember this. In any form of selling, including direct marketing—

   Delay is death

2. *Reinforce the offer.*
   Such a P.S. properly crafted is powerful. It's the most often used. It's also the safest P.S. type, providing the offer is compelling.
3. *Emphasize or introduce a premium or bonus.*
   I love this one. It's effective for every type of prospect including the wealthy. Especially the wealthy! Why? Everyone loves a valuable *free* gift! Don't you?

4. *Introduce a surprise benefit.*
   This can be effective in nudging the "fence sitter" to take action and buy your product.
5. *Emphasize price or terms of your offer.*
   Especially when your offer involves a special or bargain price or terms. When you dramatize it in the P.S., this can be highly motivating.
6. *Emphasizing tax deductibility of purchase.*
   Everyone, especially business owners and executives, enjoy taking a tax deduction and thus have the government subsidize their purchase. Tax deductibility also provides additional justification to make a purchase. Everyone feels more comfortable when they can justify their purchases to themselves or others.
7. *Emphasize guarantee.*
   Money-back guarantees can be excitingly presented. They are good raw material for a P.S. because the risk associated with any purchase is eliminated. Your prospect feels less anxiety and a greater sense of security when no money can be lost.

Examples of Winning P.S.'s

One of the best ways to learn anything is by example. I'm going to show you examples of all 7 P.S.'s For variety I'll show you several written by me as well as other copywriters.

The next time you sit down to write a letter the following examples will trigger many ideas you can incorporate in your offer.

1. Motivate the prospect to take action now

P.S. "HOW TO FIGHT CANCER AND WIN" will make a huge difference in the quality of your life. You risk nothing. The book is not the original price of $50.00, but only $29.97 and comes with a one year money back guarantee. And it comes with up to 5 free bonus reports which you may keep regardless. Order at once.

P.S. Don't let the opportunity to attend this valuable one-time only seminar worth many times its investment of only £397. Additional registrants may attend for only £197. Get up to 2 Free Bonuses worth a total of £80. Call 932-253162 now!

P.S. The HANDBOOK OF DOCTORS' NATURAL HOME REMEDIES FOR PROSTATE PROBLEMS AND SEXUAL IMPOTENCE will make a huge difference in your life. You risk nothing. You can have the book not at the original price of $50.00 but for only $29.97. You have a one-year money-back guarantee. And if you respond within 10 days you will get 3 bonus reports you may keep regardless. Order at once.

"P.S. If you don't mail your $500,000.00 SWEEPSTAKES entry, the prize that you might have won will go to someone else. That won't happen if you return the Official Entry Certificate in the envelope provided."

"P.S. Our "Summer White Sale" is only running until August 15, 1990. To make certain your Savings Certificate is valid, please post it before that date. No need to send payment now. If you prefer, we'll bill you later."

"P.S. We will not repeat this offer in 1993. Please act *now*. This offer expires on February 23rd!"

"P.S. SCIENCE NEWS in not sold at newsstands or bookstores. It is available only to those who order subscriptions and, for a limited time, through this special introductory offer."

2. Reinforce the offer

P.S. The "S" Corporation was brought into law primarily to give small business owner a few financial breaks. . . to make it easier for them to stay in business. Now, under new tax laws the "S" Corporation looks more attractive than ever. With The "S" Corporation Handbook you can gain all the benefits of owning an "S" corporation, including the big tax saving available now.

"P.S. As mentioned before, your Gift Certificate bears your name and may not be used by anyone else. A mailing like this—for a publication like *W*—must remain quite selective."

"P.S. Remember, to reserve your FREE BACKPACK and become a temporary member of the National Audubon Society, just place the token from the envelope on your RISK-FREE invitation and return it in the envelope provided. You'll be joining the group doing so much to help save our threatened planet Earth. And you'll enjoy AUDUBON magazine, free visits to Audubon Nature Centers throughout the United States, and other benefits. That's more value for less money than I've heard of in a long, long time! So, please become an Audubon Society member now!"

"P.S. You'll be pleased with your decision, your 2 magazines, your Membership and all your other benefits!"

"P.S. As mentioned earlier, this invitation is non-transferable. It is valid in your name *only*. If you decide not to accept my offer, please *do not* pass it along to anyone else. I would prefer you simply discard it. Thank you."

"P.S. Do look over the enclosed stamp sheet now, from *Pavarotti At Carnegie Hall* to *Galway's Greatest Hits,* from Sir Georg Solti to Itzhak Perlman . . . any 3 of the world's greatest artists and performances are available now for your 10-day free audition."

3. Emphasize or introduce a premium or bonus

"P.S. REMEMBER, this special offer for ORGANIC GARDENING™ magazine brings you these three free gifts. Each one is chock-full of some of the best tips money can't buy. So use the easy order card today for a start on your best garden ever."

"P.S. Remember, you will also receive, absolutely free, THE 1990s & BEYOND, an information-packed book on the last decade of the twentieth century. This 160-page, well-illustrated volume (a $7.95 value) is yours free when you join.

"P.S. Take a look at your certificate now for *news of a special gift of welcome*! 10 power crystals, from amethyst to snow quartz, plus a guide to their legendary mystic qualities. Use them to meditate or relieve stress. Or enjoy them for their natural beauty. We'll send you all 10 power crystals *free,* plus a carrying bag, when you purchase *Mystic Places.*"

"P.S. Take a look at your certificate now to see your *handsome Egyptian Paperweight!* When you keep THE AGE OF GOD-KINGS, it will be your *Gift of Welcome.* This unusual pewter-finish disk features an exquisite engraving taken from the temple of Akhenaten."

4. Introduce a surprise benefit

P.S. INCLUDED AT NO EXTRA CHARGE: Specific guidelines for most of the 166 letters; special tips on how to customize them; optional paragraphs and phrases for expanding them; and general guidelines for each of the 15 general categories of letters. ALSO: Checklist for Executive Letters; Forms of Address for VIPs; diagrams of correct letter formats; tabbed dividers; and alphabetized index—EVERYTHING YOU NEED FOR A LONG-LASTING HIGHLY USEFUL BUSINESS REFERENCE.

"P.S. Please note that your Gift Certificate has your name on it—and may not be used by anyone else."

"P.S. I nearly forgot to mention *one more unique comfort of membership*. . . our exclusive tapestry-print Floral Tote. It's stylish, sturdy, practical and—best of all—FREE (with membership). In fact, it's yours to keep, even if you choose not to remain a member."

"P.S. This offer isn't available to everyone. It isn't transferable. But, if you do decide to join and become a member of the Club, we can understand why you might want to share the news of your "no-strings" membership with a special friend or two. In that event, ask them to write me and mention your name."

"P.S. *ACT NOW AND GET THIS FREE GIFT.* To help introduce you to the world of NATURAL HOME REMEDIES, we'd like to send you "Easing Aches and Pains"—a booklet written to help you draw on your body's own natural resources to relieve the aches and pains of everyday life. And the booklet is yours *FREE* whether you decide to purchase RODALE'S ENCYCLOPEDIA OF NATURAL HOME REMEDIES or not. Supplies are limited, so please act soon. Mail the enclosed card today."

5. Emphasize price or terms of your offer

P.S. Remember, this half-price offer at $16 expires in 10 days. After this date you must pay the regular price of $32. Don't miss out. ORDER now.

P.S. Send no money now. If you are not completely delighted with the Exer-Stik, return within 30 days and owe nothing.

"P.S. This half-price offer is the lowest rate available. We may not be able to offer it again, so don't miss the opportunity. Mail your order today! Thanks—WJG"

"P.S. I think you'll discover that the Group Discount Plan makes it easier than you'd dreamed to own today's incomparable Britannica!"

6. Emphasizing tax deductibility of purchase

P.S. Your corporate shield is a valuable asset. Help protect yourself for a nominal *tax deductible* cost.

P.S. Your tax deductible investment of only $49.95 is a small price to pay to gain all the legal protection this book provides you and your business. Without a doubt, you will rest easier once you receive it.

"P.S. *Important tax benefits.* Like virtually all EARTHWATCH contributions, membership is tax-deductible. Note too that you can charge your donations to your credit card."

"P.S. Executive discount price is tax deductible as permitted by the Tax Reform Act of 1986. See page 75."

7. Emphasize guarantee

P.S. This no-risk $29.95 investment is guaranteed to give you protection personally over all your assets. Can you really afford to be without it?

P.S. You can charge THE COMPLETE BOOK OF CORPORATE FORMS to your American Express, Diner/Carte Blanche, Visa or MasterCard; if you decide to return the book, you'll receive an immediate credit or cash refund (including postage both ways). So this is truly a NO-RISK Offer.

P.S. If *Small Business Tax Saver* doesn't put tax dollars back in your pocket from the start, your subscription payment will be refunded in full. That's a promise (see enclosed letter). And the $24.95 book, *Big Tax Savings for Small Business,* is yours to keep.

P.S. There is unlimited opportunity in consulting today, and Howard Shenson's Complete Guide to Consulting Success can help you take advantage of those opportunities. Order your copy today under our unique one-full-year money-back guarantee.

"P.S. Don't forget our guarantee—if at any time you're not pleased, just let us know. The unused portion of your subscription will be promptly refunded."

"P.S. Don't wait until the expiration date on your certificate is on top of you. We guarantee your satisfaction. What can you lose? Call now TOLL FREE 1-800-228-9055."

P.P.S. Remember, to add even more zest to your first meal of Omaha Steaks™, you'll receive—ABSOLUTELY FREE—an acrylic salt shaker/pepper mill. Even if you decide not to place your order for luscious, fork-tender Omaha Steaks™ right away, the pepper mill is yours FREE. Read about it on the enclosed insert."

The P.S.'s not written by me and in quotations are from the book *Million Dollar Mailings* by Denny Hatch with a forward by Axel Andersson. The book includes 71 of the most successful mailings of the last 3 years and should be in every marketer's library. It is available from Libey Publishing Incorporated, Regenery Gateway, Inc., 1130 17th Street, N.W., Washington, D.C. 20036; price: $89.

The next time you sit down to prepare a sales letter, reread this chapter. Choose one of the P.S. categories. Write an exciting P.S. I'm sure your sales and bottom line will look better than ever!

How to Prepare 'Lift Letters' that can Double Response to Your Mailings

Including a short letter in addition to your primary letter in your direct mailings can substantially lift response. As much as 200%. That's how the term "lift letter" arose.

With strong lift letters, response increases of 20%, 50%, 100% even 200% and more have been demonstrated time and time again on my mailings and those of my clients.

This chapter reveals the secrets I have found to create lift letters.

A simple but important element of a successful lift letter is not understood by many mailers. Many of the failed sales letters which cross my desk, but are never re-mailed, contain lift letters from the sender of the sales letter.

A lift letter must come from someone other than the signer of the main letter. For credibility, this letter should also reflect a completely different style and tone than the sales letter.

Your lift letter can take many forms. The most effective types are:

1. Testimonial (from a customer, celebrity, or recognized authority)
2. Telegram
3. News release
4. Memo
5. Mini-letter

You may (a) enclose a lift letter in its own envelope; (b) clip or staple to the main letter; or (c) fold and enclose in the mailing as a last-minute insert.

For best results, the lift letter can be typewritten or handwritten. As with other direct mail, I do not recommend a typeset, slick look. Aim for a personal "me to you" appearance and feel. As to length, I have used as few as 5 short sentences to a full 8 1/2 x 11 page.

TIP

Typeset in courier. Print on a different color paper than main letter, such as pale blue, pink primrose or cream. Make sure letter is signed with a strong signature.

To increase readership, on the reverse side of the letter (or on the envelope if used) here are some suggested phrases to use as a headline. Each headline is either handwritten or set in a different style to show you some graphic layouts that are effective.

Please read only
if you are still undecided

~~~~~~~

Frankly, I'm puzzled as to why
there is even the slightest hesitation

~~~~~~~

Perhaps I did not make
myself completely understood

~~~~~~~

Here are the heart rending words of a well-known customer
~~~~~~~

~~~~~~~~

Are you skeptical? Do you want more proof?

~~~~~~~~

Looking for another professional's opinion?

~~~~~~~~

Did you notice on the enclosed brochure the guarantee on page 2?

~~~~~~~~

May I ask you a favor?

~~~~~~~~

The enclosed letter is so important and so urgent that I hope you will phone right now

~~~~~~~~

On the following pages are samples of successful lift letters. I have either written them or selected them from unsolicited letters received by me or my clients.

Lift Letter 1 (newsletter offer)

Dear Business Owner:

Suppose you were walking down a street and spotted a crisp $1,000 bill just lying on the sidewalk. Would you stoop to pick it up?

Of course. Who in his right mind wouldn't?

Yet every day, thousands of business owners pass up $1,000 opportunities that would enrich them just as much as that $1,000 bill -- because they overlook numerous ways they can be using their small companies to multiply wealth and shelter more income from taxes.

Hard to believe? Not really. As a business owner, you are in a unique position to build wealth and generate thousands in tax-free income every year. Thanks to special new rules Congress has passed to favor small business, and thanks to the freedom you have to run your business as its owner, you have more opportunities than virtually anyone else in America to build your personal fortune rapidly.

What you need most is the information on how to seize the hundreds of wealth-building opportunities available to "owners only."

And that's the whole purpose of our new newsletter, SMALL BUSINESS WEALTH BUILDER.

Every month it brings you 8 to 12 concise pages, chock full of ideas from America's foremost small business experts. These leading authorities share with you scores of ways you can use a small business to reduce or eliminate taxes ... throw off tax-free income ... compound your personal wealth tax-free ... acquire more assets ... take more money out of your business ... plan for a wealthier retirement ... get higher return on your investments both inside and outside your business ... be a stronger negotiator with suppliers, lawyers, employees and others you deal with ... everything, in short, that can help you as a business owner acquire wealth more rapidly, with less struggle and strain.

Just for trying SMALL BUSINESS WEALTH BUILDER, we'll give you a copy of the special $29.95 manual, Guaranteed Wealth Building Strategies for Small Business. It describes 211 of the most powerful ways you can use your small business to multiply wealth and shelter more of your income from taxes.

As I say, this $29.95 bonus volume will be yours to keep free, just for taking a look at SMALL BUSINESS WEALTH BUILDER.

With our complete money-back guarantee, you risk nothing. Yet you stand to gain a host of proven ideas that may just help turn your small business into that "money machine" you always dreamed it could be.

To take advantage of this special no-risk offer, just return the reply form enclosed with this note.

Warmest regards,

Ted Nicholas

Mr. Ted Nicholas
Publisher

Lift Letter 2 (seminar offer)

Dear Friend:

I heartily recommend the Ted Nicholas Marketing seminar. Why?

I've experienced Ted's program myself. From this exposure I've learned so much about success and making money, it's tough to put all of it in a short letter. But, I can tell you this.

The way I direct market products has been forever changed. In fact, my whole approach to business has been revolutionized. I've also strengthened my people and negotiating skills. Every aspect of preparing ads and sales letters has improved. Attracting new customers, the lifeblood of any business, is no longer a problem.

Let's face it. Building wealth is important to everyone. And Ted is the best teacher in the world in my opinion. But, perhaps even more important than the financial side of life, I've learned so much about real success as a human being from Ted Nicholas.

And there are many other important lessons I've learned from him. Balance between family, friends, and career. My entire family now pays more attention to our health, the greatest wealth of all. Ted, who spends at least an hour each day on enhancing his physical and mental health, has been a model for us and will be for you.

Don't miss this chance to spend time with him and his family. I urge you to do whatever is necessary to attend his 3-day seminar beginning December 2nd. And bring your employees if you are in business and your spouse, for your partner will also benefit enormously. I look forward to seeing you there.

Sincerely,

Mark Layder

Mark Layder

Lift Letter 3 (book offer)

Dear Bill:

As an M.D., I use and teach visualization therapy in my practice. I consider this therapy to be more powerful than drugs or surgery. Why?

We humans have the (often underappreciated) ability to heal ourselves using the power of the mind.

I'd like to relate a true story. You may wish to include the entire case history in your great book, How To Fight Cancer and Win. It may inspire your readers who can use this alternative approach to alleviate suffering and facilitate healing of virtually any condition.

Sara was brought in to see me at age 4 1/2. She was suffering from five angiomas, blood tumors behind her left eyeball. (Children are particularly good candidates for visualization therapy because their minds are not cluttered with negatives.)

Sara's eyesight was deteriorating rapidly. The condition was extremely serious. It was apparent the eyeball would have to be removed along with the tumors. The rapidly growing tumors were constricting the optic nerve itself and stressing vital blood vessels.

I sat Sara on my knee and explained to her as gently as I could what her problem was, and what would happen.

I began to teach Sara visual imagery. Within eleven months with continued visual imagery, Sara's vision was almost normal. Her pretty little face had lost its deformed look. She is now completely cured.

Being an M.D., you might wonder how I ever became involved with visualization therapy. After losing my eyesight due to a degenerative condition, I was forced to retire from medicine due to failing vision.

I had nothing to lose and was desperate. So I tried visualization. I developed this visual imagery technique by practicing on myself at home. I'd heard about visualization but at first was skeptical. I thought it was out of the realm of science. Finally I became convinced and a strong advocate of this type treatment. But that was after I restored 75% of my eyesight!

I recommend visualization therapy to any cancer sufferer. There simply is no risk whatsoever and the results can truly be miraculous. The power of visualization combined with the other proven natural remedies and foods included in your well-researched book will help all readers, from the healthy to cancer sufferers.

Sincerely,

Leslie Salov

Leslie H. Salov, M.D.

Lift Letter 4 (newsletter offer)

Dear Friend:

For all of us, time is money.

If the corporate legal decisions in Delaware impact upon your company or your clients, the monthly summary, PRE-CIS, becomes a time saving tool you probably cannot be without.

This service will save you, or a research assistant, many hours of time that it would normally take to review corporate cases. PRE-CIS reports on decisions involving 300-500 pages of material each month and distills them into less than 10% of that volume. The Chancery Court, Delaware Supreme Court, Federal District Court, and the Court of Appeals are all covered.

I know the value of carefully prepared legal summaries. In my years of private practice, as a professor at Delaware Law School, and as managing editor with Matthew Bender, Legal Publisher, my work has had a strong focus on decision analysis. We've worked hard on the PRE-CIS format so that you get a fast reliable overview of all corporate decisions in detail.

Try PRE-CIS and see for yourself how much easier it will be to stay abreast of important corporate litigation.

Sincerely,

In summary, the most effective lift letters are:

1. From someone other than the main letter signer.
2. Project a different voice or tone.
3. Offer a new benefit, testimonial or dramatic summary of the offer.
4. Have a curiosity provoking headline to invite readership.
5. Typed in courier or handwritten.
6. Signed.
7. Printed on a different color stock.

Prepare a strong lift letter and add to your present successful mailings. Or future mailings. You will nearly always increase response to your mailings and improve profitability.

How to Prepare Order Cards that Increase Sales

This chapter is about an important direct marketing success fundamental. Creating the often neglected order card.

An effective order card is absolutely *vital* to a successful sales letter.

Before we get started, you might wonder how I choose marketing topics to write about. Surely you've noted that I stress fundamentals. Let me explain the underlying reason.

Readers of my books and newsletters include many of the most successful marketers in the world, I'm proud to say.

There are a lot of differences between them, of course. But there is one startling similarity. What the marketing "champions" all have in common is this.

They are all avid *students of marketing.* They don't just read my work. They devour it! They insist their employees study each issue. And what they appreciate most is the emphasis on a mastery of

Basics!

The "champions" have reached their status by forgetting the basics enough times to learn from their mistakes. The not so successful sometimes question the focus on basics. Generally they may feel they already know enough about the fundamentals of successful direct response marketing and may like more coverage of "sexy" topics, such as the new electronic media, etc.

Of course, there is a time and place for coverage of new media. But when I consult with companies, small and large, you know what's missing in their marketing approaches 95% of the time? That's right, you guessed it. Implementation of the

Basics!

The basics of direct response are forgotten. Or ignored. Or just poorly implemented.

When I miss the mark in a mailing do you know what's missing? You guessed it. I've overlooked or poorly implemented a basic fundamental. Of course, I know better! But no one is immune. No marketer can review fundamentals often enough!

That's why I consider it part of my mission to emphasize excellence in regard to the marketing basics. Hopefully with more focus than anyone else in the marketing world. There is another benefit from so doing. Once you fully know the "rules" you are in much better position to deliberately break them! But it's important to know it's a conscious decision.

I'm really excited about the subject of order cards. Why? A good one doesn't require enormous extra effort. But sales results can vastly improve.

My observation is that most of the order cards I receive in numerous mailings from lists on which my name appear are poorly done. Many are confusing. And boring. And ugly. They simply do nothing to enhance sales. In fact, they often detract from sales.

Yet, no element is more important in a sales letter than the order card. After all, unless you close the sale and get a bona fide order, the goal of your mailing effort and costs are for naught.

I believe there are several key reasons why order cards are badly done, including:

1. *Writing sequence is wrong.* Order card is usually written last. The letter and envelope and brochure are most often written before the order card.
2. *Writer is "out of gas."* The emotional energy so necessary to a powerful order card is missing.
3. *Offer is often confusing.* The main effort has gone to the benefits contained in the letter.
4. *Fear of rejection.* There is a natural human tendency to avoid closing the sale, so the order instructions are timid. Or lacking.

5. *Order card doesn't sell.* Conceptually the order card is not crafted as a sales tool. Instead, it is created as though it's a "necessary evil," since the order has to be recorded somewhere.

Now let's look at what can happen to improve your order cards with this approach:

1. Get yourself *into the right frame of mind.* Assume your prospect opens your letter and reads the order card first, before the letter, as many do. Unless you sell the prospect with this document alone, your sales will be far less than they otherwise could be.
2. *Prepare the order card first.* Before the sales letter, brochure or lift letter. This sequence is very important. Why? See numbers 3-6 which follow.
3. *Make copy exciting.* You are filled with excitement for the product and, yes, the vitality necessary to all sales success is reflected in the order card.
4. *Make offer clear.* By preparing the order card early, you are forced to clearly think through all aspects of the offer early in the creative process. The result is an easy to understand offer. This clarity provides you more natural sales power.
5. *Overcome fear of rejection.* When you create an exciting order card early in the process that features benefits, it's far easier to overcome the natural reluctance in asking for the order.
6. *Make order card a sales documents.* Your order card should not be prepared just to please your accountant or order processing department. Think of your order card as a very important sales tool. It's often your final word about the product and thus an integral part of your marketing effort.

The perfect order card

Here are some tips on how your order card should be prepared.

1. *Always use a headline* on the order card. This tends to create a feeling that it's an important document. Many mailers omit a headline, which is a mistake.

   A few successful headlines I use are:

   Free Trial Request
   Free Examination Certificate
   No Risk Order Coupon
   Seminar Reservation Certificate
   R.S.V.P.
   Time Limited Reservation Certificate
   Special Order Certificate
   Free 6-month Trial Certificate
   Priority Order Certificate
   Official Entry and Enrollment Certificate
   Gift Certificate
   Membership Application
   Acceptance Card
   Free Preview Issue
   Send No Money
   21-Day Free Trial Certificate
   Acceptance Certificate
   Special Reservation Order Form
   No-Risk Enrollment Form
   Free Audition Certificate
   Send No Money—Offer Expires in 14 Days

2. *Restate the main benefit* of the product. Sometimes it's effective to include two or three benefits.
3. *Restate the features of the product.* A complete description, including dimensions, weight, and the material used in the manufacture of the product are important features which build credibility.
4. *Include a photo of the product.*

5. *Include a photo of a person.* Depending on the product, adding an appropriate human being such as the inventor, architect, author, doctor or person using the product can add sales appeal. Make sure the subject is smiling warmly and making eye contact with the reader. Subject should be dressed in business clothes and, if a man, be cleanly shaven. (While I personally like beards and mustaches, facial hair can detract and reduce credibility. Studies show people with beards and mustaches are not as trusted.) Also remember to always caption the photo.
6. *Dramatize any free gifts or bonuses* you may offer. Strong titles and descriptions really help.
7. *Include a strong guarantee.* The longer the guarantee the more orders and less returns you will have, i.e., "90 days, a full 3 months" is stronger than "21 days." A full year is better yet. A lifetime guarantee will give you the highest response.
8. *Use a certificate border.* A fancy graphic look will add perceived value and will add to the likelihood it will be retained and used.
9. *Use a different color and heavier paper stock* than the rest of the mailing. Sometimes a fancier certificate paper (which your printer can supply) can add sales.
10. *Print on one side, not both.* Mail tests show that orders are higher if the order form is printed on one side of the paper only. Leave back of order form blank. If your order information is longer than the dimensions of your BRE, fold order form in half but still print one side only.
11. *Use involvement devices.* One good approach is to use the classic choices: **Yes•No•Maybe**. Use tokens which must be inserted into die cuts on the card or stamps with photos of free bonuses or gifts. The idea is that the prospect must cut out and add items to the order card. That's how the term "involvement device" began. Involvement devices tend to increase response and are inexpensive but only when mailing quantities are large.

12. *Use window envelopes.* A label with the prospect's name and address on the order card, which serves as the address label, is an often used style because it's a proven winner. You also fulfill a basic marketing rule. You make it *easy to place an order!*
13. *Perforate guarantee.* By adding a perforated dotted line to your order card so that customer can keep it can often increase response.

TIP

Test a first-class closed-face envelope against third-class mail. If your mailing either weighs less than 1 oz. or you are offering an expensive product, a first-class mailing without teaser copy, with a live stamp and with, of course, your order card inside can sometimes pay off.

TIP

Use duplicate order forms. Perhaps the lowest cost yet most effective mailing secret you could ever be exposed to is this. Add a second order form to a successful mailing. This usually increases sales by at least 10% and up to 20%!

Following are examples of the most simple yet effective order forms from my mailings.

Order Card #1—Book Offer

The Essential Book for Every Corporation—Small or Large!

The Complete Book of Corporate Forms
by Ted Nicholas

- Reduce or eliminate corporate legal fees
- Cut time spent on corporate "window dressing"
- Simplify Record keeping process
- Handy reminder of what needs to be done year by year.
- Be prepared for IRS review of your corporate status
- Virtually all the forms you will ever need at a price less than paying a lawyer for one hour of time!

Detach and Mail Card at Right ...

30-DAY NO-RISK TRIAL

YES, please rush me The Complete Book of Corporate Forms by Ted Nicholas at $49.95 plus $4.50 for UPS shipping and handling. I understand that if for any reason I am not satisfied after examining its contents for 30 days, I may return it for a prompt and full refund—including postage both ways.

☐ Payment enclosed Charge to: ☐ Visa ☐ MasterCard ☐ American Express ☐ Diners Club/Carte Blanche

Acct. No. ______________ Exp. Date ______________

Signature (Required for Credit Card Orders) ______________

Please make any name or address corrections above

Enterprise Publishing, Inc. 725 Market St., Wilm, DE 19801 © Enterprise Publishing, Inc. MCMLXXXV

CEO Club Reservation Certificate
RSVP

Yes! Please reserve _____ seats at the special two-day Ted Nicholas Marketing Seminar at $2,997 (normally $7,500). I understand that I can bring 2 guests free. Money-back guarantee. I further understand that if at the end of Day One I am not delighted with the seminar, upon return of my materials, I will receive a prompt and courteous refund.

My guests names are: ______________ Address: ______________

Dates of Seminar (check one)

☐ New York Friday and Saturday, May 5 and 6
☐ Los Angeles Friday and Saturday, May 12 and 13
☐ Dallas Friday and Saturday, May 19 and 20

My name is: ______________ Company ______________
Address: ______________
City: ______________ State ______ Zip ______
Daytime phone number: ______________

☐ Enclosed is my check
☐ Please charge my credit card ☐ Mastercard ☐ Visa ☐ Amex
☐ I cannot attend during the above dates. While I realize there is no substitute for this live seminar, I would like to have the information. Please send me the complete set of audio tapes and workbook at $797 (normally $1,995).

Credit Card No. ______________ Exp. Date ______
Name as it appears on card ______________ Signature ______________

Nicholas Direct, Inc., P.O. Box 877, Indian Rocks Beach, FL 34635
Telephone Number: (813) 596-4966 Fax Number: (813) 596-6900

Cancellation policy: If you need to cancel, you will be given a "rain check" for a future Ted Nicholas seminar

© Copyright 1995 Nicholas Direct, Inc.

Order Card #2—Seminar Offer

Order Card #3—Book Offer

Let great things happen
to you and your career—
at no risk to you whatsoever

- *Idea-filled Complete Guide to Consulting Success only $69.95
- *One-full-year, *no questions asked*, 100% money-back guarantee
- *Money-making *Income Portfolio*, a $9.95 value, *free*—and yours to keep, no matter what

A unique value . . . a unique guarantee . . . a unique opportunity for independent-minded men and women!

Mail in the attached card or phone
1-800-533-2665 now.

Please detach here

YES, I want to make it big on my own. I'll take you up on your offer. Send me the Complete Guide to Consulting Success and the free mine-to-keep-no-matter-what *Income Portfolio*. Remember, I'm covered by your guarantee: If I return the Guide within a year, I get all my money back.

☐ Enclosed is my check payable to Enterprise Publishing, Inc.
Charge my:
☐ MasterCard ☐ Visa ☐ Amex/Optima ☐ Diners/Carte Blanche

Acct. No ______ Exp Date ______

Signature ______

Daytime phone (if we have a question on your order) ______

CONGRATULATIONS! You've made a smart move!

C(E4)

Order Card #4—Book Offer

STATEMENT OF GUARANTEE

If for any reason you feel The "S" Corporation Handbook is not for you, return it anytime up to 30 days from the day you receive it and we will immediately send you a full refund.

M.R. Buchanan
President

Please Detach Here

The "S" Corporation Handbook

FREE TRIAL CERTIFICATE

YES! I want complete details on the "S" Corporation including the tax-saving benefits I can gain and ready-to-use forms to make it happen. Rush me The "S" Corporation Handbook today. Here's my check or charge for $69.95 + $4.50 UPS Shipping. And under your Guarantee, if I decide I can't use this book, I may return it anytime within 30 days for a prompt full refund.

INCLUDE the $19.95 best-seller, How to Form Your Own Corporation Without a Lawyer For Under $50 as my FREE Bonus for ordering now.

☐ JUST send me How To Form Your Own Corporation Without A Lawyer For Under $50 at $19.95 postpaid.

☐ Check enclosed. Charge it to: ☐ MC/Visa ☐ Diner's Club ☐ Am. Exp. ☐ Carte Blanche

Save Time! Call toll-free

Order Card #5—Book Offer

With the help of this book you'll be able to:

Save money — Eliminate writing business letters "from scratch" which today cost $11.71 each in labor and overhead costs.

Save time — Cut correspondence time by 50% or more.

Increase Productivity — 20% of an executive's or business owner's time is spent on correspondence, the job you probably hate most. Avoid taking correspondence home or working overtime.

Computerize your Letters — Letters you repeat often can be entered into your computer.

Twelve Important Business Categories

Including Responding to Inquiries, Sales Letters, Follow-up Sales Letters, Buying Products and Services, Letters Promoting Customer Relations, Credit and Collection Letters, Letters Concerning Employment, Personal Letters for the Businessperson, Letters to the Media, Shareholder Relations, Formal Letters to VIP'S, Community and Personal Activities.

Retain this stub for your records

Check No. ____________

Amt. ____________

Date ____________

Iron-Clad Money Back Guarantee

It is my understanding that if for any reason I'm not satisfied after reviewing this book for 30 days after I receive it, I may return it for a prompt and courteous refund.

Free Trial Request

Please send me a copy of the Executive's Business Letter Book at $69.95+ $5.00 UPS Shipping and Handling.

☐ Enclosed is my check for $74.95.
Charge my credit card: ☐ Visa ☐ MasterCard ☐ Amex ☐ Diners/Carte Blanche

Acct # ____________

Exp Date ____________

Signature ____________

Mail to:
ENTERPRISE PUBLISHING, INC.

If address information requires correction, please make necessary changes.

30 Day No-Risk Offer

Order Card #6—Book Offer

Mail This FREE Trial Request Today!

Please rush me _____ copies of HOW TO FIGHT CANCER AND WIN by William L. Fischer.

Also send me the following free reports:
1. *The Truth About a More Exciting Sex Life*
2. *How to Take Off the Pounds and the Years*
3. *Nutritional Secrets to More Youthful Skin*
4. *How to Improve Brain Capacity Naturally*

☐ Also send the FREE report for my prompt response: *How to Increase Your Energy and Enjoy Living Longer.*

I enclose not the original price of $50, but only $29.97 (plus $3.00 shipping & handling. Ohio residents please add 6% sales tax). I understand I may examine this revolutionary new book for one full year, since I am fully protected by your 100% No-Risk Double Guarantee as stated on the reverse of this card.

Fischer Publishing Corporation
One Fischer Square, Box 368, Canfield OH 44406
Phone: (216) 533-1232 Fax: (216) 533-9860

How to Fight Cancer & Win
William L. Fischer

HOW TO FIGHT CANCER AND WIN
$29.97
Plus $3 shipping & handling

7 Time Nobel Award nominee, Dr. Johanna Budwig

☐ Enclosed is check or money order (U.S. currency only) payable to Fischer Publishing Corporation in the amount of: __________.

☐ Charge my: ☐ Visa ☐ M/C ☐ AmEx

Card # ____________

Expires ____________

Signature ____________

Are your name and address correct? If not, please make the necessary revisions to this label

Order Card #6—Book Offer

No Risk Order Coupon

Yes! Please send me:

☐ BEST DEAL. Ted Nicholas' Self-Publishing SEMINAR OF THE CENTURY on tape, 20 hours, at $317*, plus S&H, under your 3 month money-back guarantee. I have ordered within 10 days. Please include a free copy of HOW TO PUBLISH A BOOK AND SELL A MILLION COPIES. If I'm not delighted I may return them and keep the book, regardless.

☐ Send the book HOW TO PUBLISH A BOOK AND SELL A MILLION COPIES only for $89* (plus $5 S&H)

Enclosed is my check for $__________ payable to Nicholas Direct

Bill my ☐ Visa ☐ MC ☐ AMEX (*Florida residents add 7% sales tax)

CC#__________ Exp.__________ Signature__________

Name__________ Company__________

Address__________

City__________ State__________ Zip__________

Daytime Phone__________ (in case of questions about your order)

Mail to: Nicholas Direct, Inc.
P.O. Box 877
Indian Rocks Beach, FL 34635

TIP

Ideally no one will read your order card until after they read your letter. Remember, in all selling, sequence is important. When you ask for the order is important, for if it's too early sales can be lost. There is a very effective device you can use to help in this sequence. Add an inner envelope. In it place your order card and if you include a brochure, put that in as well. On the outside of this closed-face inner envelope type these words:

*"Please open **after** you have read my letter"*

Use the tips in this chapter to boost sales from mailings through more effective order cards. From now on you can convert your order cards from a "necessary evil" into what they should be—an effective sales tool.

How to Prepare a Profitable Catalogue

This chapter is devoted to marketing through catalogues—a special subject to business owners.

When you think of catalogues, most likely you have mental images of those you get in the mail. Neiman-Marcus, Harry & David, Spiegel, Hammacher Schlemmer, Tiffany, Sharper Image, Lillian Vernon, Victoria's Secret and Nightingale-Conant are among those I receive.

It may look easy. But it's tougher to make money with a catalogue than it appears. Contrary to popular belief, the majority of catalogues, especially those prepared by smaller, newer businesses are *not profitable.* And because they tend to involve a large investment, I suspect more money is lost in catalogues than any other form of direct marketing. The reasons for the lack of success by catalogue marketers include:

1. There is no coherent copy theme, which begins with the headline.
2. Offers are not benefit driven from a customer's point of view. Instead, a "manufacturer's" approach is used, i.e., *we* have been in business X years, *we* are wonderful, *we* have great quality, etc.
3. A distinct "personality" is not projected.
4. Organization of products is poor.
5. Order information is confusing.
6. Catalogue is mailed to wrong list.
7. Headlines are weak.
8. Copy is boring.
9. Catalogue does not include a letter from someone important in the company, preferably the owner or president.

10. Typefaces, colors and graphics make copy difficult to read.
11. Products offered do not have sales appeal.
12. Low quality photography or drawing is used for items selected.

Here is the direct path to *big profits* as a catalogue marketer, particularly if your budget is limited.

Let's start with products. Here is the best solution I've found. *Sell "solo" items* to develop a mailing list *before* investing in a full blown catalogue. By doing so you test products and copy in a small way, limiting investment. Later, once the product and copy appeal are proven in the marketplace, you can include them in a catalogue.

Of course, you can also eliminate products which do not sell profitably on a solo basis.

Does the "solo" approach mean you cannot start out with multiple products within a catalogue and succeed? No. Of course not. But the odds are stacked heavily against you. And you'd better be prepared to invest a substantial sum.

Now let's assume you've progressed to where you have 6 or more successful products sold "solo." And to the same audience. You now are in a good position to test a catalogue.

The very first thing to do is, you guessed it:

1. *Create a powerful headline.* By doing so, you create a theme for the product group. A selling "platform."

   For example, one of my clients is a marketer of information designed for real estate professionals. Their catalogue cover looked like many others. No strong benefit headline. The most important sales space on front of the catalogue had no headline. Just their company logo! Now, do customers care about their logo? Of course not. The only people that do are the company owners. So I created a theme for them. My headline:

   How to Be a More Successful Real Estate Professional

Did sales increase? You bet! By more than 50%! But I also rewrote a lot of the inside copy too. Undoubtedly you can appreciate how a benefit-driven headline appealed to their mail list.

TIP

For a catalogue headline, strive for the biggest benefit *you can find common to all or most of the catalogue products.*

2. The second step. *Select the products* that will be included in the catalogue. As long as the products tie into the headline theme, there is no magic number. You can have as few as 6 up to dozens of products. Of course, the danger in offering too many products is confusion. And confusion *always* reduces sales. So when in doubt, it's better to have fewer highly saleable selections rather than arbitrarily adding numerous products.

TIP

Often an offer of a "package" of everything included in a catalogue at a special price can increase your average sale. Sometimes this can be the most successful offer you can make, i.e., "The Mother Lode Offer Of Everything In The Catalogue."

3. *Prepare a letter.* The best and most successful catalogues include a letter from a key person in the company, such as the President or Proprietor. This "welcome to the catalogue" letter should appear on page 2 or inside cover.

   This letter can help to set the tone for the products and the company offering them. Your goal is to build rapport with the catalogue recipient.

   Important point. No matter the size of your company, *people like* to *deal with people* and not institutions. A carefully drafted letter helps to *humanize* your company.

A message from the Publisher Ted Nicholas:

Dear Friend,

Publishing is the most profitable field in the modern world.

You can work from home, start part-time or full-time, or keep your current job. It doesn't matter if you are young or old, black or white, rich or poor. Now, you can learn how to make more money in one day than most people make in a week!

Today, we are truly living in the information age, wherein lie the biggest opportunities. I'll show you how to succeed at publishing information products. Control your own future and your own destiny. Create a lifestyle for yourself others only dream of.

It's really simple to make a personal fortune.

All you have to do is sell books, Special Reports, disks, newsletters, videos, or audio tapes that people really need and want.

It's the kind of profit that will free you up to quit the 9-to-5 rat race. And you don't need an expensive office. It's the ideal home-based business. Avoid commuting hassles. Live anywhere in the world. Work when you want to.

The opportunities for profit from "how-to" information are virtually unlimited.

This catalog is filled with books and videos that will show you how to get involved in marketing and publishing. You can start part-time or full-time as you prefer. You'll find information on how to set up a low budget operation from product development to sales. You can begin on a shoestring just like I did.

The information in this catalog can completely change your life. You will be helped every step of the way toward the highly profitable and enormously enjoyable adventure of being an entrepreneur.

I hope you decide to become part of the very best field of endeavor that exists today.

Sincerely,

Ted Nicholas

Ted Nicholas

P.S. One of the biggest benefits of self-publishing is operating from wherever you wish, and not having to be a part of the "Big City" establishment to have a very profitable career.

Sample Letter

TIP

Make sure your letter is signed *before reproducing it. It looks and feels more personal.*

4. *Prepare the order form.* The goal here is to make it as *easy as possible* for your customer *to order.*

   Order the form so that there are clearly labeled sections large enough to accommodate handwriting. Don't forget to have lines that are wide enough and tall enough to accommodate credit card numbers and other information. This may seem like "nit picking." But cramped writing areas on order forms reduce sales! Ever try to write on a cramped order form?

TIP

Before printing your catalogue, have the order form typeset. Complete it in your own handwriting. This helps to spot problem areas. Of course, you then can correct before printing.

5. Prepare headlines for each product offered. Strive for the biggest benefit to the ultimate user of the product. As previously discussed, it's always best to *use tested headlines* from solo offers whenever possible.

TIP

If you do not have tested headlines available, and you do not write your own copy, engage the best copywriter you can afford. Have the "pro" prepare the headlines as well as other product copy.

6. *Prepare the copy for each product. Benefits* of the product in use through the product description are again the key to successful catalogue copy. Once again, use tested copy if possible derived from solo offers, card decks or full or fractional page space ads.

   Condense long copy into a shorter version. However, you can have as much as 1,000 words for each product on an 81/2" x 11" size catalogue. Or you can have multiple products on each page.

Nicholas Direct, Inc. Order Form

If, for any reason, you are not delighted with your purchase, return it in good condition within 30 days of receipt for a full refund.

4 ways to order

PHONE
Call toll-free
1-800-730-7777
24 hours a day
7 days a week

FAX
Fax this coupon to
1-813-596-6900
24 hours a day
7 days a week

MAIL
Complete this order form and mail to
Nicholas Direct, Inc.
P.O. Box 877
Indian Shores, FL 34635

E-MAIL
Got CompuServe?
Just Type GO ND

Name ______________________ Title ______________________

Company ______________________

Street Address ______________________

City ____________ State ________ Country ____________ Zip ________

Daytime Telephone *(in case of questions on your order)* ______________________

TITLE	CATALOG #	QTY	PRICE	TOTAL

Shipping and Handling Charges:
$0–24.99 .... $4
$25–49.99 .... $5
$50–99.99 .... $6
$100–249.99 .... $8
$250 and over $11
International Orders via air shipments will be adjusted accordingly.

Subtotal	
FL Residents add 7% Tax	
S&H	
TOTAL	

FORM OF PAYMENT

Enclosed is my check for $________ payable to Nicholas Direct, Inc.

Bill my ❒ VISA ❒ MC ❒ AMEX

CC# ______________________ Exp ________

Signature ______________________

Dept. X

☎ Call Toll Free 800-730-7777 or Fax Your Credit Card Order to 813-596-6900

Sample Order Form

Along with benefits include the features of the product—size, weight, color, materials used, etc. This increases credibility.

TIP

Make sure all copy is in the same voice. *There is far more sales appeal if the copy sounds as though it comes from the same person. Strive for a scenario wherein your most effective spokesperson is having a friendly conversation with your prospect.*

7. *Organize the products for maximum sales effect.* The arrangement and order in which you present products is important. Successful catalogue marketers always offer their biggest sellers *early*. If you wait to present the hottest items you can lose the chance to sell. The prospect may stop reading and toss the catalogue before getting to the hottest products.

   The best position for your hottest products is on page *3*, on a *right hand page.* Right hand pages pull more sales than those on the left. It's the furthest forward right-hand page. The next best position is page 5 and so forth. Other prominent positions are the *back cover* and the *page facing* the *order form.*

TIP

Look at the numbers. *Each time you mail a catalogue, do a postmortem. Prepare a profit and loss report for each product by page number. This enables you to keep refining subsequent catalogues for maximum profit. You also discover which products to more heavily feature and which to drop.*

To increase ease of ordering, at the bottom of each catalogue *page, add these words:*

"To order, call toll free 1–800–000–0000
or see order form on page ______."

8. *Use photographs that enhance sales.* Good photos usually work better than drawings. Spend the money to take good product photos. It's worth the extra cost to retain talented photographers.

   Sparkling photos add sizzle to your offers. Remember, *always caption photos.* If there are people in the photos, it's usually more effective if they are making eye contact with the reader.

   It's usually best to hire professional models. You can call local modeling agencies in your town or nearest city and preview available talent. Ask first for a book with sample photographs of available models.

TIP

A great way to depict your products in photographs is to show people enjoying themselves *while experiencing the benefits of the product.*

9. *Use graphics to enhance sales. Visuals* are *important* in direct selling. The appearance of your catalogue visually has a big impact on your sales. Since today far more people watch T.V. than read (unfortunately), the more you make your catalogue resemble a television show, the better. Here are some of the key things you can do:
   A. *Use full color photography throughout.* The extra print cost is usually more than paid for by increased sales.

TIP

For cost reduction, some marketers find a good solution without a drop in sales can be a blend of black and white and color pages. Some pages all black and white some all color. If your product does not absolutely depend on color photography, test blending black and white and color pages.

B. *Use graphic symbols sparingly.* Graphic designers these days tend to add too many graphic elements, such as fancy symbols, etc. Computer software makes it easier than ever to do so.

TIP

Unless a graphic symbol has a direct tie to your product, do not use at all. Symbols when used should both tie to the product and be "classic" in the sense the symbol used is not distracting to the reader. Familiar, easy to identify symbols are the least distracting. Use bullets like this:
• Or squares: ■ Or checks: ✔

C. Use easy-to-read typefaces.
- Do not use sans serif typefaces like this:

  This is a sans serif typeface

  Studies show sans serif is more difficult to read, particularly in large blocks of copy.

  The easiest typeface to read is a serif typeface like this one:

  This is Times Roman, a serif typeface

- Do not use reverse type such as this:

  This is reverse type

  Reason? Once again, it's more difficult to read.

- Never use screens behind copy such as this:

  Screened copy

  Screens reduce readership, with the exception of yellow.

A white or yellow background is best for enhanced readership.

Use screens only *outside copy areas on borders* which surround the copy. This makes the copy pop out.

- Do not use any other typeface color than *black* for a large block of descriptive copy. It's easiest to read.
- Do not use all upper case letters like this:

THE WORLD'S MOST
FANTASTIC CATALOGUE

Again, it's tougher to read. If you use upper case, use it sparingly in short words such as FREE or SALE.

Never use more *than* 2 typeface *styles in any catalogue. In body copy stay with serif classic typefaces such as Times Roman because they are easier to read. It's OK to use sans serif typefaces, such as Helvetica, in headlines.*

This is Helvetica

You can use either a matte or glossy paper stock on which to put your catalogue. Much depends on the feeling you want to communicate.

Developing a catalogue mail strategy

Your *satisfied customers* are always the *best prospects* for catalogue sales. Clearly, people who have spent money with you and are happy will trust subsequent product offers. New prospects who haven't done business with you are tougher to sell. It's been estimated that it's 16 times harder to sell to new customers than existing ones.

Perhaps the soundest catalogue game plan is this. *Send* your catalogue first *to* your *house mailing list.* If it's not profitable on your customer data base, do not mail it to strangers. If and when it is successful then test outside lists. Best possibilities are competitors who will rent to you or exchange lists.

If your catalogue is not profitable now, it's best to concentrate your efforts on developing a new, more powerful one to mail to your data base. Of course, you can always drop the catalogue idea altogether, and instead concentrate on single product offers.

Contrary to popular belief, experienced direct marketers are aware of this powerful truth. It's far easier to make a single product ("single shot") offer work in direct mail than a catalogue. Reason? You can write longer copy. And the buying decision is by necessity more focused and less confusing than any multiple product offer.

TIP

Often tests show a successful catalogue can be made more successful by enclosing it in an envelope instead of as a self-mailer. When doing so, always include a benefit-filled sales letter.

TIP

When fulfilling inquiries with a catalogue, always insert in an envelope. Use a rubber stamp on the outside of the envelope which reads:

"Here is the information you requested"

TIP

The easiest and cheapest way to increase catalogue sales by 10%–20% is to include an extra order form within it! The order form can either be bound in or loose. Try it. You'll be delighted!"

I'll look forward to hearing about your next catalogue "home run!"

How to Make Card Decks Pay

For years I've successfully sold millions of dollars worth of products and services via card decks. Yet, most marketers who try card decks cannot make them pay out.

The reasons why so few make money are a well kept secret. I'll *reveal* the real *secrets* of *how to succeed with card decks* in this chapter.

"Do people really look through a big, thick batch of cards in a deck and actually respond?" I'm often asked that question. The answer is an emphatic

YES!

Many busy people enjoy quickly reviewing many exciting products offered in card decks. It's a quick way to "shop" through a variety of products. But, as with any other method of delivering sales information to a prospect, you *must do it right* to succeed.

In case you don't know what a card deck is, let's define terms. A card deck offer is a product description on an individual card about the size of a postcard placed within a deck along with 50–100 other cards. These cards are wrapped in cellophane or plastic to keep them together in a deck.

There are many choices to select from when considering where to place your card deck offer. In fact, there are over 500 card decks published in the U.S. at the present time. A good source of contact information about card decks is a Standard Rate and Data Directory found in a good library.

Card decks are potentially a *very profitable* medium *for you.* They could be your best media investment. Why? They are a relatively low-cost way to reach large numbers of prospective customers. It's not unusual to reach *100,000* plus people at a rate of $10 to $20 per thousand. Or, just $1,0000–$2,000 to reach a big audience! Thus, you can target and send your offer to a *larger number* of carefully selected *prospects for less money* than nearly all other direct marketing methods.

But why are most marketers who test card decks spectacularly unsuccessful? What are the pitfalls you should avoid?

Let's look at the reasons as I see them.

Avoid these common mistakes

1. ***Placing selling copy on just one side of card.***
Most marketers *use only one side* of the card for selling copy. The entire reverse side of the card is commonly used just for the address to whom the response is sent. The effect is to reduce the potential size of sales copy by 50%! Remember the old adage. The more you tell, the more you sell. This is especially applicable in a card deck wherein you have a limited area you can fill with copy.
2. ***Using weak or untested copy.***
Typically, those testing a card deck prepare new copy employing a less than top flight copywriter. A card deck is *not* the ideal place to test new copy. *Or an unproven copywriter.* Because card decks are so inexpensive, unsuccessful marketers often employ young, unseasoned copywriters without sufficient experience with their "feet to the fire."

   Since you have less space than an ad or sales letter to devote to copy, you really need top flight copywriting talent.
3. ***Using an untested offer.***
It's far better strategy to test and prove the sales appeal of an offer when using long copy, such as in a sales letter or full page space ad.
4. ***Card deck is sent to the wrong mailing list.***
As with all other forms of direct selling, you must *mail your card* to the *right audience.* A sufficient number of appropriate prospects must be the majority of people who make up the card deck mailing list to make the offer cost effective.

   Because card deck advertising is relatively cheap, marketers make far more mistakes in selecting the card decks mailed to unresponsive lists for their product or service.

5. ***Graphics do not enhance the sales power of your message.***
   Once again, a card deck is not the ideal place to test graphics, which are a very important element of a successful offer. Typefaces, headline layout, photos, etc., are better tested in a space ad or sales letter.
6. ***Two-step (lead generating) and one-step (sales generating) ads are not tested against each other.***
   Some card decks work better on a two-step basis and others on a one-step. And vice versa. Results vary from offer to offer and must be tested.

Here are the little known techniques which reveal exactly how I've made card decks pay for 23 years. Employ these tips and watch your sales explode!

How to Make a Card Deck Offer Succeed

A. ***Run sales copy on both sides of the card deck.***
   It's much more important to provide a *longer sales message* filled with benefits on both sides of the card than to devote one entire side of potential sales with a reply mechanism.

   If your offer and copy are compelling, your prospects will respond *using their own envelope.* Or they will call the toll free telephone number you list. But only if they have been sufficiently sold.

   The secret is to have twice as much selling copy than the strategy used by other marketers who fail.

B. ***Use tested copy.***
   Test out the card deck *copy* in a *long copy medium*, such as a sales letter or space ad.

   Here is the key point. If the offer does not work when you are not limited for selling space, it surely will *not* work in a card deck. When you do have a successful offer, use the same headline. Boil it down to its strongest benefits for use in your card deck. And only put profitable products and offers in card decks.

If you are creating a new offer for the card deck, write the copy yourself. Or hire the best copywriter you can possibly afford.

When preparing a card deck offer, *do not waste time* and *money* with *copywriters* who do *not* have a *successful track record* in print media. Reason? Whenever you employ relatively short copy, as in a card deck, you need an "Olympic Champion" copywriter. A copywriting effort by a novice will almost surely fail.

Tip

If you are testing a promising new copywriter's work, use a long copy medium. The best medium is a sales letter where length is not even an issue. Plus, you can test a small segment of a mailing and keep costs down. If a copywriter cannot prepare a successful sales letter, there is no way he/she can create a card deck that works.

C. ***Use a tested offer.***
Price your *product* in accordance with *what* has *worked best* in other media. If a *bonus* and *guarantee* are included in your tested long copy offer, *incorporate* it exactly *in* your *card deck offer.*

D. ***Mail your card deck offer to the right prospects.***
Use the *same* or *similar mailing lists* that are proven to give you a profitable response to space ads or sales letters. Conversely, if it is not profitable to mail sales letters to certain mail lists, a limited copy card deck surely won't work.

E. ***Use tested graphics.***
Use the *same graphic elements* previously used in a successful space ad or sales letter. For example, *repeat* the *same headline* typeface. As to body copy, it's safe to use Times Roman, which has best stood the test of time. Use two or three columns in body copy for ease of reading. I've tested "ragged" right and justified right hand columns. Results were the same, so use whichever you prefer or fits copy best.

F. ***Test lead generating card deck offer against one which asks for the sale.***
It is, of course, *easier* to *get* a *prospect* to "*raise their hand*" in responding to an offer request. In such a case, your response is to mail a long copy sales letter which sells the benefits of your offer and asks for the sale. A card deck can be the ideal vehicle for lead generation due to its limited copy characteristics.

Again, the ideal copy approach is to include a proven headline. Then your body copy asks the prospect to respond for more information.

Against the two-step approach, *test* a *one-step offer* which immediately goes for the sale.

Experienced direct marketers have been puzzled for years why I have so many successful one-step offers running in card decks. The underlying reasons which I've never written about before are revealed in this chapter. Now you can experience the same success by employing the strategies that work.

I've also included actual examples of successful "one-step" and "two-step" card deck offers, which demonstrate the techniques I've just discussed.

Put the secrets of successful card decks to work for you and watch your sales grow from this little understood, yet extremely powerful, medium.

This card has been successfully running for many years in a variety of card decks which are mailed to executives and entrepreneurs

Beat New Tax Law with Your Own "S" Corporation

New handbook shows how you can beat tax reform... gain limited liability... without double taxation

Limit your liability and avoid double taxation. These important advantages and many others are now available to you when you form an "S" Corporation. Individual tax rates are lower than corporate tax rates for the first time in decades. That's why the "S" Corporation strategy is the most significant tax loophole under the new tax law

Let's look at the facts. There is no income tax whatsoever at the corporate level—you pay at the new lower personal rate. You would have all the benefits of a corporation. You can operate even as a one person business if you like.

That's why there has been a recent surge of "S" Corporations. If this strategy appeals to you, a new publication makes it clear and simple. *The "S" Corporation Handbook,* by Ted Nicholas (author of the best seller, *"How to Form Your Own Corporation Without a Lawyer for Under $50).*

Front

Back

EIP 10/88

The handbook covers how to:

- Completely avoid corporate tax.
- Discover when an "S" Corporation becomes your best personal tax shelter. Losses are taken on your personal return—yet you retain all corporate advantages including limited liability easy transfer of ownership, and continuity.
- Own investments including real estate and securities in an S Corporation when 100% of your income can be from rents, dividends, and other passive sources without losing status.
- Put children through college with IRS help.
- Personally sell property tax free to your new S Corporation.
- Tax deduct your kids' allowances.
- Hand your children a $120,000 graduation present.
- Give your spouse a tax deferred $144,000.
- Have up to 35 stockholders and still retain S status.
- Have proper timing on making the S Election.
- Insert buy-sell agreements so that you can easily get back stock of any shareholder who dies, is divorced, or wishes to sell.
- Build wealth without more work.
- Avoid accumulated earnings tax.
- Structure your holdings for maximum advantage.

For ease of ordering, call toll-free 1-800-533-2665.
Or complete the order card and mail at once.

☐ Please send me one copy of *The S Corporation Handbook* by Ted Nicholas at $69.95, plus $5.00 shipping and handling. If for any reason I am dissatisfied, I can return it within 30 days of receipt for a prompt and courteous refund.

☐ Also, send me a copy of *How To Form Your Own Corporation Without a Lawyer for Under $50* for $19.95.

☐ Enclosed is my check. Charge my:
☐ Diners Club ☐ Carte Blanche

Card No. ____ Exp. Date ____

Signature ____

Name ____ Company Name ____

Address ____

City ____ State ____ Zip ____

Daytime Phone (in case we have a question about your order) ____

Make check payable and mail to:
Enterprise Publishing, Inc.
725 Market Street, Dept. EN-8XI
Wilmington, DE 19801

I1004

FILL OUT THIS CARD COMPLETELY AND MAIL IT ALONG WITH ANY OTHERS OF INTEREST IN THE ENCLOSED POSTAGE PAID ENVELOPE.

This unique selling proposition (U.S.P.) continues to pull sales in space ads, sales letters, and card decks mailed to small business owners

What Will You Do When Your Personal Assets Are Seized to Satisfy a Judgement Against Your Corporation?

Every single one of the many tax benefits you receive from owning a corporation could be wiped out overnight. How? The IRS could visit and claim you have not kept proper corporate records.

And banks, insurance companies and various government agencies require notarized authorizations to grant loans, enter into leases and even sell assets.

In a small, one person business, it seems silly to keep records. Isn't it just a waste of time? NO! Recordkeeping is part of the price you pay to receive all the advantages of incorporation.

You could hire a lawyer to keep your records — just like the big corporations do. And to have one form prepared, you'll pay $100 or more, even though your lawyer's secretary may complete the standard forms.

There is now a way for you to solve your corporate recordkeeping problems. Without a lawyer. Without the high fees. And without spending a lot of your valuable time. It's THE COMPLETE BOOK OF CORPORATE FORMS by Ted Nicholas, author of the bestselling book, HOW TO FORM YOUR OWN CORPORATION WITHOUT A LAWYER FOR UNDER $50.

SEE OTHER SIDE FOR MORE DETAILS

Front

Back

EAP-10/88-DMI

Virtually every form your corporation will ever need is prepared for you, and there are simple easy to follow instructions for each document. Each form can be completed in minutes. And you have permission to reproduce any form in the book.

Here is just a sampling of what you'll receive:

- Minutes of Stockholders' and Director's meetings.
- Minutes of Special Meetings.
- Forms authorizing your expenses and salary. And much more.

Even if you are behind in keeping accurate corporate records, this book will help you catch up. Just complete a few blanks to document your companies' activities. It's legal and it works. And best of all, if you use just one of the forms in the next year, you will more than justify your modest investment in it. K-1043

© Enterprise Publishing, Inc. MCMLXXXVIII

Please rush me ____________ copy(s) of THE COMPLETE BOOK OF CORPORATE FORMS by Ted Nicholas at $69.95 plus $4.50 for shipping and handling. I understand my purchase is covered under the Enterprise 30-Day Money Back Guarantee if not satisfied.

☐ Check enclosed.

☐ Visa ☐ MasterCard ☐ American Express

Account No. ____ Exp. Date ____ Initials ____

Name ____

Company ____

Address ____

City ____ State ____ Zip ____

Day-time phone (in case we have a question about your order) ____

Mail to: Enterprise Publishing, Inc., Dept. EO-8XK
725 North Market Street, Wilmington, DE 19801

This offering is endorsed by the **Entrepreneurs of America**. EOA members are entitled to a 20% courtesy discount on Enterprise books and other benefits. For complete membership information, call the EOA toll-free: 1-800-553-3932.

This card deck offer produces both direct sales and leads. Those who inquire are sent a letter, brochure and within two weeks receive a follow-up telephone call

Instant Incorporation WHILE-YOU-WAIT™

Often, it's urgent to form a corporation immediately. Reasons include closing a deal, tax savings or to limit personal liability. Now, all you need do is pick up the phone and have your credit card ready. No lawyer necessary. You can be incorporated — including name reservation — while you hold the line! Patented system makes it easy for you. Your cost? Only $35.00 (plus filing fees, usually $71.00).

See other side for more details...

Front

Back

Your incorporation will be handled individually, with care. Our nationally known corporate service organization has been established for over 15 years. We've set up over 70,000 corporations and incorporate in any state, specializing in the well-known Delaware corporation. ©The Company Corporation 1988

Call toll-free now:

1-800-228-2677

Or write: EAP-10/88-DMI

The Company Corporation
725 North Market Street, Dept. EO-8ZY
Wilmington, DE 19801

This offering is endorsed by the **Entrepreneurs of America**. For complete membership information, call the EOA toll-free: 1-800-553-3932. Y-1017

How to Prepare a Brochure that Sells

This chapter is about an important concern of every business owner—brochure preparation.

No matter the type of business, all should use brochures to help bring in business.

Therefore, every business, not just a direct response company, needs to know how to put together brochures and fliers that sell.

Yet, most brochures fail to produce profitable sales. Indeed, many produce such a poor response they often can be a financial disaster.

I'll discuss reasons why often they don't work. And the secrets of making them work like crazy. But first let's define terms.

Exactly what is a brochure?

A *brochure* is a sheet of paper imprinted with information that is used to sell a company's product, service or image.

Length can be anywhere from 2 pages to 20 pages, or even more. A single 8½ x 11" sheet printed on one or both sides can be called a brochure. But it can also be called a flier. I'll use these terms interchangeably.

Avoid these 7 common mistakes. How Many Do You Make?

Here are the most common mistakes made in brochures and fliers.

1. ***Poor headlines***
   Often entrepreneurs use weak or oblique headlines. Or they like seeing their product name or company in the headline so much sales impact is lost. This particularly depresses sales when the product trade name is such that the reader cannot relate immediately to a benefit in a headline. Remember, the most powerful sales promise in any headline is to answer the question, "What's in it for me?"
2. ***Boring copy***
   Instead of copy filled with appealing benefits of the product, brochures are often written using dry, stilted "manufacturer's" language, i.e., "We have been in business —— years. Our craftsmen are wonderful, etc." This is a "me" message, which does not sell.

   No one ever buys anything unless there is a strong, emotional, benefit-driven appeal in the sales message.
3. ***Disorganized***
   Whether you offer a single or multiple products, for a large response you must arrange graphics, photos, benefits, and order information in an easy-to-follow organized manner.
4. ***Poor graphics***
   Dark screens, lots of reverse type, sans serif typefaces in body copy, too many italicized words and other errors often make brochures difficult to read.
5. ***Order information is omitted***
   It's amazing but true. The purpose of a brochure is to sell your product. Or company. Or both. Yet, many brochures and fliers used by companies, large and small, do not include basic order information! This is often the case with direct mailers. Since a separate order card is included, it's assumed duplicate order information is not necessary because it's already elsewhere within the mailing. This is a big mistake.

Often brochures and fliers become separated from sales letters or are passed along to someone else who may want to order but cannot find exactly where and how! And from whom!

6. ***Photographs used disadvantageously***
   Many marketers use poor photos or those which do not clearly tie the product to the headline or theme. Another common mistake is not to caption each photograph.
7. ***Lacking theme***
   A brochure or flier loses sales impact unless a strong copy theme is clearly reflected throughout. The theme helps convey the "personality" of the company offering the product or service.

How to prepare a profitable brochure

1. ***Write a powerful headline***
   Your headline should be artfully created. You can't go wrong with the tried and true strategy of making your lead the biggest benefit of using your product. Often you can simply duplicate the headline from the sales letter which should accompany the brochure.

   Always include a good letter to accompany a brochure when mailed to a prospect or customer. Your sales result will be better every time! In some cases you will see a huge difference.
2. ***Maintain a congruent theme***
   Whether you offer one or several products in the brochure, for maximum impact and credibility, the body *copy* should *tie* to *the central theme*. For example, if you happen to be a software marketer of tax information and were planning a brochure with a headline, "How to Slash Your Business Taxes," your sales results will be far better if all the products in the brochure helped the prospect with tax saving tips instead of offering unrelated products.

3. ***Employ exciting copy filled with benefits, benefits, benefits***

   It is very important to *include features* in your brochure copy. Always include factors such as color, dimensions, weight, materials used in manufacture, etc. This helps build credibility.

   However, as with sales letters and space ads, the *biggest sales hot buttons are always benefits.* The benefits of using the product or service are what must be stressed to maximize sales impact.

   As to length, keep it as long as necessary to tell a complete story. But, as with sales letters, don't include a single wasted word.

   Repeat your strongest benefits. Don't worry about losing impact with repetition. Repeat the benefits of your product in already used sales letters, even if it accompanies the brochure.

   Also include customer testimonials in the brochure, which are among the strongest ways to enhance the sales power.

4. ***Use graphics that increase sales***

   A. *Typeface:* Use serif typefaces on body copy for ease of reading. Stick with Times Roman or another classic typeface. Sans serif is OK for headlines. Use *no more* than *two typefaces* in the brochure.

   B. *Paper:* Use a white or cream semi-gloss or glossy (coated) stock. Your brochure will then have a classy look and feel. Ask your printer for samples.

   C. *Screens:* Do *not* use any screens *behind blocks of copy.* Unless the background is yellow, you reduce readership. The best use of *screens* is *surrounding copy areas.* This helps to "punch out" the copy so it stands out.

   D. *Layout:* Do not crowd together too much copy, photographs, and illustrations. Leave plenty of "white space" for a clean, uncluttered look.

E. *Colors:* Regardless of your field, your products, as well as photos of people in your brochure, will *always look better in full color.* Therefore, if your budget allows, use full color. However, with some items such as information products, you can do almost as well with one color in addition to black. Use primarily black ink for the body type against a white or light background. Headlines are OK in other colors.

The use of full color is almost a necessity with certain products and services such as cars, art prints, vacation resorts, clothing and jewelry.

5. ***Photographs help sell***

Photographs can often enhance the sales power of your brochure or flier. As the old saying goes, "A picture is worth a thousand words."

But always include a *caption* under every photograph. If you include a "head shot" of a human being, the caption can simply be the person's name who is subject of the photo.

When showing people using your product, the *caption should clearly state what is happening.* Assume nothing. For example, "Mr. and Mrs. John Smith are enjoying a Sunday ride with their family in the new Nickmobile voted the best new car of the decade."

6. ***Include order information***

To maximize sales from your brochure, you must *make it as easy as possible to order from you.* Be sure your brochure clearly states:

A. Price of your product(s)
B. Shipping and handling charges (if any)
C. Telephone number
D. Fax number
E. Company name and address
F. Credit cards you accept

Use the foregoing techniques. You'll dramatically increase the sales power of your brochures and fliers.

Here are the Best Books Ever Written on Marketing

Every super successful marketer I know is constantly working to improve skills. Why? You must be a perpetual student to become a master in any field. Those who never achieve their potential in life simply do not exercise their innate capacity to learn and grow.

Continuing education through books is perhaps the best way known to expand your knowledge. But what books should you read?

My personal library contains over 100 highly acclaimed books on marketing and copywriting.

You may want to read many books to select your own favorites. However, to possibly save you time and money, I've selected 13 books considered the best ever written. Every serious marketer should study and refer to them over and over, as I do.

Here are the "lucky 13 library" which are musts for every marketer.

Confessions Of An Advertising Man by David Ogilvy

Perhaps more than any founder of a large ad agency, Ogilvy understands direct marketing. And he communicates his wisdom clearly and effectively.

You will learn how to:

- Prepare better headlines
- Enhance the graphics of your space ads and direct mail
- Use photography in ways that increase the pulling power of your promotions
- Select typefaces that help sell your product

- Use reverse type selectively
- Improve your creativity
- Find good copywriters

You'll find the ads written by Ogilvy himself to be especially useful in studying powerful copy techniques. My favorite is his ad for Rolls Royce with the classic headline, "At 60 Miles An Hour the Loudest Noise in this New Rolls Royce Comes From the Electric Clock."

The Robert Collier Letter Book by Robert Collier

This book, first published in 1931, is a classic. It clearly shows why Collier was considered the best copywriter in the world during the first half of this century. Virtually all the techniques he used then are just as powerful now. Perhaps even more so. The wisdom in this book shows you how to:

- Improve the pulling power of your sales letter
- Use word pictures that make people want your product
- Put a hook into your letters
- Get news interest into your letters
- Discover motives that make people buy
- Six essentials in any offer
- Take the guess out of advertising
- Raise money by mail

Collier's book is filled with useful tips on every page, an indispensable guide for any great marketer. It is one of my top selections.

My Life in Advertising/Scientific Advertising
by Claude Hopkins

Hopkins' book is used like a bible in marketing circles. First written in 1923, its lessons are just as relevant today. Hopkins will help you improve your results from your advertising investments through his unique approach. You'll discover how to:

- Tell your full story
- Use art in advertising
- Develop marketing strategies
- Offer samples effectively
- Get distribution
- Test campaigns
- Lean on dealers

Hopkins' copywriting style will keep you glued to the page as you discover all the gems he offers.

How to Make Your Advertising Make Money
by John Caples

This book is jam-packed with wisdom and usable strategies. Caples is perhaps the best known for his classic ad headline, "They Laughed When I Sat Down at the Piano—But When I Started to Play." In the book Caples presents proven techniques that include:

- Twelve ways to find advertising ideas
- How to write headlines that make money
- How to write small ads that make money
- 303 words and phrases that sell
- How to write sentences that sell
- How to write sales letters that make money
- Sales appeals that last forever
- How direct response can help general advertisers make money

- Tips on copywriting:
  (A) 12 ways to get started
  (B) 11 ways to get going
  (C) 14 ways to improve copy

I had the pleasure of receiving a valued piece of correspondence with Caples before he died. I asked him if he would consider writing an ad for my book "How to Form Your Own Corporation Without a Lawyer For Under $75." He wrote back and said he felt he couldn't improve what I'd written. But I'm not sure; perhaps he told other copywriters the same thing.

Making Ads Pay by John Caples

The "lucky 13 library" contains a second book by Caples that is also very valuable. Included is information which shows you:

- Seven steps to successful advertising
- Which appeals succeed? . . . which fail?
- How to think up ideas
- Ten ways to write the first paragraph
- Ten ways to make ads believable
- Six ways to prove it's a bargain
- Nine ways to make it easy to buy
- Six ways to make people buy now

Caples has such an engaging writing style as he compellingly presents all his strategies.

The First Hundred Million by E. Haldeman-Julius

The best book ever written on the relationship between the name or title of a product, and the resulting sales. While this book covers the sale of books, the lessons derived apply equally to selling any product. Therefore, no seller of anything, especially an information product, can afford to be without this book.

It's fascinating to see proof from numerous tests that human nature does not change. The same appeals that worked in 1928 work equally well today. The book covers topics including:

- What America wants to read can lead you to saleable products of all kinds
- Are Americans afraid of sex?
- The quest for self-improvement is eternal
- People want fun and laughter and how to create products to meet their wants

The enormous value of this book, more than any other ever written before, is that Haldeman-Julius reveals the statistical impact and results from all his advertising. He shows you the actual sales totals of books before and after title changes. Get this book. You will be thrilled and delighted.

How to Make More Money with Your Direct Mail

by Edward N. Mayer, Jr.

Former president of James Gray, Inc. and the Direct Mail Advertising Association, Mayer reveals secrets of how to:

- Add a personal touch to increase direct mail results
- Improve the looks of your mailings
- Seven cardinal rules of direct mail success
- Twenty kinds of direct mail letters
- Keep your list from getting stale
- Get your full money's worth at the post office
- Get action from your prospects
- Use color to increase results
- Interpret what testing tells about eighteen direct mail problems

Mayer is considered by many of the professionals in direct marketing today to be one of the most brilliant practitioners ever in this field. And I wholeheartedly agree.

The Mirror Makers by Stephen Fox

This well-written but little known book is the best history of American advertising and its creators I've ever read.

It's both fascinating and instructive to study the early beginnings of advertising.

Samples of early ads are the best reflection of the thinking and how it evolved up through today. The lives and impacts of the early pioneers in American advertising are discussed. Albert Lasker, John E. Kennedy, Claude Hopkins, Raymond Rubican and the first woman copywriter of real importance in American advertising, Helen Lansdowne Resor, all made indelible contributions to the field of advertising.

This book will help make you a smarter marketer by better understanding the history of your craft.

The Greatest Direct Mail Sales Letter of All Times
by Richard S. Hodgson

This book is really an encyclopedia of sales letters. It will help you better understand:

- How winning sales letters are created
- Why sales letters succeed
- How to create your own great sales letter
- Consumer mail order letters
- Circulation and book promotion letters
- Fund raising letters
- Business to business direct mail
- Inquiry and lead getting letters
- Retail and services letters
- Personalized letters
- How to start a letter
- How to close a letter
- Tips from the experts

It's so instructive to see many examples of great sales letters from some of America's creative geniuses. You'll learn to write better copy by modeling these letters.

The 100 Greatest Advertisements

by Julian Lewis Watkins

There is much to glean from great ads which pulled profitable results for long periods of time. These full-page space ads, run for years in newspapers and magazines throughout the U.S., show how you can sell virtually anything in a space ad. Products depicted include cars, correspondence courses, soft drinks, toothpaste, shaving cream, soap, diamonds, insurance and, of course, books.

You'll get lots of new ideas from the advertisements included here.

Million Dollar Mailings

by Dennison Hatch, founder and editor of "Who's Mailing What," with a foreword by Axel Andersson, the legendary direct marketer who conceived the idea for the book.

This new publication contains 71 fully illustrated mailings of today. To qualify for inclusion, the mailing has to be a "control" for 3 years or longer.

60 direct marketing superstars reveal their thinking behind mailings which have been the most powerful during the last decade. Discover how to:

- Apply 26 design tips to lift response
- Interrupting—the key to successful advertising
- Use double post cards profitably
- Use direct mail profitably, and why it is the second largest medium with $25.6 billion spent on it. (Only newspapers receive a larger share of the advertising pie—approximately $27.9 billion)

These winning ad creations are all winners of an "Axel" award, named in honor of Axel Andersson. Every part of the mail offer is included in the book (and photographed beautifully), including order card, envelope, brochure, and lift letters.

I debated on whether to include any of my books on the list. At first I was not going to. But some close friends in direct marketing felt the "greatest marketing books" would not be fully represented unless I did. Since I would be the last person to argue this point and for the benefit of subscribers who do not have them yet, I've included two of my books.

The Golden Mailbox—How to Get Rich in Direct Marketing by Ted Nicholas

This book approaches direct marketing from both the creative and business aspects. Of course, unless these two elements are in sync, you cannot succeed. The ideas apply to marketing any product or service. The book shows you:

- The steps to a successful ad
- Which ads will work?
- If it works, don't fix it
- Make choices not guesses
- Write copy that sells
- How to effectively test
- Develop consumer products
- Create your own future
- Thinking small for big success
- Markets ripe for picking
- Ads versus direct mail

In case you are interested, this book is also perhaps my most autobiographical to date.

How I Sold $200 Million Dollars Worth of Products and Services by Ted Nicholas

This 644-page book contains **every** successful ad, brochure, sales letter, and card deck I've ever written. Each offer is graded from one to five stars for performance. One star is at least break even. Five star is a home run, a highly profitable ad.

As mentioned, there are sections on:

- Print ads in magazines and newspapers
- Sales letters
- Card decks
- Brochures

Many of the world's best marketers have written me indicating they use the "$200 Million" book as a "starter" when writing copy. You surely are aware how difficult it can be to begin an ad when staring at a blank sheet of paper.

Several people at my $7,500 seminars wanted to pay $5,000 for the book. Price is only $287.

In my opinion, every successful marketer should spend at least $15,000 to $25,00 each year on **continuing education**. This includes books, tapes, seminars, and travel costs. I actually spend more than $25,000 per year. If you can't afford anything like this level of expenditure right now, devote 5%–10% of your income to increasing your knowledge. There is no better investment.

The total cost to buy all the books I've discussed is about $500!! The wisdom contained in this mini-library is worth hundreds of thousands of dollars, perhaps millions to you. So I urge you to get them all.

A good bookstore can order most of these books for you, although some might take a little more effort. Most of the rest of these books can be supplied to you by a nice fellow, Carl Galletti, a copywriter who also runs a small business which sells hard to locate books on advertising. He can probably supply any hard to find marketing book or tell you where to find it. He has a catalogue, too. Carl can be reached at 609–896–0245, One Paddock Drive, Lawrenceville, NJ 08648.

Of course, my books are available from Nicholas Direct.

An extra special book treat

As I was riding a stationary bike recently (I have the habit of reading while exercising), I was feeling so grateful for all the contributions that books have made to my life. Autobiographies in particular have been a great source of emotional fuel. So I decided to add one more book I heartily recommend.

Up From Slavery by Booker T. Washington

If you've read it before, I urge you to re-read it with today's eyes.

While not being a marketing or business book, it surely will inspire you to be both a more successful human being as well as business person.

Its most important lesson—the value of constant learning.

You will also see the relationship between reading good books and success in life perhaps more clearly than ever before.

This autobiography, written by one of the greatest men of this century will lift your spirits to new heights.

When you feel down, as is part of the human condition, just pick up this book and you'll be moved beyond your present condition.

Whenever I feel life's problems are really tough, at times even overwhelming, I pick up this book. The spirit of this great human being—born a slave, without education, and who taught himself to read—will help put any problem you now face into better perspective.

I can't recommend it too highly.

What about seminars, tapes and newsletters?

There are many seminars presenting marketing information which may sound good. But often the theories do **not** work in the real world.

The very best seminars on any subject are conducted by *peo-*

ple who are doing what they teach. On a daily basis. "They walk the talk." But they are rare gems throughout the world as there are only a handful of marketing teachers who have proven theories to share.

You're going to have a great time studying these books while you enhance your knowledge and marketing skills.

Isn't it terrific being in such a profitable business that is also a lot of fun?

39 Hot Direct Marketing Success Rules by Ted Nicholas

This chapter contains valuable information about what to do to succeed in direct marketing. I've put these secrets in the form of rules.

When you spend over $100,000,000 of your own money on direct marketing, as I have, you acquire an education not possible by any other method. You learn which things work. You also learn what doesn't.

As you'll immediately see, these rules defy conventional wisdom, which is dead wrong most of the time.

These "secrets" will help you succeed. They will also help you survive and avoid going broke.

There are notable exceptions to all rules about direct marketing. However, based on experience you would be safe 99% of the time if you heed them.

1. ***Spend up to 80% of your time on the headline of a space ad or sales letter.***
   Reason? 50% to 80% of the sales success of your advertising message is a direct result of your headline. That means your message loses up to 80% of its effectiveness without a strong headline! Another reason to invest this time is that the offer's positioning is determined by the headline theme. (Your letter headline can often be used as the teaser copy for the envelope.) Most copywriters do not spend nearly enough time on headlines. I write as many as 250 headlines before I select the final one for a campaign.
2. ***Use either "ragged" right or justified right margin*** for each column of copy when you have a space ad set in type.

   I've tested both and I have seen no effect in response rates.

3. ***Use Courier typeface in sales letters.*** Some call it old-fashioned, but my experience shows that Courier outpulls any other type style. The typewriter "me to you" look "feels" more personal and urgent.
4. ***Use highly salable products as free bonus gifts.*** Bonuses always increase sales with one exception. I once made the mistake of using a failed product as a bonus with disastrous results. Remember this! If you can't sell it, you can't give it away successfully!
5. ***Always use a headline at the top of your sales letter.***
Never use a company logo or your name and address at the top of a sales letter. It is a "me" message and depresses response. Use logo at the end of a letter on the last page. Exception: if you are writing to an audience who would be positively influenced by your name or credentials, e.g. a famous doctor writing to other doctors.
6. ***Never change a word of winning copy for anyone until you test it.***
Especially "for copy acceptance reasons." I learned the lesson the hard way. A magazine' s legal department asked me to change 3 words in a 1200 word full-page ad, which I did. The response dropped to 1/10 of the former level! My recommendation: if it's working, don't change even a comma. If someone insists on changes, just pull the ad. Remember, because a *winning ad often challenges conventional thinking*, it seems to attract requests for change. But don't do it. Once you agree to do it with a given media you've lost control of the creative process. And your sales will usually plummet.

7. ***Copyright all your sales materials.***
   Your winning ads are worth their weight in gold. You are bound to have people who try to copy your success. For your protection on every letter, space ad, brochure, etc., add the copyright symbol, a small "c" in a circle like this, ©, along with the word "copyright", your name and year. It should look like this:

   © Copyright 1995 John Smith Corporation

8. ***Test a photograph in your space ads.***
   It often improves response. But it must support and tie into the headline and copy. For highest response, always include human beings rather than just objects in copy. Children are the biggest attention-getters of all. Remember the old saying, which happens to be true, "A picture is worth a thousand words."
9. ***Use a caption under every photo.***
   The eye is drawn to a photograph. If you don't at least identify who is in the photo, at minimum you will lose many readers who will stop reading your sales message.
10. ***In photos of people make certain they are looking directly into the camera.***
    Eye contact with the reader is a good involvement strategy.
11. ***Do not use more than 17 words in a headline.***
    Why? Based on my tests, I've never been able to make a headline work that is longer than this!
12. ***Use the two most underused and powerful words more often in your copy.***
    Free and *You.*
13. ***Do not use "I", the biggest turn-off word in copy, at all or very sparingly.***
14. ***Always use a "drop" first letter in a space ad.***
    This helps get the reader's eye from the headline into the body copy. Here is an example of a drop first letter.

    Look at the bargain!

15. ***Use subheads which are strong enough to be headlines.***
    They both help keep the prospect reading, plus break up large blocks of copy which appear to require so much effort reading is discouraged.
16. ***Do not use a screen behind any copy area.***
    (Except for yellow behind black, which can make copy more readable. A screen in any other color diminishes readership.) Use screens only for things you don't particularly want readership, such as some obscure regulation you may need to include in your offer. However, a screen within borders outside blocks of copy can help copy stand out.
17. ***Never print body copy in any color other than black.***
    Black is easiest to read. Colors should only be used for headlines or sub-headlines.
18. ***Eliminate the word "that" in your copy.***
    After copy is written, see if you can eliminate the word "that" as many times as you can. The word "that" is perhaps the most overused word in copy. It's boring and tends to weaken strong sentences.
19. ***Be provocative. If copy doesn't bother or offend someone it usually doesn't work!***
    When getting feedback on new copy from colleagues, advertising media and prospects, if everyone likes it, watch out! Nearly every time I write a breakthrough ad or sales letter it pulls orders and also bothers someone. Reason? *Great copy gets attention by being provocative.* And interrupting usual thinking habits.
20. ***Never use sans serif typeface on any body copy in a space ad.***
    All studies show it's more difficult to read. Sans serif in a head line is OK.
21. ***Forget rules of grammar when writing copy.***
    As copywriter John Kennedy in 1920 said, "Good copy is salesmanship in print." The prime goal in copy is to sell. Sentence fragments are OK.

22. ***Use short words, short sentences and short paragraphs in writing copy.***
    Keep 75% of words 5 letters or less. Keep sentences to an average of 8 to 17 words. Paragraphs no more than 5 sentences. But vary the length, otherwise it will seem repetitive and boring.
23. ***Use quotation marks around headlines.***
    Studies show 27% more people will read the headline. It increases the feeling that something important is being stated.
24. ***Use upper and lower case letters in a headline.***
    Do not use all caps, a frequent mistake by marketers and graphic designers in an attempt to make headlines stand out. *Upper and lower case is easier to read.* That's why any good newspaper or magazine sets their headline this way.
25. ***Read copy out loud.***
    The best test of copy tone, flow and persuasiveness is to say it out loud. This is what your reader does in his/her head. You will always be able to improve copy when you do this because the rough spots stand out.
26. ***Handwriting great copy is best way to improve your copywriting skills.***
    When you come across someone else's effective copy, especially a control piece that is working for a period of time, hand write it, word for word. You will be exposed to the writer's thinking process. You'll also gain a deeper sense of how ideas should flow to a logical conclusion.
27. ***Get into a peak emotional state before you write.***
    You cannot write great copy if you are exhausted, harassed or down mentally. Make sure to get a good night's sleep. Exercise moderately before starting. Eat sparingly. Take the time to count your blessings. Turn off the phone and make sure you are not interrupted. For mega-success, also do the Ted Nicholas "Yes" exercise (to be sent to any reader upon request).

28. ***When writing copy, imagine you are talking to a friend or loved one.***
Credibility, tone, and warmth in copy comes from the feelings you generate through the words you write. *Be as honest and sincere* as you possibly can be. *Maintain enthusiasm* about the product's benefits as though you are sharing with a friend.
29. ***Never put a period at the end of a headline.***
Do not punctuate at all except when asking a question. A period causes a reader to pause and possibly stop reading any further.
30. ***Break the last sentence on the page in a sales letter.***
Do not end the last sentence on any page. Break the sentence. Below it add the words "Please turn to page 2 (etc.)" to help keep the prospect reading.
31. ***Make sure your printer provides ink coverage that is as dark as possible on all your printed materials.***
Your response can drop by as much as 10% if the ink coverage in a letter has the all too common "grey" appearance. This is tough to read. *The easiest way I know to increase mail response* is by having the ink coverage made darker. *I've seen response increase by 10%* just by getting it "blacker"!
32. ***Make the signature used in a sales letter clear and bold.***
Use a fine felt tip pen for the original and always, always print signatures in *reflex blue.* Not black, red, green, etc., reflex blue! Prospects look at the signature and respond less well to a "wimpy" appearance, which suggests uncertainty or lack of confidence.
33. ***Use hand written margin notes*** on a sales letter to draw attention to important points.
34. ***Cross out and change prices and words*** in a sales letter to emphasize points, such as a special price.
35. ***Underline words in a sales letter*** for emphasis. But don't overdo it. About 10 words a page is ideal.

36. ***Test a handwritten P.S.,*** which can often increase response.
37. ***Price your products using a 7 as the ending number.***
    (i.e. $49.97, $77.77, $317, $597, $1,997, etc.) My tests, as well as those of other marketers, find 7 attracts the most sales.
38. ***Write long copy.***
    Don't limit what you write about the benefits of your product. Copy can never be too long. Just too boring! So present your benefits with emotion combined with human interest and don't worry about the length. Remember the old true saying, "The more you tell, the more you sell."
39. ***Always include your name, address, telephone number and product price on brochures*** or fliers contained within your mail package.
    If the brochure is passed along or becomes separated from the sales letter the recipient can still order.

What happens if you don't follow the 39 rules?

You could wind up in a prison! Or at minimum, fined and put on probation. Figuratively, of course! Let me explain.

One night after a seminar appearance in Phoenix, I was talking with several other direct marketing speakers who had attended my presentation.

We were discussing what an uphill battle it can be at times to change the mind-set of attendees. Most people, of course, have already bought the numerous myths taught by college professors who have never invested a penny of their own money but who lecture on what it takes to be a successful marketer.

My rules work. They are based on hard-won knowledge and experience earned in the real world.

We thought it would be fun to create a special kind of prison called Direct Marketing "Hell." Anyone who knowingly broke my rules after they were taught them would be sentenced. Of course, the length of punishment would depend on the severity of crime.

The conversation between three inmates of Direct Marketing Hell might go something like this:

> "How long are you in for Jeff?" asks Bill.
>
> Jeff somberly answers, "I got 3 months. I really messed up. I used more than 17 words in a headline."
>
> "Bill laments, "That's sad. But you know what? I got 2 years just for not adding a P.S. to a sales letter."
>
> "That ain't nothing," interrupts Gary. "I committed the most serious crime. It's a capital offense. They gave me life without parole. I mailed a sales letter and ran an ad and guess what? Neither had a headline!"

So dear reader, break the rules at your peril! Remember, failing to use Courier in your letters, while seemingly a minor crime, could get you a 3-month sentence.

Message to Friends who want to Become Millionaires

This chapter is a real change of pace. It's dedicated to your friends and loved ones.

As your success grows, many people will ask for your assistance on their business endeavors. I'm sure you will do all you can to help. So to give you food for thought, I've devoted this chapter to advising would-be millionaires!

People often approach me to help mentor their business success. For example, recently John, a friend, called. John is a mid-level manger in a large company. The conversation went something like this:

> **John:** "I'm getting bored with my job. Direct marketing looks like a great way to build wealth. I'm interested in getting rich. I would like to learn all I can from you. Perhaps be a protege. I know a lot of what you teach is in your books, tapes and live seminars. However, at the moment I don't have any money to invest in these materials and programs."
>
> My reaction to people with such an approach is usually to seek more information. After John granted me permission to ask some personal questions, here is how the conversation proceeded.
>
> **Ted:** "I notice you're driving a new 1995 automobile. Do you mind telling me what your payments are?" **John:** "$395 a month."
>
> **Ted:** "Approximately what did you spend on your week's vacation this past year?" **John:** "$1800."
>
> **Ted:** "You live in a new apartment building. What is your current monthly rent?" **John:** **"$750** a month."

Undoubtedly you see where my questions lead. I wanted to get a sense of John's values. The foregoing answers already communicate volumes about John.

I think it's safe to say he will *never* become a millionaire. Not as long as he continues to think the way he does. And most Americans unfortunately share the same values.

The big problem? A profound lack of understanding of what it takes to succeed. The most important element in anyone's potential business success is

Education!

The price of business success is very simple. A good education.

I feel that education in the U.S. is greatly under-valued by nearly everyone. Except by super successful entrepreneurs!

This may sound self-serving. But there is no other way of communicating the reality. As a marketer of "how to" information, a source of constant fascination to me is that my very *best customers* are also the *most successful.* Subscribers of my newsletter, Direct Marketing Success Letter, and buyers of my videos, audio tapes and books I'm proud to say are among the best-known marketers in the world. And the richest!

The underlying reason for their outstanding success?

They value education so much they seek and pay for it.

They know knowledge about their career is an asset more priceless than gold. And unlike money, jewels, real estate, stocks, all of which can be lost or taken away, what you know is yours forever.

Education can *never* be taken away. The super successful seem to instinctively know this. So they've become perpetual students. Always interested in learning something new. Constantly reading. And listening to tapes. Seeking out seminars conducted by doers who "walk the talk."

Those who are unsuccessful have bought into ideas that are not advancing their wealth production. Instead of investing in their own knowledge, they prefer to spend their money on cars, boats, planes, apartments, vacations, gadgets, etc.

The unsuccessful are unaware of this reality. It's impossible to succeed big in any field without a lot of knowledge.

There are just two ways to get the reality tested information you need which works in the real world:

1. The school of hard knocks—trial and error method.
2. Books, tapes, seminars offered by those who have proven themselves.

Back to John. He tells me he really wants to hear my honest views. It's been said that "when the student is ready the teacher appears." I believe John. Here, then, is the advice I gave my friend.

Ted: "I'm going to give you ideas and suggestions. If you follow them your future success is guaranteed.

However, there is a catch. Your comfort level may be affected. Many ideas won't feel right at first. The recommendations are unconventional. Chances are you've never in your life received advice like I'm about to give you—from anyone. So some of it might sound strange and make you uncomfortable. That's OK. It is to be expected. As we learn and grow our belief systems must be re-examined. And if necessary, changed.

1. The first thing you need to do on your path to success is completely ***stop acting*** on the ***advice of friends, relatives*** and ***teachers.*** However well-meaning they are, their advice will ***not*** be helpful. Unless they are self-made millionaires. One must have lived and experienced being an entrepreneur. Otherwise no one can understand what is required.

   Indeed, you may have to find new friends. Negative ones can really hold you back. If you have a supportive mate or spouse, terrific. If you don't, a tough decision will have to be made. There may be no choice but to leave the relationship.

   You ***must*** have support. Negative people are influential. More than you realize. Don't just walk away from them. Run!

2. Begin immediately to ***get out of debt.*** Since your car payments are too big in relation to your income, ***sell your car at once.*** If you can do without a car and walk for awhile, great.

   My father taught me a great lesson. Automobiles are the biggest financial liability anyone can have. No investment you will ever make loses its value so quickly.

   If you feel you need a car, get a used one. Pay cash for it. Fortunately, the U.S. is one of the few countries in the world where you can get a good used car cheap.
3. ***Move to a one-bedroom apartment***, or ***look for a roommate or two*** to share your apartment costs. Since you are single and have a two-bedroom apartment, you can easily slash your rent by half or more.
4. ***Vacation creatively.*** Instead of going to an expensive resort for a week, this year go to 2 or more good seminars that will advance your knowledge.

I'm sure you can do more to slash overhead. You could reduce or eliminate the big cost of interest your debts are causing. But, just by the suggested steps you will immediately have over $900 per month! Every saved cent can and should go toward your direct marketing education! It will be the best investment you have or will ever make.

You can begin investing in your long-neglected but potentially most valuable asset—

Yourself

5. ***Start a success library*** of your own. At minimum buy these books. Study and read them as soon as you can.

   Confessions Of An Advertising Man by David Ogilvy
   The Robert Collier Letter Book by Robert Collier
   My Life in Advertising/Scientific Advertising by Claude Hopkins
   How To Make Your Advertising Make Money by John Caples
   Making Ads Pay by John Caples

The First Hundred Million by E. Haldeman-Julius
How to Make More Money with Your Direct Mail by Edward N. Mayer
The Mirror Makers by Stephen Fox
The Greatest Direct Mail Sales Letter of All Times by Richard S. Hodgson
The 100 Greatest Advertisements by Julian Lewis Watkins
Million Dollar Mailings by Dennison Hatch
Atlas Shrugged by Ayn Rand
The Fountainhead by Ayn Rand
How I Found Freedom in an Unfree World by Harry Browne
Ageless Body / Timeless Mind by Deepak Chopra
The Mysterious Cause and Cure of Illness by Jonn Matsen

Plus, get the following products from my company as soon as possible:

- *The Golden Mailbox—How to Get Rich in Direct Marketing* by Ted Nicholas
- *How I Sold $200 Million Worth of Products and Services* by Ted Nicholas
- *Direct Marketing Success Letter*—all back issues
- *Ted Nicholas Self-Publishing Seminar Tapes*
- *Ted Nicholas Direct Marketing Seminar Videos*
- *Ted Nicholas Magic Words Seminar Tapes*—Million Dollar Sales Lectures

6. ***Join the following organizations:***
   Toastmasters. Regardless of what field you choose, when you learn to speak clearly and confidently it will help you.
   Direct Marketing Association, New York. Get their mailings and go to some of their seminars.
   Local Direct Marketing Association if you have one in your area.

7. ***Get on good mailing lists.*** Well-run direct marketing companies' mailings are important. Getting on their mailing lists is part of your education. Ask to be put on the following companies' lists, or buy something from them.

   Phillips Publishing
   Agora Publishing
   Nightingale Conant
   DELL Computer
   Reader's Digest
   The Company Corporation, Wilmington, Delaware
   Fischer Publishing, Canfield, Ohio
   Nicholas Direct, Inc., Indian Rocks Beach, Florida

8. ***Subscribe to these magazines:***

   Direct Marketing
   Direct Mail News
   Economist
   Entrepreneur

9. ***Subscribe to these newsletters:***

   Health and Healing, Phillips Publishing
   Forecasts and Strategies, Phillips Publishing
   Who's Mailing What, Target Marketing
   Direct Marketing Success Letter

10. ***Seminars to attend:***

   DMA Seminars
   Dan Kennedy Seminars
   Jeff Paul Seminars
   Gary Halbert Seminars
   Peter Lowe Seminars
   Dan Peña Seminars
   Ted Nicholas Seminars

TIP

When money is really tight, offer to work at seminars which interest you in return for free attendance. Many promoters will happily hire you to help sell tapes, etc.

A note of caution. Be wary of whose advice you choose to follow at seminars or on tape. Most college professors and ad agency people are not teaching reality. They teach theory which often sounds good but does not work in the real world. Entrepreneur speakers who invest their own money in their own companies and who teach what they do every day are special. What they offer you is *invaluable.*

11. ***Learn to write sales copy***. The most financially lucrative skill you can possess is the ability to write effective sales copy. There are two ways to learn.
    A. *Get a part-time job in commission sales.* New York Life or CIGNA Insurance, Amway, Mary Kay, Fuller Brush, Encyclopedia Brittanica, Kirby Vacuums, can all be excellent training ground for direct marketing. But, here is the key. Find an organization with a good sales manager to train you. Capable trainers often exist within leading direct sales organizations.
    B. *Practice.* (After you read the previously mentioned books.) You don't have to be a great creative writer. But, you do need to develop sales skills. Good copy is "salesmanship in print." An excellent way to develop skill is to take a piece of successful copy you like that is working, such as an ad or sales letter. Write it out in long hand. It's great practice. You'll also begin to get a good feel for the writer's thinking process.

12. ***Get a part-time job in a mail order company***. Here is an approach you can use that almost never fails. Find out who the direct marketing companies are in your area. Choose one or two with whom you'd like to work. Approach them. Explain how you can help them. Make this nearly impossible to resist offer. Include in your proposal this statement. You will help the employer make or save money. Or you'd rather quit or be let go anyway. And mean it. Offer to work *free* for at least two weeks! You will have a lot of takers. There would be absolutely no risk on the employer's part.

    After you are hired, learn all you can about what it takes to operate the business.
13. ***Start your own mail order business in your spare time***. What to sell? Choose a product or service that is now under-marketed. Acquire the rights to the product (see separate chapter on this topic). I recommend you begin by offering a free special report. Choose a hot subject you know, can learn or acquire the rights to. You then can sell a product to those who request your special report.
14. ***Take a low-level job with a worthwhile company***. Many college graduates and MBAs can't get a job today. One of the big reasons is their unwillingness to take a lower level job which they consider "beneath" them.

    That's precisely one of the reasons which underlies why minorities make up the biggest portion of the new millionaires in the U.S. They are willing to take any job no matter how humble. Just for the chance to work and earn money!

    There are many such examples. Sam Yeoung, a 23-year-old man originally from China took an entry level job at McDonald's 1 1/2 years ago. His pay? Minimum wage. Within 6 months he was the assistant manager of the restaurant. Then he became manager. Today he is a district manager earning a six-figure income. Next year he will open his own MacDonald's. My guess is he'll be a millionaire in less than 5 years.

Do you think a typical American-born college graduate would take such a position? No way! Instead, they might spend months, even years, collecting unemployment. The new millionaires create their own career. The real opportunity makers have learned how to capitalize on the smallest chance.

There are no bad jobs! Take any job. And do it extremely well, as best you can. Result? You'll create the ultimate job security. How? You'll make yourself indispensable to the business.

15. ***Join the U.S. Marines!*** Recently a survey showed that 77% of the CEOs of Fortune 500 companies were former Marines. (Of course I'm not biased, but I also happen to be a former Marine.)

    Do you think there is any relationship between CEOs rising to the top of their organizations and the world-famous discipline learned in the "Corps?" Of course there is!

    Besides, John, I've never met anyone who couldn't use some more discipline. Have you?

16. ***Do whatever is necessary to succeed*** **.** When the going gets tough, as it inevitably will at times, stop whimpering, "I'm doing the best I can." This is not good enough for a truly successful life. And it isn't worthy of you.

    There is only one thing good enough.

You must do what is necessary.

When the banks turned Dan Peña down nearly 200 times, he kept contacting the next one. He got the financing. Today he is worth $200 million. Would you have given up at 6? or 12? or 50?

Colonel Sanders began at age 66 with assets of a broken down jalopy and a chicken recipe. He went to nearly 2,000 restaurants and was turned down. He kept going. When he was asked what he would have done if the 2,001st turned him down, he said, "I

> would have gone on to the 2,002nd!" Most people would have quit long before this. When would you have stopped?
>
> I started my first business with savings of $800 and debts of $96,000. Numerous people turned me down. My bank also rejected my proposal. They told me I was crazy, the idea would never work. But I would not be denied. I knew I would find willing backers. And I did.
>
> Most of the reason for my success today as a marketer, copywriter and entrepreneur is *not* more talent than others. What is the reason? I dig deeper than most people. I write 200 or more headlines for every product to find the right one. Others write 2 or 3 and expect a miracle. I study products strictly from the buyer's point of view. I write more copy drafts. I'm willing to try more tests and to fail more often than others. But here's the secret. I succeed more often, too!
>
> The real secret is to:
>
> ***Work harder at doing whatever is necessary!***
>
> "You, John, must do whatever is necessary to succeed. You will become a millionaire or whatever else you want to become! It's just inevitable."

As you read these words, you may be feeling that the path to direct marketing success is steeper than you first realized. And that sacrifices have to be made.

Here is the reality. There is a price to pay for success. And a price to pay for lack of achievement. You, like all of us, have a choice. To succeed in a big way, gratification may have to be delayed.

But the good news is, it's worth it! I believe there is no wasted energy in the universe. During those tough times when things look bleak, which happens in all our lives, I give myself a reminder for just as night follows day the results will come.

Yes, once you pay the price for success, the rewards will come. And keep coming forever! You will become as wealthy as you desire.

People all over the world will seek you out to buy your products. Invite you to speak. Offer you large sums to help them—be their partner. Present you with more opportunities than you could ever pursue.

And life is long. Gratification won't be delayed forever. There is plenty of time to own fancy cars, enjoy luxurious vacations, mansions, jewelry, whatever you want. You'll be able to live the lifestyle you choose anywhere in the world.

So dear reader, the above is what I offer my friends. And yours.

Part III

Advanced training materials for those who wish to enhance their magic word power

Magic Words that Bring You Riches

(The Advanced Home Study Course)

Dear Friend,

The single *most important activity* in your life is your *ability to communicate.*

It's astonishing. Just use certain special words.

Result? You will invariably get everything you want in life. The words work like magic! Discover which are the powerful words and which turn people off and block your path to success.

Ted Nicholas is a master communicator—one of the most successful writers and speakers in the world. Ted's 14 best-selling books include HOW TO PUBLISH A BOOK AND SELL A MILLION COPIES and THE GOLDEN MAILBOX—HOW TO GET RICH DIRECT MARKETING YOUR PRODUCT.

But Ted wasn't always a big success. He struggled for years, laboring 12 hours a day, 7 days a week. He searched for the *key* to *mega success.* When he found it, his life changed.

The key is words! Certain *words assured successful outcomes.* After refining these words, earning large sums of money and gaining other riches *became remarkably simple* and *easy.*

Ted's new home study course reveals all his secrets. It's called MAGIC WORDS THAT BRING YOU RICHES. It includes an amazing course on tape, "HOW TO BECOME A MAIL ORDER MILLIONAIRE"! You get the *exact words* that have been *proven* to work best in virtually every situation. Everything you need is included.

From small beginnings to great wealth

Ted Nicholas was born in modest circumstances. Self-educated and starting with no money, he is perhaps the highest paid communicator *per word* in the world. Today he earns as much as $500,000 from a simple 1,000 word ad. Ted has earned as much as $3,500,000 in a single year. His profit from a book can exceed $20,000,000. And all because he discovered the magic words that work best.

Ted started without capital and with a $90 classified ad. Then he sold $500,000,000 worth of products and services. He will show you how *you can start with little or no money, too!*

You don't even have to work full time to earn big money. Discover how you can earn an additional $10,000 to $30,000 a month from home, on a part-time basis! Have lots of free time to pursue hobbies, spend quality time with your family, loved ones and friends. Or just relax. Enjoy a lifestyle of which others only dream.

Sell your product *worldwide* from your *easy chair as easily* as you now sell locally. This is just one of many benefits you'll get from this amazing home study course.

Hear every word presented live and *unedited* at Ted's seminar that cost people $7,000 to attend. And Ted is considered one of America's very best public speakers. You can learn at your desk, while you drive, jog or relax at home.

On the MAGIC WORDS THAT BRING YOU RICHES Home Study Course you'll discover:

- How to become a mail order millionaire—a step-by-step guide.
- 6 easy ways to find hot new product opportunities. You can have a million dollar new product idea every half hour!
- Put Ted's *5 secret principles* to work in your life which assure *success* and *make failure impossible!*
- 27 magic words that help you sell anything to anyone.
- Grab attention in your ads by learning the *latest secrets* of *writing powerful headlines.*

- 17 magic words that get advertising on national magazines absolutely free!
- What *opportunities* found in the *U.K. can easily be duplicated in the U.S.* (and vice versa) with *almost guaranteed profits.*
- *7 compelling sub headlines* (the actual words) that will *make* your ads more powreful.
- *5 magic phrases*, word for word, to place on your envelopes that *almost guarantee your sales letter will be opened.*
- How to *raise all the money you need,* yet *limit* your *financial risk.* (Remember, Ted began with a $90 ad, and so can you).
- Determine which new products have the *highest probability* of *success.*
- 23 magic words that help you get the *rights* to a *hot* existing *product* with a track record of *success* for as little as *$250.*
- Create *direct mail letters* and space ads with the highest probability of success.
- Select the *right media* in which to advertise among magazines, newspapers, catalogs, radio, T.V., card decks, or the hottest new media—electronic bulletin boards!
- Unleash the power of today's *best low-cost/no-cost marketing strategies.*
- *Secrets* of *pricing products* for maximum profit.
- Prepare the *ideal sales letter* for your product that is *almost irresistible.*
- Learn the *art* of *testing*—the real key to marketing success.
- *Legally protect* your *products, ads* and *sales letters* at no cost. Prevent others from cashing in on your success.
- Get *free publicity* in newspapers and on radio and T.V.
- Determine the *most ideal business* in the world for you.
- Run *small classified ads* and build a mail order business, perhaps the *ideal retirement activity.*

Unsolicited Comments About Ted Nicholas' Work

"Have attended many seminars, including those at the university gaining my Economics degree. None has taught me as much as I have learned from you. It's simply the best—the experience of a lifetime."

C. Neophytou
London, England

"Although I've been in marketing for over 30 years, I've learned more in these three days than I believed possible. Thank you for the opportunity."

Gil Evans
Palm Harbor, Florida

"Your Marketing information on tape is worth more than 10 times its cost. In 30 days your techniques earned me $15,000.00."

Francois Blot
Chantilly, France

"There's probably no human alive who knows more about how to make magazine advertising pay off than Ted Nicholas. For the record, Ted Nicholas has my absolute highest recommendation! Ted you have just given the most valuable seminar I ever attended."

Gary Halbert
Key West, Florida

"You really put your money where your mouth is. With your sincere interest in really helping your seminar attendees."

Norman Rentrop
Bonn, West Germany

"Ted: Not only was your seminar fantastic for newcomers, it was equally valuable to those who are already established. Your expertise has shown me how we can increase sales on our existing products, and create new products and take them to new heights as well. Thanks for sharing your life experiences with us. It's the greatest form of education I know. Thanks again."

Deanna Polk
Hagerstown, Maryland

"Your home study course reveals the most valuable information for entrepreneurs in the world today! Top Secret—worth millions of dollars in the right hands."

Blade Thomas
Malibu, California

"Ted Nicholas has made fortunes for himself and others with his direct marketing knowledge. Treat any advice you get from this man as nuggets of the purest direct marketing gold, for that's what he's giving you."

Gary Bencivenga
Garden City, New York

"I'm a lawyer by education. Ted Nicholas inspired me to get into my own business. His home study course helped me write the first full-page ad I've ever attempted. Best marketing ideas I've heard . . ."

Mark Warda
Clearwater, Florida

Here is more of what's included in the Magic Words Home Study Course

- How to raise all the capital you'll ever need.
- How to successfully test your product.
- The best 10 free bonuses that pull orders like crazy.
- The little known price point that sells best.
- 7 best places to find hot products.
- The one ingredient to seek in any new product.
- Today's 10 hottest trends offering the most profitable business opportunities.
- How to negotiate for rights to successful products, word for word.
- The low cost/no cost marketing secrets of getting free publicity.
- 3 secrets to classified ads that make money.
- 5 secrets that make small display ads profitable.
- 6 little known secrets to raising money.
- 8 tips when meeting investors that help you get financing nearly every time.
- Best money making opportunities in business.
- 3 big advantages that give you an edge as a business owner.
- How to prepare the ideal sales letter that will bring in sales like crazy.
- 5 secrets of a profitable sales letter.
- 4 tips on how to prepare to write ad copy and even what to do first that most people overlook.
- How to choose the best form of business—proprietorship, partnership or corporation.

If you were paying the usual fee to attend a live Ted Nicholas seminar, your investment would be significant. (Many people have happily paid $7,500 per person plus travel expenses to attend.)

But your investment will not be $7,500. Or $3,750. Or $1,000. Or even $500.

Your total investment, including all the elements of the MAGIC WORDS THAT BRING YOU RICHES Home Study Course, for a limited time only is just $97. That's not a misprint. But you must act now!

Two Free Bonuses for Early Response

Plus, if you order immediately, we'll send you two free video tapes, normally $80.

Video 1—"How to Buy Magazine and Newspaper Advertising at up to 80% Discount." Learn the one simple action that saves 17.5% instantly, 5 questions to always ask and how to negotiate the best deal. (This session alone could be worth hundreds of thousands, even millions, of dollars to you.)

Video 2—"9 Secrets of a Successful Space Ad." This video also has 27 best headline words and the secrets of creating headlines that make sales soar and shows you precisely what copy sells best. (This recently revised list, proven by tests, works as though by magic and will earn you all the money you really want!)

Limited availability

This amazing offer is part of a limited test and may be withdrawn at any time. To avoid disappointment, order now.

Money-Back Guarantee

Review the MAGIC WORDS THAT BRING YOU RICHES Home Study Course in your own home for 30 days. If you are not completely satisfied for any reason, return it undamaged for a prompt and courteous refund. What could be more fair?

Please complete the enclosed application and mail now. And thank you.

Sincerely,

B. J. Waller

B. J. Waller
President
Nicholas Direct

P.S. Imagine. You get the MAGIC WORDS THAT BRING YOU RICHES Home Study Course by Ted Nicholas on tape plus 2 free videos normally $80 if you order immediately. And all for just $97! And this offer is fully guaranteed for 30 days.

P.P.S. If you don't yet have Ted's new book, MAGIC WORDS THAT BRING YOU RICHES, it's a must. One reviewer calls it the "ultimate marketing book." And it is. See the Free Examination Certificate for a great offer!

P.P.P.S. Your investment may be tax deductible. Please check with your tax advisor.

Application for Home Study Course

Yes! Please accept my application for **MAGIC WORDS THAT BRING YOU RICHES** Deluxe Home Study Program. I understand that this offer is limited and may be withdrawn at any time. If I am not delighted with the course, I may return it undamaged after examining it for 30 days and receive a prompt and courteous refund.

Items includes in the Deluxe Home Study Program: Value

"MAGIC WORDS THAT BRING YOU RICHES" Home Study Program Audio Tapes and Workbook. These tapes include the tape series, **HOW TO BECOME A MAIL ORDER MILLIONAIRE.** Discover the simple way to become financially successful no matter what business or profession you are in or product you are selling.

Retail Value of Tapes $497

For a limited time only, your investment is just	$ 97

Please check blocks which apply:

☐ Please include two FREE videos with my order: "9 SECRETS OF A SUCCESSFUL SPACE AD," and "HOW TO BUY MAGAZINE AND NEWSPAPER ADVERTISING AT UP TO 80% DISCOUNT."

☐ Enclosed is my check for $97 plus $8 shipping and handling, total $105

☐ Please add to my order a gift copy of Ted Nicholas' book, 'MAGIC WORDS THAT BRING YOU RICHES"—322 pages—at the special low price of only $19.77 (Book alone is $23.77 postpaid)

☐ Please charge my credit card: ☐ Mastercard ☐ Visa ☐ Amex

______________________________ ____________
Credit card No. Exp. Date

______________________________ ____________
Name as it appears on card Signature

Name____

Address______________________________________

City____________________ State____________ Zip ________

Daytime Phone No.______________________________

(in case we have a question on your order)

Call, mail or fax to:

Nicholas Direct, Inc.
1511 Gulf Boulevard, Suite 1
P.O. Box 877 Dept MWB2
Indian Rocks Beach, FL 34635
Fax: (813) 596–6900
Telephone: Toll Free 1–800–730–7777

*Canadian orders, add $12 for air mail shipping and handling. Other internation orders, $20 will be added for air mail.

Application for Home Study Course

Yes! Please accept my application for **MAGIC WORDS THAT BRING YOU RICHES** Deluxe Home Study Program. I understand that this offer is limited and may be withdrawn at any time. If I am not delighted with the course, I may return it undamaged after examining it for 30 days and receive a prompt and courteous refund.

Items includes in the Deluxe Home Study Program: Value

"MAGIC WORDS THAT BRING YOU RICHES" Home Study Program Audio Tapes and Workbook. These tapes include the tape series, **HOW TO BECOME A MAIL ORDER MILLIONAIRE.** Discover the simple way to become financially successful no matter what business or profession you are in or product you are selling.

Retail Value of Tapes $497

For a limited time only, your investment is just	$ 97

Please check blocks which apply:

☐ Please include two FREE videos with my order: "9 SECRETS OF A SUCCESSFUL SPACE AD," and "HOW TO BUY MAGAZINE AND NEWSPAPER ADVERTISING AT UP TO 80% DISCOUNT."

☐ Enclosed is my check for $97 plus $8 shipping and handling, total $105

☐ Please add to my order a gift copy of Ted Nicholas' book, 'MAGIC WORDS THAT BRING YOU RICHES"—322 pages—at the special low price of only $19.77 (Book alone is $23.77 postpaid)

☐ Please charge my credit card: ☐ Mastercard ☐ Visa ☐ Amex

______________________________ ____________

Credit card No. Exp. Date

______________________________ ____________

Name as it appears on card Signature

Name______________________________

Address______________________________

City______________ State____________ Zip ________

Daytime Phone No.______________________

(in case we have a question on your order)

Call, mail or fax to: Nicholas Direct, Inc.
1511 Gulf Boulevard, Suite 1
P.O. Box 877 Dept MWB2
Indian Rocks Beach, FL 34635
Fax: (813) 596–6900
Telephone: Toll Free 1–800–730–7777

*Canadian orders, add $12 for air mail shipping and handling. Other internation orders, $20 will be added for air mail.

Application for Home Study Course

Yes! Please accept my application for **MAGIC WORDS THAT BRING YOU RICHES** Deluxe Home Study Program. I understand that this offer is limited and may be withdrawn at any time. If I am not delighted with the course, I may return it undamaged after examining it for 30 days and receive a prompt and courteous refund.

Items includes in the Deluxe Home Study Program: Value

"MAGIC WORDS THAT BRING YOU RICHES" Home Study Program Audio Tapes and Workbook. These tapes include the tape series, **HOW TO BECOME A MAIL ORDER MILLIONAIRE.** Discover the simple way to become financially successful no matter what business or profession you are in or product you are selling.

Retail Value of Tapes $497

For a limited time only, your investment is just	$ 97

Please check blocks which apply:

☐ Please include two FREE videos with my order: "9 SECRETS OF A SUCCESSFUL SPACE AD," and "HOW TO BUY MAGAZINE AND NEWSPAPER ADVERTISING AT UP TO 80% DISCOUNT."

☐ Enclosed is my check for $97 plus $8 shipping and handiing, total $105

☐ Please add to my order a gift copy of Ted Nicholas' book, 'MAGIC WORDS THAT BRING YOU RICHES"—322 pages—at the special low price of only $19.77 (Book alone is $23.77 postpaid)

☐ Please charge my credit card: ☐ Mastercard ☐ Visa ☐ Amex

__________________________ __________
Credit card No. Exp. Date

__________________________ _______________
Name as it appears on card Signature

Name______________________________________

Address______________________________________

City________________ State__________ Zip _______

Daytime Phone No.____________________________
(in case we have a question on your order)

Call, mail or fax to: Nicholas Direct, Inc.
1511 Gulf Boulevard, Suite 1
P.O. Box 877 Dept MWB2
Indian Rocks Beach, FL 34635
Fax: (813) 596–6900
Telephone: Toll Free 1–800–730–7777

*Canadian orders, add $12 for air mail shipping and handling. Other internation orders, $20 will be added for air mail.

Application for Home Study Course

Yes! Please accept my application for **MAGIC WORDS THAT BRING YOU RICHES** Deluxe Home Study Program. I understand that this offer is limited and may be withdrawn at any time. If I am not delighted with the course, I may return it undamaged after examining it for 30 days and receive a prompt and courteous refund.

Items includes in the Deluxe Home Study Program: Value

"MAGIC WORDS THAT BRING YOU RICHES" Home Study Program Audio Tapes and Workbook. These tapes include the tape series, **HOW TO BECOME A MAIL ORDER MILLIONAIRE.** Discover the simple way to become financially successful no matter what business or profession you are in or product you are selling.

Retail Value of Tapes $497

For a limited time only, your investment is just	$ 97

Please check blocks which apply:

- ☐ Please include two FREE videos with my order: "9 SECRETS OF A SUCCESSFUL SPACE AD," and "HOW TO BUY MAGAZINE AND NEWSPAPER ADVERTISING AT UP TO 80% DISCOUNT."
- ☐ Enclosed is my check for $97 plus $8 shipping and handling, total $105
- ☐ Please add to my order a gift copy of Ted Nicholas' book, 'MAGIC WORDS THAT BRING YOU RICHES"—322 pages—at the special low price of only $19.77 (Book alone is $23.77 postpaid)
- ☐ Please charge my credit card: ☐ Mastercard ☐ Visa ☐ Amex

________________________ __________
Credit card No. Exp. Date

________________________ ______________
Name as it appears on card Signature

Name____________________________________

Address__________________________________

City________________ State__________ Zip ______

Daytime Phone No._________________________

(in case we have a question on your order)

Call, mail or fax to:

Nicholas Direct, Inc.
1511 Gulf Boulevard, Suite 1
P.O. Box 877 Dept MWB2
Indian Rocks Beach, FL 34635
Fax: (813) 596–6900
Telephone: Toll Free 1–800–730–7777

*Canadian orders, add $12 for air mail shipping and handling. Other internation orders, $20 will be added for air mail.

Application for Home Study Course

Yes! Please accept my application for **MAGIC WORDS THAT BRING YOU RICHES** Deluxe Home Study Program. I understand that this offer is limited and may be withdrawn at any time. If I am not delighted with the course, I may return it undamaged after examining it for 30 days and receive a prompt and courteous refund.

Items includes in the Deluxe Home Study Program: Value

"MAGIC WORDS THAT BRING YOU RICHES" Home Study Program Audio Tapes and Workbook. These tapes include the tape series, **HOW TO BECOME A MAIL ORDER MILLIONAIRE.** Discover the simple way to become financially successful no matter what business or profession you are in or product you are selling.

Retail Value of Tapes $497

For a limited time only, your investment is just	$ 97

Please check blocks which apply:

☐ Please include two FREE videos with my order: "9 SECRETS OF A SUCCESSFUL SPACE AD," and "HOW TO BUY MAGAZINE AND NEWSPAPER ADVERTISING AT UP TO 80% DISCOUNT."

☐ Enclosed is my check for $97 plus $8 shipping and handling, total $105

☐ Please add to my order a gift copy of Ted Nicholas' book, 'MAGIC WORDS THAT BRING YOU RICHES"—322 pages—at the special low price of only $19.77 (Book alone is $23.77 postpaid)

☐ Please charge my credit card: ☐ Mastercard ☐ Visa ☐ Amex

____________________ __________
Credit card No. Exp. Date

____________________ __________
Name as it appears on card Signature

Name____________________________

Address__________________________

City____________ State________ Zip _____

Daytime Phone No.____________________
(in case we have a question on your order)

Call, mail or fax to: Nicholas Direct, Inc.
1511 Gulf Boulevard, Suite 1
P.O. Box 877 Dept MWB2
Indian Rocks Beach, FL 34635
Fax: (813) 596–6900
Telephone: Toll Free 1–800–730–7777

*Canadian orders, add $12 for air mail shipping and handling. Other internation orders, $20 will be added for air mail.

How Ted Nicholas Works With Clients

In response to readers who want to retain Ted Nicholas as a speaker, copywriter and/or marketing consultant, here are his fees.

1. Speaking engagements. Since each situation is different, it's best to Fax number below with description and date of event. Ted will then contact you.
2. (A) Copywriter/Consultant: $15,000 plus 5% of sales per project. $7,500 due upon engagement; $7,500 when copy is completed.

   or

   (B) No up-front fee. 25% stock in company. Option for 10% more stock upon sale or public offering of company.

   or

   (C) Daily consulting fee of $3,850 plus first class travel.

Should you have an interest in communicating with Ted about a project, please send a one-page Fax with brief description.

Ted Nicholas may be contacted via:

Nicholas Direct, Inc.
Phone: (813) 596–4966
Fax: (813) 596–6900
Address: P.O. Box 877
Indian Rocks Beach, FL 34635